Contending

for the

Gospel

For the Glory of Christ
and the Sanctity of His Church

Mike Gendron

Acknowledgements

—◦◦◦—

Any Christian husband knows that in order to do one's best, he needs his wife's encouragement, faithfulness and support to the work God has called him to accomplish. God has blessed me with a precious helpmate who has served with me in ministry for over 30 years. I am forever thankful for Jane and for all the help and wisdom she has provided as we have labored together to bring glory to our Lord Jesus Christ through His Gospel.

I am also thankful to several dear friends who have helped make this book a tool that will hopefully equip and edify the saints to be faithful and effective witnesses for our Lord Jesus Christ. John Manning has been a dear brother-in-Christ and accountability partner for many years. I appreciate his expertise in laying out the format of this book and his theological insight to what I have written.

Our sovereign Lord also raised up a faithful supporter of the Proclaiming the Gospel ministry to devote her time and expertise to editing this book. Carolyn Bivans's work has been greatly appreciated, and I am thankful for the many hours she has invested to proofread the text and make suggestions.

I would also like to acknowledge the many brothers and sisters in Christ, throughout the world, who have been using our evangelistic resources as they labor in the fields white for harvest. May God continue to receive all praise and honor and glory for the work He is doing through His servants.

CONTENTS

INTRODUCTION

—◆—

We can be wrong about a lot of things in this life and still survive, but if we are wrong about whom we are trusting for our eternal destiny, we will pay for that fatal mistake forever. At the moment we take our last breath, our eternity is irrevocably sealed. There are no second chances, no excuses and no calls for mercy (Hebrews 9:27). For this reason, there is not an issue of greater importance than investigating where we will spend eternity. Everyone will live forever either in the glories of heaven or in the torments of hell. Why then do people rarely seek the answers from the Word of our Creator, our most trustworthy authority? The true God who spoke all of creation into existence is the same God who spoke through 40 authors to give us His infallible Word. In the Scriptures, God speaks with one voice to reveal one Savior who offers one way to be saved from sin.

Whose Word Should We Trust?

In the garden of Eden, Adam and Eve lived in perfect union with God. God's voice was the only one they heard until Satan spoke through a serpent. Satan questioned Eve by asking, "Has God indeed said...?" (Genesis 3:1). Then the serpent attempted to invalidate God's Word with a fatal lie, "You will not surely die" (Genesis 3:4). Eve had a critical decision to make: to trust God and His Word or believe the word of someone else? Her fatal decision to trust Satan's word instead of God's Word led her and Adam into sin, and caused both spiritual death (separation from God) and physical death. "Through one man sin entered into the world, and death through sin, and so death spread to all men, because all sinned" (Romans 5:12). All of Adam's descendants inherit his sin nature and are born spiritually dead. Adam was not originally subject to spiritual or physical death, but because of his sin, death became a reality for himself and his posterity.

Nothing has changed in human history. Man is still facing the same decision Eve faced. Should I believe God and His Word or the voice of another? Today there are many voices that people choose to believe instead of God's Word. Many put their faith in the words of religious leaders, scientists, philosophers, or their parents. In doing so, they ignore the warning of Paul: "Let God be true, but every man a liar" (Romans 3:4).

Many of my dear friends and family members are practicing Roman Catholics. I often ask them questions regarding the official traditions and doctrines of their church. Rather than answer my questions, they usually respond, "Oh, I don't believe that." So common and casual is this statement that I'm reminded of a plentiful smorgasbord offering a variety of favorite and not-so-favorite dishes. As one approaches, he may pick and choose only those items that suit his taste. Yet Catholic teaching does not allow this. Many Catholics may not be aware that by definition a dogma is an infallible teaching of the Roman Catholic Church and must be believed by all Catholics under the penalty of anathema (eternal condemnation). This really becomes a dilemma when dogmas oppose the Bible.

For over 30 years of my life, I believed the words of Catholic priests and popes. I was blindly deceived because I did not know the truth. But God in His grace and mercy gave me a desire to read His Word, and I transferred my faith from fallible men to our infallible God.

A number of professing Christians treat the Bible the same way many Catholics treat their dogmas. They choose scriptures to believe, while ignoring or spiritualizing the rest. The key question for those who do not use the entire Bible as the authority for truth is, "How do you determine in which part to believe?"

When we are influenced by the opinions, philosophies and traditions of men, we have a tendency to create our own god rather than acknowledge the God of the Bible. Why not go to the source of all truth, to the One who is truth and whose Word is truth? Seek the one who created life rather than a fallible human being whose opinions are only as trustworthy as the next man's.

So Great a Salvation!

Indifference to the offer of "so great a salvation" will leave us with no escape on the day of judgment (Hebrews 2:3). God's Word explains why: "Because I called and you refused, I stretched out my hand and no one paid attention. Then they will call on me, but I will not answer; They will seek me diligently but they will not find me, because they hated knowledge and did not choose the fear of the Lord. They would not accept my counsel, they spurned all my reproof." (Proverbs 1:24, 28-30). How utterly sobering are these words of almighty God! Yet, He is glorified before angels and men not only in His infinite mercy and grace, but also in the unrestrained fury of His justice.

How precarious is the state of ignorant people who live in the constant danger of this eternal misery. No matter how pious, religious, devout or moral they may be, if they have not been born of God (John 3:3), they will experience God's sin-avenging wrath and judgment. They will be given immortal bodies capable of enduring suffering and torment eternally [that would surely cause instant death in a mortal body] (Revelation

20:15). They will be thrown into a furnace of fire where there will be weeping and gnashing of teeth (Matthew 13:50). They will quickly discover the eternal fire of hell is kindled with the anger of almighty God (Deuteronomy 32:22). There will be no intermission or relief, for they will be tormented day and night forever and ever (Revelation 20:10). How terrifying it will be to be judged by a sin-avenging God!

Rescuing Those Who Are Perishing

May this book and the Word of God give us a growing compassion for those who are perishing. Can there be any higher calling than warning people of the fatal sin disease they inherited? Can there be any greater act of love than offering them the only cure that will save their soul? I know of none! We should grieve for the unconverted as if we see them suspended over hell and one after another is falling in. We who have been graciously entrusted with the glorious Gospel of God's saving grace should shout it from the rooftops. Let us not make the Lord's great commission our great omission! Let us engage people with the Gospel throughout the day. If they only have a few minutes to spend with us, offer them a Gospel tract which reveals the greatest news they will ever hear about the greatest gift they could ever receive from the greatest Man who ever lived. Sow the imperishable seed of God's Gospel in the fertile soil He prepares!

In this book, the glorious Gospel of our Lord and Savior Jesus Christ is examined and affirmed from the Word of God, which is the supreme authority in all matters of faith. It is God's inspired Word that provides truth and hope, not the uninspired words or opinions of man. It is my desire that as you study the eternal truths of the Gospel, you rejoice in your worship of the Lord Jesus Christ and grow in your desire to proclaim, defend and live His Gospel. May we all echo the words of the Apostle Paul, "For I am not ashamed of the gospel, for it is the power of God for salvation to everyone who believes, to the Jew first and also to the Greek" (Romans 1:16).

It has been said that when you contrast truth with error, the truth shines even brighter. That is the approach I have taken in this book. I will contrast the objective truth of God's inspired, inerrant Word with the subjective, uninspired, errant teachings and traditions of men. May the glorious light of God's Gospel shine bright!

Mike Gendron
Proclaiming The Gospel
info@ProclaimingTheGospel.org

Chapter 1

THE FOUNDATION FOR THE GOSPEL

⧯⧯⧯

At the very beginning of His earthly ministry, The Lord Jesus Christ commanded everyone to repent and believe in the Gospel. He declared, "The time is fulfilled, and the kingdom of God is at hand; repent and believe in the Gospel" (Mark 1:15). There is no greater call to humanity than the one given by the Creator of the universe. The salvation of mankind, that is offered in the Gospel, is the theme of the entire Bible from the beginning to the end. In the most profound way, the very nature of the Gospel, as described in the Bible, is what separates it from all religious writings and traditions.

The Bible is unique in its message of salvation in that it claims to reveal God's only way of salvation from the one and only God of the universe. It is not "a" way, but "the" way. Jesus Himself said, "I am the way, and the truth, and the life; no one comes to the Father but through Me (John 14:6). He is the way for those who are lost, the truth for those who are deceived and the life for those who are dead in sin. The One True God offers forgiveness and eternal life in paradise as a free gift of His grace, through faith alone, in the Lord Jesus Christ alone. All other religious books declare man must merit salvation through works, religious rituals or some form of law keeping.

For many, this begs the question: Why should I believe the Bible over other religious writings? Why should I be convinced that the Bible is in fact God's Word and the supreme authority for knowing truth?

The answer to these questions is truly the foundation for the authority of the Gospel. Without such divine authority, the words of Jesus and His apostles, and the Old Testament writers before them, are but empty declarations and no different from the religions of the world.

Why Should Anyone Believe the Bible?

There is so much evidence that the Bible is indeed God's Word and that we can trust it to guide us through life and prepare us for eternity. The Bible is dramatically different from all other religious books and is set apart by the following characteristics:

Unique in its Divine Origin

The authors claimed their writings were inspired by God. "Holy men of God spoke as they were moved by the Holy Spirit." They claimed they spoke for God. "Thus says the Lord" occurs nearly 500 times (2 Timothy 3:16; 2 Peter 1:21). The Bible, as some say, is not a collection of mystical thoughts and religious experiences. It does claim to be the Word of God and His message to mankind. With such claims, the Bible should meet the highest standard for accuracy.

Unique in its Unity and Harmony

God commissioned 40 different authors from all walks of life, over a time span of 1,500 years, on 3 continents, to write the 66 books of the Bible. From Genesis to Revelation, the writers are united in truth and harmony, to reveal a complex narrative about God's redemption of man through the atonement of the Lord Jesus Christ.

Unique in the Reliability of its Transmission

In 1948, a shepherd made the greatest manuscript discovery of all times near the Dead Sea. Entire manuscripts were found that were copied over 2000 years ago and were essentially the same as our modern copies, proving they were transmitted over many centuries with extraordinary precision. The manuscript support for the accuracy of the original writings far exceeds that of other writings of antiquity.

Unique in its Indestructibility

The Bible has withstood intense scrutiny by thousands of skeptics and has survived continuous attacks by emperors, kings, and dictators. They all failed in their attempts to destroy its message. God's Word has stood firm for thousands of years and will stand forever!

Unique in its Historical and Geographical Accuracy

Archeologists continue to unearth evidence of ancient people, places, and cultures described in the Bible. Virtually every discovery has confirmed the truth of the Scriptures. The faith of people who visit Israel is affirmed by what they experience.

Unique in Scientific Accuracy

Modern technology continues to unfold the mysteries of the universe that were recorded in Scripture thousands of years ago. The God, who created the universe and set in motion the laws that govern it, is the same God who inspired the writers to record these fascinating mysteries.

Unique in its Prophecy

The Bible contains over 2500 prophecies that foretell specific details about the Messiah, Israel, nations and cities. Two thousand have already been fulfilled without error. When the Bible was written, 30 percent of it was prophetic.

Unique in its Painfully Honest Accounts of its Heroes

Whereas some religious writings may sugarcoat certain periods of history or its religious leaders, the Bible reveals Moses, the lawgiver, was a murderer, David, Israel's most loved king and spiritual leader, was an adulterer, Paul, was the worst of sinners, and Peter, was a betrayer of the Lord Jesus. In all historical accounts throughout the pages of the Bible, man is described as flawed and in need of redemption—the very gift offered in the Gospel.

Unique in its Influence and Popularity

No other book has impacted society and culture so impressively or has changed lives so dramatically. The Bible is the most circulated book in history. It has been read, studied and quoted by more people than any other book. It is the most translated book ever – 2,454 languages covering 98 percent of the world's population.

The Bible is so amazing! It brings truth where there is deception, understanding where there is ignorance, confidence where there is doubt, order where there is confusion, and light where there is darkness. Instead of trusting what man says God says, we can go directly to what God says.

Who Determined the Books of the Bible?

Over the 1500 years that the books of the Bible were written, there were some writings that claimed "biblical authority" but were not included in the canon of Scripture. The canon is an officially accepted list of books. The canon was determined by God and discovered by man.

The Catholic Church claims it was given the authority to establish the canon at the Council of Hippo in A.D. 393. However, the church did not create the canon; it simply recognized the letters that were already accepted as Scripture by the first century church. Long before church councils were ever convened, church elders were constantly evaluating and deciding which of the many writings of their day carried apostolic authority. We have proof that letters were circulated and accepted before the canon was formally established. Paul wrote: "After this letter has been read to you, see that it is also read in the church of the Laodiceans" (Colossians 4:16).

The Roman Catholic Bible contains not only the 39 books of the Old Testament and the 27 books of the New Testament, but also the apocryphal books Tobit, Judith, Wisdom, Ecclesiasticus, Baruch and Maccabees. These books were never part of the early church canon because they contain historical and geographical errors, proving they were not divinely inspired. The apocryphal books also teach doctrines which are at variance with the inspired Scriptures. For example, 2 Maccabees 12:43-45 teaches the efficacy of prayers and offerings for the dead. Ecclesiaticus 3:30 teaches that almsgiving makes atonement for sin and justifies cruelty to slaves (33:26, 28). Christ and His apostles quoted frequently from Old Testament books but never from these apocryphal books. Furthermore, they were never included in the Jewish canon, which is of utmost significance because God entrusted His Word to the Jews. Paul wrote: "(The Jews) were entrusted with the oracles of God" (Romans 3:1-2). The entire Old Testament was affirmed in the Jewish community by means of the Holy Spirit long before any council sat in judgment.

All the Old Testament books are quoted in the New Testament except Esther, Ecclesiastes and the Song of Solomon. None of the books of the Apocrypha, which the Catholic Church added to its canon in the 16th century, are quoted.

To collect various letters and books of Scripture into one volume was the task given to Christians already converted to Christ by the Word of God. These early Christians did not give us the Word of God. The Word of God gave us these early Christians. They were under conviction and illumination of the Holy Spirit from the writings of the Apostles and the oral teachings of Jesus long before any council pieced together the Bible. Hence, the Word of God established the Church. Early

Christians were convinced and persuaded that it was the Word of God because the Holy Spirit convicted them.

The actual gathering together of the Scriptures into one volume took place in God's providence, under the supervision, persuasion, and conviction of the Holy Spirit. Christians labored together to separate the actual Word from false writings. The early Christians pooled their cognitive convictions and brought together a Canon of the text to end speculations and dismiss false writings.

Jerome completed his version of the Bible, the Latin Vulgate, in 405. In the Middle Ages, the Vulgate became the de facto standard version of the Bible in the West. The manuscripts clearly identified certain books of the Vulgate Old Testament as apocryphal or non-canonical. Jerome described those books not translated from the Hebrew as apocrypha; he specifically mentions that Wisdom, the book of Jesus' son of Sirach, Judith, Tobias, and the Shepherd, "are not in the canon". In the prologue to Esdras, he mentions 3 and 4 Esdras as being apocrypha. In his prologue, he said of the Books of the Maccabees, that the Church "has not received them among the canonical scriptures".

We know the Bible was complete and "once for all delivered to the Saints" in the first century (Jude 3). The Old Testament Canon was closed about 425 B.C., 425 years before Christ. The last book was written by Malachi. There was no question which books were inspired by God. The writers were well known as spokesmen for God and claimed to be speaking and writing the inspired Word of God. Secondly, there were no errors of history, geography, or theology in the writings.

The New Testament had similar tests to determine a book's canonicity. First, was the book authored by an Apostle or someone closely associated with an Apostle? They knew who the Apostles were, and they knew who their close associates were.

The key question about the book's inspiration was tied to Apostolic authorship or one closely associated. For example, the Gospel of Mark was written by Mark, and Mark was not an Apostle but a close associate of Peter. The Gospel of Luke and the Book of Acts were written by Luke, who was not an Apostle but a very close associate of Paul. The Apostles were known to the people, their associates were known to the people, and when Apostles wrote and claimed inspiration, the people were secure in the veracity of their writings.

Another test applied by the Early Church was the test of content. Did the writings square with what the Apostles taught? In those early years of the Church, heretics such as the Gnostics tried to slip in phony books, but none of them ever made it. If it didn't square with Apostolic doctrine, it didn't pass. And the doctrinal aberrations were very easy to spot.

A third test was this: is the book regularly read and used in the churches? In other words, did the people of God readily accept it? Did they read it during worship and make its teachings a part of their daily living? A final test was to determine if the book was recognized and used by succeeding generations after the Early Church.

There was also a formidable group of spurious books that came in the New Testament period. They all failed to make the canon because they couldn't pass the test of authenticity. Christ has put His stamp of authority on the Scripture. The early Church clearly discovered the canon of God's Word under the guidance of the Holy Spirit. To add anything to Scripture, or to reject the inspiration of Scripture, is to not only to ignore the warnings of Scripture and the teachings of Christ and the Apostles, but also to bring yourself into the very dangerous place where you are susceptible to the curse of God.

The New Testament writers confirm the authenticity and authority of the other writers. Paul cites Luke's Gospel as Scripture (1 Timothy 5:18). Peter referred to Paul's writings as Scripture (2 Peter 3:15-16). Paul commanded the Thessalonians to have his letter read to all the brethren (1 Thessalonians 5:27). John promised a blessing to all those who read the Revelation (Revelation 1:3). To the Colossians Paul wrote, "have this letter read in the church of the Laodiceans (Colossians 4:16). As long as the apostles were alive, everything could be verified. They were eye witnesses to all that Christ said and did.

The councils of Hippo 393 and Carthage 397 simply approved the list of 27 NT books which had already been recognized by the early church. They neither added to the number or took away from it.

Scripture Is The Supreme Authority for Knowing Truth

The 66 books that make up the Bible, God's Holy Word, are rich with truth, wisdom, and a clear offer and explanation of salvation that is found in Christ alone through faith alone. But is the Bible the sole authority? Are there other sources equally important that must be considered when understanding the Gospel?

The Bible gives overwhelming evidence as to why Scripture must be always our sole authority for faith. The Word of God is pure, perfect, inerrant, infallible, living, truth, light, holy, eternal, and forever settled in heaven. It illuminates, cleanses, saves, frees, guides, converts, heals, quickens, judges, and sanctifies. It also brings conviction, gives knowledge, gives wisdom, produces faith, refutes error, searches the heart, equips for every good work, and is used as a weapon. The Word of God is exalted even above the very name of God.

> I will bow down toward Your holy temple
> And give thanks to Your name for Your lovingkindness
> and Your truth;
> For You have magnified Your word according to all
> Your name.
>
> (Psalm 138:2)

Elevating tradition to the level of authority was common with the religious leaders during Jesus' earthly ministry. Consider this exchange between the Pharisees and Jesus.

> Then some Pharisees and scribes came to Jesus from Jerusalem and said, "Why do Your disciples break the tradition of the elders? For they do not wash their hands when they eat bread." And He answered and said to them, "Why do you yourselves transgress the commandment of God for the sake of your tradition? For God said, 'Honor your father and mother,' and, 'He who speaks evil of father or mother is to be put to death.' But you say, 'Whoever says to *his* father or mother, "Whatever I have that would help you has been given to *God*," he is not to honor his father or his mother.' And *by this* you invalidated the word of God for the sake of your tradition. (Matthew 15:1-6)

For Christians, the Scriptures provide the only objective basis for authority while the indwelling Holy Spirit provides illumination, conviction and discernment. This dual authority, the Spirit of God working with the Word of God, is sufficient in all matters of faith and Christian living. Consider the biblical justifications for the authority of Scripture alone.

> All Scripture is inspired by God and profitable for teaching, for reproof, for correction, for training in righteousness. (2 Timothy 3:16)

Since Scripture is used to correct and reprove, then it must be the authoritative standard by which everything else is judged for its truthfulness. Jesus said, "Scripture cannot be broken"(John 10:35), meaning, it cannot be annulled or made void. It cannot be set aside in favor of the traditions of men.

The character of God is on the line when it comes to Scripture.

God is not a man, that He should lie,
Nor a son of man, that He should repent;
Has He said, and will He not do it?
Or has He spoken, and will He not make it good?
(Numbers 23:19)

Since God has spoken, His inspired Word is authoritative. Submitting to the authority of God's revealed Word will guide us in His perfect will.

Christ used the authority of Scripture to rebuke Satan's attempt to deceive Him. Look at the entire exchange recorded in Matthew 4:1-11. He gave prepositional statements to accurately convey the truth that Satan attempted to distort. Jesus was our perfect model for rebuking deception, and He did so with Scripture, not the writings of men.

Jesus used the authority of Scripture to rebuke false teachers. In Matthew 22:23-33, He responds to a question posed to Him by the Sadducees regarding the resurrection. The Sadducees differed from the Pharisees in that they rejected human tradition but rather relied more on rationalism. Jesus responds to their trick question firmly backed by the authority of Scripture—God's eternal Word:

But Jesus answered and said to them, "You are mistaken, not understanding the Scriptures nor the power of God (Matthew 22:29).

The integrity of the Gospel must be maintained and proclaimed for true conversions.

Repentant sinners are saved by hearing and believing the Word.

So faith *comes* from hearing, and hearing by the word of Christ. (Romans 10:17)

In Him, you also, after listening to the message of truth, the Gospel of your salvation—having also believed, you were sealed in Him with the Holy Spirit of promise, who is given as a pledge of our inheritance, with a view to the redemption of *God's own* possession, to the praise of His glory. (Ephesians 1:13-14)

Jesus prayed for Christians to be sanctified (set apart) by the truth of His Word:

Sanctify them in the truth; Your word is truth. (John 17:17)

Christians must separate themselves from apostate churches and false teachers. God uses division to show those who have His approval (1 Corinthians 11:19). That approval, or testing, is determined by the Word of God.

Our Lord made it quite clear that His Word, and His Word alone, not the tradition of men, is what sets us apart as His disciples.

So Jesus was saying to those Jews who had believed Him, "if you continue in My word, *then* you are truly disciples of Mine; and you will know the truth, and the truth will make you free". (John 8:31-32)

Christ rebuked the religious leaders for nullifying the Word of God with their tradition. In this passage, Jesus states how the religious leaders twist and distort the Word of God by their tradition.

He was also saying to them, "You are experts at setting aside the commandment of God in order to keep your tradition. For Moses said, 'Honor your father and your mother'; and, 'He who speaks evil of father or mother, is to be put to death'; but you say, 'If a man says to *his* father or *his* mother, whatever I have that would help you is Corban (that is to say, given *to God*),' you no longer permit him to do anything for *his* father or *his* mother; *thus* invalidating the word of God by your tradition which you have handed down; and you do many things such as that". (Mark 7:9-13)

Any tradition that nullifies the Scriptures must be exposed and renounced so others will not be deceived. The Scriptures were written to all Christians, not to popes and the Magisterium to be interpreted for lay people. Anytime we allow others to interpret God's Word for us, we leave ourselves open to deception.

The Apostle Paul commended the Bereans for using the Scriptures, not tradition, to verify the truthfulness of his teaching. Since an apostle who penned over half the New Testament was tested by the Bible, all religious teachers must be tested using the same Scriptural authority. The Bereans received the message with great eagerness and examined the Scriptures every day to see if what Paul said was true (Acts 17:11).

After considering all other sources of authority we must always ask, as did the Apostle Paul, "But what does the Scripture say?" (Galatians 4:30). Since it is impossible for God to lie, His Word must be the standard by which we discern truth from error (Hebrews 6:18).

We are from God; he who knows God listens to us; he who is not from God does not listen to us. By this we know the spirit of truth and the spirit of error. (1 John 4:6)

The writers of Scripture claimed they were transmitting the very Word of God, infallible and authoritative to the highest degree. God's Word is sufficient to function as the sole, infallible rule of faith because the Bible does not refer to any higher rule of faith. Everything that we must know, understand and believe to become a Christian is found in the Scriptures. In the following text, the Apostle Paul makes it clear what is and what is not the source of authority in the preaching of the Gospel. It is "the Scriptures," not tradition.

> Now I make known to you, brethren, the Gospel which I preached to you, which also you received, in which also you stand, by which also you are saved, if you hold fast the word which I preached to you, unless you believed in vain. For I delivered to you as of first importance what I also received, that Christ died for our sins according to the Scriptures, and that He was buried, and that He was raised on the third day according to the Scriptures. (1 Corinthians 15:1-4)

Those who reject the supreme authority of Scripture are prone to be deceived. God foreknew that the teachings and traditions of men would become corrupt and would lead many astray. In His wisdom, He left us with His written Word, the only objective, absolute authority for truth, to lead us back to Him. It is pure, powerful, perfect, inerrant, infallible, living, holy, eternal, and forever settled in heaven. It illuminates, cleanses, frees, guides, converts, quickens, judges, sanctifies, brings conviction, gives wisdom, produces faith, and refutes error. Can you describe tradition in the same way God describes His Word? God forbid that anyone would add anything subjective to the objective standard God has given us!

Remember: Scripture is what God says; religion is what *man says* God says.

Chapter 2

THE MESSAGE OF THE GOSPEL

—◦◦◦—

The Gospel of God is the most profound doctrinal truth woven throughout Scripture and holds the key to our eternal destiny. There is no message more important in all of human history. It demands our utmost attention because it reveals the gracious gift of salvation that can only be received one way.

The message of the Gospel must always drive home the reality of God's holiness and the sinner's helpless condition. God is the eternal Creator of everything. He is perfectly holy and requires perfect obedience to His Law. Man has sinned by breaking God's Law and the consequence for sin is death and separation from God. Man can do nothing to save himself. The hopeless condition of sinners points them to Jesus Christ as a merciful Lord who purchased full atonement for all who will turn to Him in repentance and faith. Jesus Christ came to earth as both God and sinless man. After living a perfect life He died on a cross to pay sin's penalty and to reconcile us with God. He rose from the dead and is alive today. Sinners must repent with godly sorrow for their sins and believe in Jesus Christ as Lord and Savior.

The Gospel message answers the divine paradox that is presented in the form of two questions.

1. How can a righteous, holy and just God, who must punish sin, let sinners go unpunished?

2. How can a loving, merciful and gracious God, who created us, punish anyone with everlasting torment?

The Gospel reveals that all of God's attributes work in harmony through a sinless substitute who bears the sinner's punishment vicariously. God's holiness, righteousness and judgment were satisfied when Jesus Christ, His eternal Son, made atonement for believer's sins. God's attributes of love, mercy, and grace are demonstrated by saving sinners who repent and believe His Gospel.

Lest we be found in error and led astray by a distorted, deceptive, counterfeit or partial truth, let us examine the essential aspects of the Gospel message directly from God's Word.

What Must I do to be Saved?

Can you think of a question any more important than the one asked by the Philippian jailer, "What must I do to be saved?" Is there any other issue in life more critical or urgent than determining where one will spend eternity? The guard of the Philippian jail must have known he was facing eternal punishment to even ask the question. He must have known that God will deal with sin either with His wrath or with His grace. The answer Paul and Silas gave to his question was very clear and profound, "Believe in the Lord Jesus and you will be saved" (Acts 16:30-31). Later, we will see what it means to believe in the Lord Jesus.

Faith Alone Saves, but Faith that Saves is Never Alone

In the book of James, Scripture addresses a widespread problem that exists even in the church today. Many profess to know Christ but do not possess Christ because they have never been born again. They are victims of the worst kind of deception, believing they are Christians when they are not. The most terrifying words professing Christians could ever hear would be Jesus saying, "Depart from me, I never knew you" (Mat. 7:23). That's why James exhorts his readers to "be doers of the word, and not hearers only, deceiving yourselves" (James 1:22).

James is making it clear that a mere profession of faith does not result in salvation. But he is not teaching that salvation is earned by works. In fact, he already wrote in chapter one: "Every good gift and every perfect gift is from above, coming down from the Father of lights" (1:17). Faith and salvation are included in that perfect gift of God's grace (Ephesians 2:8-9). That is why he says, "show me your faith apart from your works, and I will show you my faith by my works" (James 2:18). Since faith is an invisible relationship between God and man, its only visible evidence are the works produced by faith. James is declaring that genuine faith will be accompanied by good works. We are justified by faith alone, but faith that justifies is never alone! Those with God-given faith have also been given a new heart and a new nature that produces a changed life, which, in turn, bears fruit for the glory of God (John 15:4-8).

True believers may have times of unfruitfulness in their lives, but the pattern and direction of their lives will be characterized by an increasing pattern of righteousness and a decreasing pattern of sin. This process of sanctification is not about *sinless perfection*, but a *righteous direction*. Righteous behavior is what distinguishes counterfeit faith from genuine faith. We enter into salvation by faith apart from works (Ephesians 2:8-9), but after we are saved, we do the works God has prepared for us (Ephesians 2:10).

Some will ask why James appears to contradict Paul, who wrote: "For by grace you have been saved through faith. And this is not your own doing; it is the gift of God, not a result of works, so that no one may boast" (Eph. 2:8-9). We need to explain that Paul is dealing with the **means of salvation**, whereas James is dealing with the **outcome of salvation**. Paul is dealing with the **nature of justification**, while James is dealing with the **nature of faith**. When Catholics say that James 2:24 is the only place in the Bible where the words "faith alone" appear together, we must explain that James is not teaching how to be justified. He is declaring that believers are vindicated by their works as a demonstration of their living faith.

We also need to know that the word "justified" has two meanings. One is an act of God's grace, whereby He pardons and declares a person righteous. It is a legal or forensic declaration by God to those who have faith. Paul wrote: "having been justified by faith, we have peace with God through our Lord Jesus Christ" (Romans 5:1). The other meaning is "to vindicate" or "to show" that someone is righteous. Abraham was justified (vindicated) "when he offered up his son Isaac on the altar" (James 2:21). His obedience to God vindicated, or displayed, his genuine faith. Abraham did not need to be legally declared righteous again because God had justified him by faith many years before (Genesis 12:1-7; 15:6).

Faith and Repentance Unto Salvation

It has often been said that repentance and faith are two sides of the same coin: distinctively different yet inseparable. They are both sovereignly granted by God at the moment of conversion (Acts 11:18; Ephesians 2:8-9; Philippians 1:29). Once received, these divine gifts continue to be manifested throughout the life of believers (Romans 12:1-2; Hebrews 12:1-2). It is biblically inconsistent and theologically problematic to suppose that anyone could believe in the Lord Jesus, yet not repent. After all, repentance includes turning from unbelief to belief in the Lord Jesus (Matthew 21:32). Genuine saving faith is always accompanied by repentance. Paul testified to both Jews and Gentiles of "repentance toward God and faith in our Lord Jesus Christ" (Acts 20:21). Faith that is not grounded in repentance is not genuine God-given faith. Those who refuse to repent should fear God's wrath in the day of judgment (Matthew 11:20-24).

Followers of Jesus Christ are familiar with the word "repentance", but many are unsure of its biblical meaning or its role in the salvation of sinners. Some would argue passionately that it must be coupled with faith as the only saving response to the Gospel. Others say that repentance is not necessary for the salvation of sinners, only faith (2 Tim 2:25). Consider the importance of repentance in the ministry of our Lord Jesus. The very first word of His very first sermon was "repent" (Mat. 4:17). He later declared that He had come to call sinners to repentance (Luke 5:32). His last sermon to His apostles before ascending into heaven, included a command to preach repentance for the forgiveness of sins (Luke 24:47). This leaves no doubt to the Savior's position on repentance.

The Importance of Repentance

In Peter's first two sermons, he commanded his listeners to repent for the forgiveness and expiation of their sins (Acts 2:38; 3:19). On another occasion, when Simon the magician sinned by trying to buy God's power with his money, Peter called him to "repent from his wickedness" (Acts 8:22). Peter also taught that repentance is necessary for salvation: "The Lord...is patient with you, not wanting anyone to perish, but everyone to come to repentance" (2 Pet. 3:9). This beautiful insight into the long-suffering and compassionate nature of God shows the importance of repentance. Our Lord gave specific instructions to the apostles on how to evangelize and then sent them out into the world preaching that "men should repent" (Mark 6:12).

Repentance Defined

The widely-accepted and standard Greek-English Lexicon of the New Testament provides an excellent definition of the common Greek word *"metanoia"* used for repentance in the New Testament. It means "to change one's way of life as the result of a complete change of thought and attitude with regard to sin and righteousness." We find in its meaning a conviction that produces action. Such a change is profoundly noted by Paul's description of the Thessalonians: "You turned to God from idols to serve a living and true God" (1 Thessalonians 1:9). These saints displayed three elements of repentance:

- a turning from sinful behavior
- a turning to God
- a desire to serve Him

It is impossible to turn to God without turning away from sin. People who continue to live in habitual sin and think they are saved must be warned that Jesus saves us from our sin, not in our sin.

One of the most gifted preachers of the 17th century, Thomas Watson, defined repentance as a "grace of God's Spirit, which enables a sinner to be inwardly humbled and visibly reformed." Repentance moves a man to recognize the wickedness of his sin, which produces godly sorrow and a broken and contrite heart (Psalm 51:17). Convicted by the Holy Spirit, the sinner acknowledges his sinful nature, confesses his sins and makes a heartfelt plea for God's forgiveness (Psalm 51:1-4; 1 John 1:9; Luke 18:13; Proverbs 28:13). Scripture says that a truly repentant person hates the sin he once loved and is ashamed of it (Ezekiel 36:31; Romans 6:21). He forsakes his wicked ways and turns to God (Isa. 55:7; Acts 26:20). Repentance produces a genuine desire to be victorious over sin and a longing for the day he will be forever delivered from it (1 John 3:3).

Repentance Produces Change

Repentance produces not only a change in mind, but it also leads to a changed heart and life (Isaiah 55:7). Intellectually, repentance sees sin as an affront to our holy God and Creator. The sinner understands that his sin has separated him from God and caused enmity with God. God's Word instructs him to turn to Christ as his only hope. No one can cling to their sin and to Christ because "the mind of sinful man is death, but the mind controlled by the Spirit is life" (Romans 8:6).

Emotionally, repentance is accompanied by sorrow, because sin has greatly offended our loving and gracious God. This sorrow, in and of itself, is not repentance, because people can have sorrow and not repent. Judas is an example of one who felt great remorse but did not repent (Matthew 27:3). When repentance is produced from godly sorrow, according to the will of God, it leads to salvation (2 Cor. 7:10). God's kindness is meant to lead sinners to repentance, but a stubborn and unrepentant heart stores up His wrath for the day of judgment (Romans 2:4-5).

Volitionally, repentance produces a transformation of the will, which will be evidenced by a change in direction and purpose (Romans 6:6; 12:2). The change in behavior is not repentance; it is the fruit that repentance brings forth. The Lord Jesus gave an example of this fruit when "the men of Nineveh repented at the preaching of Jonah" (Matthew 12:41). After Jonah preached, the Ninevites' king issued this proclamation: "'Let everyone call urgently on God...so that we will not perish.' When God saw what they did and how they turned from their evil ways, He had compassion and did not bring upon them the destruction He had threatened" (Jonah 3:8b-10). According to Jesus, who is our ultimate authority for faith, their repentance produced fruit; they turned from their evil ways.

Whenever God grants repentance, a vivid contrast is observed between the life that was once dominated by the power of darkness and the new life in Christ Jesus (Colossians 1:13; Titus 3:3-7; 1 Peter 4:1-4). The law is a tutor to bring men to Christ through repentance and faith (Galatians 3:24). Each conversion will be vindicated by works of repentance and obedience (Acts 26:20; Romans 6:17). God saves us the way we *are*, but He never leaves us the way we *were* (1 Thessalonians 4:3). Those whom God loves, He reproves and disciplines to bring them to repentance (Revelation 3:19). Salvation is not just delivery from the punishment of sin, but also from the power of sin. Those who are saved through Christ will turn from sin to be saved from it. This can only be done in the power of the

Holy Spirit, who converts slaves of unrighteousness to slaves of righteousness (Romans 6:16-18).

Repentance is a Divine Command

Our Lord began His earthly ministry with the command: "Repent and believe the Gospel" (Mark 1:15). He also commanded the churches at Ephesus, Sardis and Pergamum to repent (Revelation 2:5,16; 3:3). Sinners are commanded to turn from sin to the Savior to escape the coming judgment. Nonetheless, the call to repentance is the critical truth that is most often left out of Gospel preaching and evangelism. It is noteworthy that Luke's account of the Great Commission includes a mandate to preach repentance (Luke 24:47).

Paul wrote, "God…commands all men everywhere to repent, because He has appointed a day on which He will judge the world in righteousness" (Acts 17:30-31).

We also see our Lord speaking through the prophet Isaiah, "Turn to me and be saved, all the ends of the earth! For I am God, and there is no other" (Isaiah 45:22).

God's Judgment of Unrepentant Sin

Tragically, there are many who live with no fear of God. They delight in His love, mercy and grace while ignoring His justice and righteousness, which are the foundation of His throne (Psalm 89:14). They dismiss the righteous indignation He displayed by judging sin with a global flood (2 Peter 3:5-6). They ignore the many passages in the Bible that speak of God's judgment and fierce anger towards sin. In Isaiah 66:15-16, it is written:

> "The Lord will come in fire and His chariots like the whirlwind, to render His anger with fury, and His rebuke with flames of fire, for the Lord will execute judgment by fire and by His sword on all flesh, and those slain by the Lord will be many."

God has no pity on unrepentant sinners. "I indeed will deal in wrath, My eye will have no pity nor will I spare; and though they cry in My ears with a loud voice, yet I will not listen to them" (Ezekiel 8:18). These words should terrify everyone who does not know God's only way of escape.

In hell, there is no mercy and no escape from the terrifying wrath of God. Once people enter, their doom is fixed forever, their anguish is never ending and the devil is ready to torment them in the flaming pit that was created especially for him (Matthew 25:41). They will realize they are there because they believed Satan's lie instead of God's truth. The dreadful consequences of dying under the curse of God with unforgiven sin is too much to fully comprehend. No one should enter into eternity without the Lord Jesus Christ. We must call sinners to repent and believe the Gospel while they still have life. Today is the day of salvation! God does not promise anyone tomorrow.

Jesus is The Object of Saving Faith

It is also essential to consider the object of faith. In Scripture, faith always requires an object. It is never *wishful thinking* or *faith in faith*. What I find fascinating is this: the instrument (faith) that once condemned man is the same instrument (faith) that God uses to justify man. When our first parents shifted their faith from God's Word to Satan's lie, the resulting act of disobedience was condemnation (Romans 5:16). Now when anyone shifts their faith from the word of another to the Word of God, the result is justification (John 5:24; Romans 5:1). The instrument of faith is the same, but the object is obviously different. When man disobeyed God's first command in the garden, it brought judgment and condemnation (Genesis 2:17). When man obeys the Lord Jesus Christ's first command "Repent and believe the Gospel", it brings justification and salvation (Mark 1:15). When the object of a man's faith is Jesus Christ and His Word, he receives the gift of His righteousness and a permanent right-standing before God (Romans 5:17-18; Hebrews 10:14).

We Must Trust Christ's Righteousness

Jesus Christ is the object of saving faith in which we trust, and it's His righteousness that we obtain. The righteousness of Christ is man's only passport to heaven. His righteousness is what every man will need on judgment day (Matthew 5:48). Yet the unbelieving world does not know that God's righteousness requires perfect righteousness (Romans 10:1-4). All those who suppress God's truth in unrighteousness will stand before the judgment seat in the filthy rags of their own righteousness and suffer God's wrath forever (Isaiah 64:6; Romans 1:18).

One of Satan's most popular and fatal lies seduces gullible people who have not spent much time in the Bible. He deceives many with a works-righteousness salvation. They flatter themselves by thinking they can appease God with all they have done. They believe their good works will outweigh their bad deeds on judgment day. Nothing could be further from the truth. Apart from Christ, every man stands condemned to divine justice. "He who does not believe has been judged already, because he has not believed in the name of the only begotten Son of God" (John 3:18). At the judgment seat of Christ, every mouth will be stopped and no one will be justified by the deeds of the law (Romans 3:19-20).

The Law Reveals that our Righteousness is Not Enough

The law of God clearly shows that, "Now it is evident that no one is justified before God by the law, for 'The righteous shall live by faith'" (Galatians 3:11). The law was not given to justify us but to condemn us by exposing our sins and rebellious acts against God (Romans 7:8-11). The law was given to stop our boasting and show us how desperately we need God's mercy. Even if we were nearly perfect in obeying the law, we would still be cursed. "For whoever keeps the whole law and yet stumbles in one point, he has become guilty of all" (James 2:10). The law was given to break our stubborn pride and to lead us to Jesus Christ as our only hope of acquittal. "The law was our schoolmaster to bring us unto Christ, that we might be justified by faith" (Galatians 3:24).

What the Lord Jesus Christ Commands and Promises

As noted before, Jesus began His earthly ministry and commanded everyone to "repent and believe the Gospel." To those who respond, He promises justification. It is critical to understand what justification is and is NOT. Below is a contrast between what the Roman Catholic Church teaches and what Scripture teaches regarding this important doctrine of justification.

CATHOLICISM TEACHES	SCRIPTURE TEACHES
Justification is God's act of making man righteous by good works and obedience	Justification is God's act of declaring a sinner righteous by faith
Infused sanctifying grace through the sacraments makes the believer acceptable to God	Christ's imputed righteousness makes the believer acceptable to God
Justification is achieved by faith plus good works	Justification is received by faith alone
Justification is granted the sinner when he is actually made just	Justification enables God to see the sinner as if he were just
Justification can be increased by receiving more sacraments	Justification cannot increase since the ground is the perfect righteousness of Christ
Justification is affected by sin	Justification is a permanent verdict and is not affected by sin
Final justification is not determined until death	Justification comes at the moment of faith in Jesus Christ
The ground of justification is the righteousness of the person	The ground of justification is the righteousness of Jesus Christ
Sanctification and justification are similar	Justification precedes sanctification
Emphasis is on the sacraments	Emphasis is on God's verdict

Who Holds the Keys to Salvation?

Within the Roman Catholic tradition, doctrines have developed that give the papacy authority to delegate the power to forgive or retain sins through a sacramental system of penance and absolution. The Catholic Encyclopedia states, "The power to confer or withhold forgiveness might well be viewed as the opening and shutting of the gates of heaven." It was used both as "admission to" as well as "excommunication from" the kingdom. The power to "bind and loose" also gives the Popes authority to pronounce doctrinal judgments, making disciplinary decisions in the Church and even canonize saints. This authority and power prescribes what and who Catholics must believe and how and when they must worship. But is this what the Bible teaches?

Two thousand years ago, Jesus said to Peter, "I will give you the keys of the kingdom of heaven; whatever you bind on earth will be bound in heaven, and whatever you loose on earth will be loosed in heaven." This reference to the "keys of the kingdom" is found only in Matthew 16:19; however, the authority to "bind and loose" is given to all the disciples in Matthew 18:18. Many biblical scholars believe the "keys" are symbols representing the authority to govern and minister theocratic principles on earth. However, the interpretation of this verse has been the subject of debate for hundreds of years.

The Vatican teaches that Peter's keys have been handed down to his successors throughout the centuries. This has given credence to the papacy to govern the kingdom of God, which they believe, is the Roman Catholic Church. As a result, Peter and his successors are said to have special spiritual powers as Christ's representative on earth.

Proponents of the Roman Catholic tradition point to history as supporting evidence for their interpretation of the "keys of the kingdom." However, most of their historical support comes from tradition dating back only to the fourth century.

An accurate historical and grammatical interpretation must consider the use of terms at the time of the writing of the original text. The concept of the kingdom and the keys must be understood from their usage in the first century. Peter and the disciples understood the kingdom to be the visible rule of Christ over the earth, not the spiritual rule of Christ over His invisible church (Acts 1:6; Rev. 20:2-5). The king would rule from Jerusalem, free Israel from political bondage, and destroy her enemies. After Israel rejected the offer of the kingdom, Christ began to teach about it from a different perspective. He taught that part of God's plan would be a mystery, invisible, and progressive. This part would be both present and future, and could be entered only by regeneration. The kingdom would not be limited to Israel, but a new entity called the church, would now proclaim the good news of God's redemptive rule.

Previously, in Luke 11:52, Jesus denounced the Pharisees for misrepresenting God and the Scriptures with a religion of their own making. As a result, they were shutting the kingdom of heaven in men's faces. "Woe to you experts in the law, because you have taken away the key to knowledge. You yourselves have not entered, and you have hindered those who were entering." Israel's religious leaders were rejecting God's plan to usher in the kingdom at that point of time. Yet the Lord knew this would be the case, for He has always declared the end from the beginning (Isaiah 46:10).

Therefore, after the events of Pentecost, when the church was formed, Christ's teaching and the indwelling Holy Spirit gave the disciples a clearer understanding of this aspect of God's plan. The real authority of the keys given by Christ is ultimately in the revelation of God's principles from the Scriptures for His theocratic kingdom. Men of God were able to discern the correctness of doctrine and practice using the whole counsel of God (Acts 17:11).

The ultimate power to open and close the gates of heaven is the Gospel, which "is the power of God for the salvation of all who believe" (Romans 1:16). Peter's first proclamation of the Gospel on the Day of Pentecost, in Acts 2, opened the door of the kingdom to thousands. Since then, the disciples, and all Christians who have succeeded them, have been opening and closing the doors of the kingdom with the Gospel. Those who hear it and believe it are forgiven (loosed) of their sin and enter the kingdom, while those who reject the Gospel remain unforgiven (bound) of their sins and cannot enter the kingdom (John 3:36).

The contrast between the Catholic interpretation of the "keys of the kingdom" and the historical-grammatical interpretation is significant. One centers around the teachings of men and is based on tradition and reason, while the other centers around the Word of God and is based on His revealed will and reign.

Chapter 3

THE PERSON OF THE GOSPEL

—⟞∞⟞—

R eligious polls taken in America show that most Americans say they believe in Jesus. However, a much smaller percentage of people say they are born-again Christians. How can so many people be deceived or deluded? It is no wonder the Apostle Paul exhorted his readers to "examine yourselves as to whether you are in the faith" (2 Cor. 13:5). We are to test ourselves and encourage others to do the same. The test: have we believed the true Jesus as He is revealed in the Scriptures or a "Jesus" who has been created by the imagination of men?

If anyone hears the message about Christ and His Kingdom and does not understand it, the evil one comes and snatches it away (Matthew 13:19). But the one who hears the Word of Christ and understands it will share the good news with many others, bringing them to a saving knowledge of Christ (Matthew 13:23). The good news is the Gospel of Jesus Christ which has the power to save all who believe it (Romans 1:16). What a clear and profound message from the Paul's letter to the Romans:

> If you confess with your mouth Jesus as Lord, and believe in your heart that God raised Him from the dead, you will be saved; for with the heart a person believes, resulting in righteousness, and with the mouth he confesses, resulting in salvation. For the Scripture says, "Whoever believes in Him will not be disappointed."

For there is no distinction between Jew and Greek; for the same Lord is Lord of all, abounding in riches for all who call on Him; for "Whoever will call on the name of the Lord will be saved". (Romans 10:9-13)

Many Catholics do not understand who Christ is because the official teachings of the Roman Catholic Church paint a different picture of Him than what is revealed in the Sacred Scriptures. The Catechism of the Catholic Church (CCC), paragraph 2027, declares that we attain our own salvation and co-operate in saving our brothers through prayer and good works. Was Christ merely "the gate opener" of heaven, or was He the Savior? If we can attain our own salvation, then why did Christ have to die for us? Is Christ the only sinless Mediator between God and man, or does He share that role with Mary as Roman Catholicism teaches? When Mary was "taken up to heaven, she did not lay aside her saving office, but by her manifold intercession, continues to bring us the gifts of eternal salvation" (CCC 494).

Is Jesus the only Way to the Father, or are Muslims, who reject the deity of Christ, also part of God's plan of salvation as Catholicism teaches (CCC 841)? Should we believe the Dogmas of the Catholic Church that nullify the sufficiency of His perfect sacrifice, His grace, and His Word? Rome teaches, "In the supremely wise arrangement of God, sacred Tradition, sacred Scripture and the Magisterium of the Church are so connected and associated that one of them cannot stand without the other" (CCC 95).

There are distinctive truths about Jesus Christ declared in Scripture that set Him apart from any and all religious figures. Essential and foundational to the Gospel is an accurate understanding of Jesus Christ, the eternal Son of God.

Jesus is the Eternal God

Throughout the Bible, the divine nature of Jesus and His eternal existence is proclaimed.

In the beginning was the Word, and the Word was with God, and the Word was God. And the Word became flesh, and dwelt among us, and we saw His glory, glory as of the only begotten from the Father. (John 1:1, 14)

We see from these verses that He is distinct from God and at the same time God. He is the eternal Son of God, the second person of the triune God. John later affirmed that Jesus Christ "is the true God" (1 John 5:20). Even the doubting apostle Thomas addressed the resurrected Jesus as "my Lord and my God" (John 20:28). Paul said of Jesus, "In Him all the fullness of Deity dwells in bodily form" (Col. 2:9). Those who believe Jesus is one of many gods or that He was a man who became God have been woefully deceived and must repent of these fatal lies.

Jesus is Our Creator

Paul wrote, "By Him all things were created...all things have been created through Him and for Him" (Colossians 1:15-16). "All things came into being through Him, and apart from Him nothing came into being that has come into being" (John 1:3). Since mankind is the Lord's crowning work of creation, our only rightful attitude toward Jesus should be one of complete dependence, worship and submission. Those who recognize their accountability to their Creator and trust Him become a new creation (2 Corinthians 5:17). They are re-created "according to God, in true righteousness and holiness" (Ephesians 4:24).

Jesus is Sovereign Lord

All authority has been given to the Lord Jesus, and He rules over His entire creation (Psalm 103:19; Matthew 28:18). The sovereign authority given to Jesus by His Father is absolute and universal. During His earthly ministry, He demonstrated His authority over diseases, demons, sin, death and nature. He also has the judicial authority to condemn men to eternal death or give them eternal life. Professing Jesus as sovereign Lord is not an option but an essential confession for salvation. Paul declared: "If you confess with your mouth Jesus as Lord, and believe in your heart that God raised Him from the dead, you shall be saved...whoever calls upon the name of the Lord shall be saved" (Romans 10:9-13). Confessing Jesus as Lord should result in humble submission to His divine authority (Philippians 2:10-11).

Jesus is the Way

Those who are lost need to know the way. Jesus is *the* Way and not *a* way. When people follow Jesus Christ, they can be certain they are "going right", but if they follow any other way, they may never know they are "going wrong." The Lord Jesus came "to seek and to save that which was lost" (Luke 19:10). Lost sheep will listen for the voice of the Good Shepherd, and they will follow Him (John 10:3-9). He is the door the sheep must enter to be saved (John 10:9).

God's one and only way to eternal life is through His Son (John 14:6). That is why the most frequent command the Lord gives in the Gospels is "Follow Me!" His mandate is given "because narrow is the gate and difficult is the way which leads to life, and there are few who find it" (Matthew 7:14). Oh, there is another way which seems right to men, but it leads to death (Proverbs 14:12). Those who do not follow Jesus spend their lives wandering aimlessly on the broad way which leads to destruction (Matthew 7:13). Following Jesus is the only sure way to keep people from going to hell; however, there is absolutely no way to rescue anyone out of hell (Hebrews 9:27).

Jesus is the Truth

People need truth because we are easily taken "captive through philosophy and empty deception according to the tradition of men and the elementary principles of the world" (Colossians 2:8). For this reason, Jesus came into the world to bear witness to the truth (John 18:37). Our Lord said, "If you abide in My Word, then you are truly disciples of Mine; and you shall know the truth, and the truth shall make you free" (John 8:31-32). Jesus sets people free from the bondage of religious deception.

Jesus is the personification of truth, and His Word is truth (John 14:6; 17:17). He and His Word are so connected that those who reject His Word are also rejecting Him (John 12:48). The personification of truth can only be known in truth by those who seek the truth from the only infallible source for truth. We need a trustworthy standard for truth because Satan leads the whole world astray through his false teachers (1 John 5:19; Revelation 12:9). The only way to discern God's truth from Satan's lies is to abide in God's Word. To use any other standard is a fatal mistake.

Jesus is the Life

Jesus is the life we need because everyone is born into this world spiritually dead. The spiritual death we inherit from Adam leads to eternal death unless we are born again (Romans 5:12). It is for this reason Jesus announced, "Unless one is born again, he cannot see the kingdom of God" (John 3:3). A description of this second birth is explained by Paul: "When you were dead in your transgressions... He made you alive together with Him, having forgiven us all our transgressions (Colossians 2:13). When one is born again, he receives the very life of Christ, who can never die again (Romans 6:6-9). Jesus declared, "He who has the Son has the life; he who does not have the Son of God does not have the life" (1 John 5:12). The Lord Jesus sovereignly gives life to whom He wishes. At the very moment repentant sinners receive the love of the truth and believe, they pass out of death into life (John 5:21-24). The life Jesus promises is eternal, everlasting, never-ending life in His presence (1 John 2:25).

Jesus is the Only Mediator

A mediator is necessary whenever two parties are at enmity with one another. The Lord Jesus is the only one qualified to mediate between His Father and sinful man. He is God's perfect man and man's perfect God. "There is one God, and one mediator also between God and men, the man Christ Jesus" (1 Timothy 2:5). "When we were enemies we were reconciled to God through the death of His Son" (Romans 5:10). He changes the relationship that repentant sinners have with God from one of hostility to one of peace and harmony. "For He Himself is our peace, who... broke down the barrier of the dividing wall, by abolishing in His flesh the enmity... through the cross" (Ephesians 2:13-16). Only in Christ Jesus can those who were formerly far off be brought near by the blood of Christ. Only in Christ can the sin that separated us from God be removed (Isaiah 59:2). Only in Christ can believers be permanently reconciled to God (Romans 8:31-39). He is God's Perfect Man and man's Perfect God.

Jesus is the Only Savior

The Lord said, "Besides me there is no Savior" (Isaiah 43:11). Peter proclaimed: "There is salvation in no one else; for there is no other name under heaven that has been given among men, by which we must be saved" (Acts 4:12). Jesus, the eternal God, is the only Savior, because finite man could never pay his own, or another's eternal debt for sin. The Bible makes this clear. "No man can by any means redeem his brother or give to God a ransom for him; the redemption of his soul is costly, and he should cease trying forever" (Psalm 49:7- 8). The redemption of a sinner's soul requires that every sinner must turn to Christ for salvation. This was the ministry our Lord gave to Paul sending him to turn people "from darkness to light and from the dominion of Satan to God, that they may receive forgiveness of sins and an inheritance among those who have been sanctified by faith in Me" (Acts 26:18).

Knowing the attributes and claims of the Lord Jesus Christ, we are all faced with this vital decision. What will we do with Him? "He who believes in the Son has eternal life; but he who does not obey the Son will not see life, but the wrath of God abides on him" (John 3:36). Those who trust and follow Jesus choose:

Life over death

Justification over condemnation

Freedom over bondage

Light over darkness

Peace over hostility

Joy over despair

Sight over blindness

Truth over deception

Those who deny that Jesus is who He said He is make a fatal mistake. Our Lord said, "Unless you believe that I am He, you will die in your sins" (John 8:24).

May God help us all to grow in the grace and knowledge of our Savior, not only to glorify Him, but to proclaim Him wholly and clearly to those who are being deluded or deceived.

What Jesus Christ Accomplished

Understanding the nature and identity of Jesus Christ is foundational. The next question is equally important: What did He accomplish?

The Scriptures reveal that Jesus is the Savior who appeared "to take away sin once for all by his sacrifice" (Hebrew 9:26). As we have seen, Jesus is the only one qualified to save us. He has to be both God and man. Only as God could His sacrifice produce the infinite value needed to save all men for all time. Only a man could be our kinsman-redeemer. And only a man who lived a sinless life could die for someone else. Otherwise he would have to die for his own sin. It is clear that God provided the only way possible for us to be saved. He became man, lived a perfect life, and willingly paid the death penalty for sin that His justice demanded.

Scripture is clear regarding Christ alone as the only means for salvation and the only mediator between God and man. "There is no salvation in anyone else, for there is no other name in the whole world given to men which we are to be saved," (Acts 4:12). There is no other mediator between God and man: "God is one, one also is the mediator between God and men, the man Christ Jesus" (1 Timothy 2:5). The importance of believing who Christ is can best be summed up by the words of Christ Himself, "You will surely die in your sins unless you come to believe who I am" (John 8:24). Those who believe salvation can be obtained by adding to the perfect, finished, and all-sufficient work of the Lord Jesus Christ must repent and come to the cross with empty hands of faith, bringing nothing but their sins (2 Tim. 2:24-26). Adding human achievement to grace nullifies God's saving grace which is the only way God saves sinners (Rom. 11:6).

What Did Jesus Have to Do to Save Sinners?

The forgiveness of sins is a marvelous and humbling act of mercy and grace by our great and holy God. In our proclamation of the Gospel, it is important that we never overlook the importance of sharing all that the Lord Jesus had to do to save sinners completely and forever.

A question I often ask people who attend various churches is this: Why did Jesus have to die? Few people give the right answer from Scripture. Most will say, "Because He loved us." It is true that love was His motivation for dying, but it does not explain why He had to die. Some will say, "He died to forgive us." Then I will ask, "Why couldn't He just forgive us without dying?" It is because His holy law demands death as the punishment for sin (Romans 6:23). "The soul who sins shall die" (Ezekiel 18:4). The sinless Savior went to the cross to die as a substitute for sinners, who deserve the death penalty for their sins. Divine justice had to be satisfied, because our holy and righteous Judge in heaven must punish every sin that has been, and ever will ever be, committed. There is not one sin that will ever go unpunished. Any judge who pardons law-breakers by letting the guilty go free is not a righteous judge.

Jesus was born to die. "The Son of Man came...to give his life as a ransom for many" (Mark 10:45). He was delivered up to be crucified according to the definite plan and foreknowledge of God (Acts 2:23). This was to demonstrate His righteousness, so that He might be just and the justifier of the one who has faith in Jesus (Romans 3:26). Since God's laws were broken and His righteous wrath was provoked, it had to be satisfied by Christ before divine forgiveness could be applied to sinners. Dying as a substitute for sinners, the Lord Jesus paid the eternal debt for sin. He satisfied the demands of justice while appeasing God's wrath, so that He could extend mercy and grace to those who trust Him. God's perfect Son satisfied divine justice when "God made Him (Christ), who knew no sin, to be sin" for those who would trust Him (2 Corinthians 5:21). He cancelled the record of debt that stood against us with its legal demands (Colossians 2:14).

For those who die having rejected the Lord Jesus Christ as their Savior, divine justice will be satisfied in the eternal fires of hell. Since all sin is committed against an infinitely holy and majestic God, the punishment must be infinite. Therefore, the wrath of God is poured out in an everlasting fire. No tears can quench the flame of God's anger. Unrepentant sinners will be in the fiery furnace forever. There is no escape because God is "a consuming fire" (Hebrews 12:29). He "feels indignation every day" toward the wicked, because He has "hated wickedness" (Psalm 7:11; 45:7). Anyone who rejects God's only provision for their sin is choosing to suffer God's eternal wrath. Tragically, there are many who stubbornly refuse to seek wisdom from God's Word. "Whoever trusts in his own mind is a fool, but he who walks in wisdom will be delivered" (Proverbs 28:26). Christ Jesus is not only "wisdom from God", but also, "righteousness and sanctification and redemption" to those who trust Him (1 Corinthians 1:30). "There is therefore now no condemnation for those who are in Christ Jesus" (Romans 8:1). What a glorious Savior!

Following are eight important accomplishments of our great God and Savior that we can discuss when sharing the Gospel and fulfilling our role as ambassadors for Christ.

1. *Righteousness had to be perfected*—Jesus lived a perfect and sinless life so that His righteousness could be given as a gift to those who believe (Romans 5:17). His righteousness is man's only passport into heaven, because there are none righteous. Condemned sinners can only be justified by faith in Christ (Romans 3:9-26).

2. *Divine justice had to be satisfied*—God poured out the full measure of His righteous wrath upon His Son, who bore the sins of His people on the cross (1 Peter 2:24). Sin could not be overlooked. Justice had to be served. The holy character of God would not allow a change to His standard of justice or to dismiss the charges against men. Sin had to be punished with death (Romans 6:23).

3. *Blood had to be shed* —The scarlet thread of blood began in the garden right after Adam and Eve tried to cover their sin with the works of their hands. Since life is in the blood and the punishment of sin is death, blood had to be shed as a covering for sin until Christ shed His precious blood. Without the shedding of blood there is no forgiveness of sins (Hebrews 9:22). The blood of Jesus cleanses us from all sin (1 John 1:7).

4. *Sins had to be forgiven*—Finite men can never cancel the eternal debt for sin, which is why hell is eternal. It took the eternal Son of God to become a man to forgive the eternal debt. He canceled the certificate of debt consisting of decrees against us, which was hostile to us; and He has taken it out of the way, having nailed it to the cross (Colossians 2:13-14).

5. *Redemption had to be paid* —Since all men are born as slaves to sin, a ransom had to be paid to set them free from sin's bondage and power. The Lord Jesus paid the ultimate price of redemption with His precious blood (Ephesians 1:7; 1 Peter 1:18-19). Jesus entered the holy place once for all, having obtained eternal redemption (Hebrews 9:12).

6. *Reconciliation had to be achieved*—Reconciliation was necessary because sin had separated all men from God. He is the one mediator that brings reconciliation between repentant sinners and our holy God (1 Timothy 2:5). Those who were far off have been brought near through Jesus Christ (Ephesians 2:13).

7. *Resurrection had to be witnessed*—If Christ was not raised from the dead, the Christian faith would be without hope. Death would not have been conquered, and the deity of Christ would not have been validated. His resurrection assures the resurrection of every believer (1 Corinthians 15:54-55). Jesus said, I am the resurrection and the life; he who believes in Me will live even if he dies (John 11:25).

8. *Salvation had to be secured*—Every believer is secure in Christ, who promises an inheritance which is imperishable and undefiled and will not fade away (1 Peter 1:4-5). The glory of salvation is assured because of God's omnipotent power and promises.

As we consider the ultimate sacrifice of our precious Savior and all that He endured for our salvation, let us encourage one another to be more faithful to His great commission. The reason there is a Great Commission is because sinners need the Gospel.

Our Lord's Victory Cry, "It Is Finished!"

The night before the Lord Jesus Christ went to the cross, He prayed to His Father that He had "finished the work you have given me to do" (John 17:4). When we consider all that He had to do to save sinners, His victory cry, "It is finished," speaks volumes. Righteousness had to be perfected, divine justice had to be satisfied, blood had to be shed, redemption had to be paid, sins had to be forgiven, reconciliation had to be accomplished, death had to be conquered, salvation had to be secured, and heaven had to be opened. All this was perfectly accomplished so that eternal life could be offered as a free gift of God's grace to those who trust the all-sufficient Savior.

Only when sinners realize their hopeless and helpless condition can they begin to understand the glorious promises revealed in the Gospel of Jesus Christ. Everything that man could never do was completely accomplished by our Lord Jesus Christ. His mission to seek and to save the lost culminated on the cross. The work of salvation was finished. The eternal sin debt was paid in full. Since it was an eternal debt, it was impossible for man to pay. But God forgave us "all our trespasses, by canceling the record of debt that stood against us with its legal demands. This he set aside, nailing it to the cross" (Col. 2:13-14).

Jesus "appeared once for all at the end of the ages to put away sin by the sacrifice of himself" (Hebrews 9:26). Yet Catholicism rejects the Word of God by teaching that a Catholic must do "something more to make amends for the sin: he must 'make satisfaction for' or 'expiate' his sins. This satisfaction is called 'penance'" (CCC, par. 1459). What a terrible deception this is for faithful Roman Catholics who look to their church, rather than the Bible, for truth! By adding to the perfect and sufficient work of Christ they have nullified God's grace, which is the only means by which God saves sinners (Rom. 11:6). The very purpose Christ became our kinsman redeemer and suffered an excruciating death was to expiate sin, once and for all, by His perfect sacrifice.

Roman Catholicism also rejects another finished work of Christ: the purification of sins. God's Word declares "when He had made purification of sins, He sat down at the right hand of the Majesty on high" (Heb. 1:3). Those who trust Christ alone are purified from *all* sin, by His blood (1 John 1:7). Catholicism denies the efficacy of Christ's blood and instead offers a place called "purgatory." It states: "every sin, even venial, entails an unhealthy attachment to creatures, which must be purified either here on earth, or after death in the state called Purgatory" (CCC, par. 1472). How can a religion which names the name of Christ reject His precious blood for a fictitious place that robs Him of His glory?

After finishing His all-sufficient work on the cross, Jesus now offers His righteousness as a gift to all who believe (Rom. 5:17). The only way to receive the gift is by faith in Christ alone. Those who are blinded by religious deception must do what the Apostle Paul did. He exchanged his religion for a relationship with Christ. He wrote: "I count everything as loss because of the surpassing worth of knowing Christ Jesus my Lord. For his sake I have suffered the loss of all things and count them as rubbish, in order that I may gain Christ and be found in him, not having a righteousness of my own that comes from the law, but that which comes through faith in Christ, the righteousness from God that depends on faith" (Phil. 3:8-9).

The Finished Work of Christ for His People

Here is a portion of what Jesus accomplished in His finished work of redemption. Each point is a glorious truth for meditation and contemplation. What a glorious and all-sufficient Savior we have in Christ Jesus!

He testified to the truth; listen to Him! (John 14:6; 18:37; Acts 3:22)

He came to give life to people who are spiritually dead. (John 14:6)

He gave us access to the Father. (John 14:6; Matthew 27:51)

He gave His life as a ransom for many. (Matthew 20:28)

He bore our sins in His body on a tree. (1 Peter 2:24)

He died for the ungodly. (Romans 5:6)

He gave Himself up for us as a sacrifice to God. (Ephesians 5:2)

He died so that we may live together with Him. (1 Thessalonians 5:9-10)

He gave Himself for us to purify His people. (Titus 2:14)

He died for sins, once for all, to bring us to God. (1 Peter 3:18)

He exchanged our sin for His righteousness. (2 Corinthians 5:21)

He has forgiven all our sins. (Colossians 1:14)

He purified us from all sins. (1 John 1:7; Hebrews 1:3)

He has reconciled us to God. (Ephesians 2:14-18)

He redeemed us from the power of sin. (Galatians 3:10-14)

He saved us from condemnation. (John 3:18, 5:24)

He delivered us from darkness into His kingdom. (Colossians 1:13)

He satisfied divine justice for our sin. (1 John 2:2)

He made us into new creations. (2 Corinthians 5:17)

He is the only Name by which man can be saved. (Acts 4:12)

Chapter 4

THE EXCLUSIVITY OF THE GOSPEL

———⟨∞⟩———

What is the greatest attack on the church today? That was the weighty question asked of the speakers at a conference I attended. I promptly responded, "The greatest attack we are seeing today is on the exclusivity and purity of the Gospel." The exclusivity of the Gospel declares all other faiths are false, because no one can come to God except through the atoning death of Jesus Christ (John 14:6; Acts 4:12). The exclusivity of the Gospel also humbles the pride of self-righteous people and calls them to repentance.

This is why many pastors are compromising the Gospel. They want to make it more inclusive in order to draw a larger following, gain more influence, and be loved by more people. This man-pleasing Gospel makes people comfortable in their sin, but it has no power to save them. It has become popular because it exalts man and his importance and diminishes God and His significance. It also emphasizes God's love while ignoring His holiness, justice, and hatred of sin.

Tragically, those who embrace this diluted Gospel are woefully deceived and remain dead in their sins. Equally tragic is the willingness of born-again Christians to put up with another Gospel. Paul exhorts them to repent of such apathy with a sharp rebuke: "If someone comes and proclaims another Jesus than the one we proclaimed, or if you receive a different spirit from the one you received, or if you accept a different Gospel from the one you accepted, you put up with it readily enough" (2 Corinthians 11:4). The only thing worse than a Christian without discernment is one who has discernment but refuses to use it to challenge professing Christians in their unfruitful lives. Those who have been deceived will not know it unless they are lovingly confronted with the truth. They must be reproved in order to become sound in the faith (Titus 1:13).

Many Christians are unaware of their responsibility to judge and test all things. Paul commended the Bereans for rightfully judging his teaching. "They received the word with great eagerness, examining the Scriptures daily, to see whether these things were so" (Acts 17:10-11). The apostle John exhorted Christians to make judgments concerning doctrinal and spiritual issues: "Beloved, do not believe every spirit, but test the spirits to see whether they are from God; because many false prophets have gone out into the world" (1 John 4:1). Clearly, all Christians are called to judge righteously by using the Word of God as the plumb line for discerning truth from error. And judge we must, because the "father of lies" deals in half-truths, and his fatal lies are often coated with a thin veneer of truth to deceive the unsuspecting (John 8:44).

Spiritual discernment is a discipline and a privilege that only born-again Christians can exercise. Paul wrote: "But the natural man does not receive the things of the Spirit of God, for they are foolishness to him; nor can he know them, because they are spiritually discerned. But he who is spiritual judges all things." (1 Corinthians 2:14-16). The ability to make judgments is a mark of Christian maturity. "Solid food is for the mature, who because of practice have their senses trained to discern good and evil" (Hebrews 5:14). By practicing discernment, we are able to guard and protect the Gospel for the next generation.

As we practice discernment, we must make sure our motives are Christ-honoring. Our objective must be to obey God's

Word in the spirit of love for the purpose of helping, healing, correcting, warning and sharing in the spirit of love. When our motives are pure, people will be encouraged to love the truth and hate what is false (Psalm 119:104). Pure motives will result in contending for the purity of the Gospel and the sanctity of our Lord's Church!

There is no more critical issue in the Church today than guarding the purity of the Gospel. It is the rudder that must guide the Church through stormy waters that have been stirred up by every wind of doctrine (Ephesians 4:14). Churches that do not provide a steady diet of God's Word will become entertainment centers for goats instead of sanctuaries for the Shepherd's sheep (Matthew 25:32). When doctrinal truth is being withheld, ignored, denied, or rejected, it will produce fertile ground for deception. The only way people will know if they have true faith or a false hope is to discern the true Gospel from a false Gospel. It is the responsibility of every born again Christian to make disciples and challenge false converts to examine their faith.

The Battle for Truth

Let us be mindful of the words of A.W. Tozer, who wrote: "So skilled is error at imitating truth that the two are constantly being mistaken for each other. It is therefore critically important that the Christian take full advantage of every provision God has made to save him from delusion—prayer, faith, constant meditation of the Scriptures, obedience, humility and the illumination of the Holy Spirit" (*That Incredible Christian*).

We need to ask God for courage and boldness as we rely on the power of His Word. May we all become more like the apostles who were strong, bold, fearless, dogmatic, unaccommodating of error, courageous, intolerant of sin, inflexible concerning the Gospel, controversial, willing to die for the truth and fully devoted to Christ. We are no longer to be children, tossed here and there by waves and carried about by the trickery of men, by craftiness in deceitful scheming (Ephesians 4:14). During these times of great deception, the Body of Christ must respond with a theological, biblical worldview that defends the glory and honor of our Lord Jesus Christ. We must protect the purity of His Gospel for the sake of His elect.

Claims of Exclusivity Are Resisted and Ridiculed

Claims of exclusivity are often met with great resistance in societies where different religious paths are accepted as equally valid. Christians who communicate the exclusivity of their faith will experience this in a variety of ways. They are either dismissed, ridiculed, mocked, or considered intolerant. These responses to the Gospel have been occurring for 2000 years. Paul wrote: "we preach Christ crucified, to Jews a stumbling block and to Gentiles foolishness" (1 Corinthians 1:23).

Why is there so much antagonism toward the Gospel of Jesus Christ? It is because people do not want to be told there is only one way to heaven in a society deeply influenced by pluralism and postmodernism. Yet when it comes to the Gospel, Christians must contend for its purity and exclusivity (Galatians 1:6-9). The call for ecumenical unity among all "professing Christians" must be met with determined opposition. We know that "truth" is exclusive and cannot be compromised because "No lie is of the truth" (1 John 2:21). Truth is as incompatible with error as light is with darkness. Any teaching which contradicts or opposes biblical truth is false, and it must be exposed for what it is. As Christians, we cannot be passive or indifferent towards any distortion of the Gospel. We must contend earnestly for the faith (Jude 3).

The Gospel is exclusive because it is about only one Person and two historical events (1 Corinthians 15:1-4). It reveals the good news of man's redemption, which was accomplished by the eternal Son of God incarnate, through His atoning sacrificial death and glorious resurrection from the dead. The

Gospel is a unique and eternal message (Revelation 14:6). It is the same message for every generation and must be proclaimed, protected and defended. The exclusivity of the Gospel affirms the exclusivity of the Lord Jesus Christ.

Only One Savior

The apostle Peter proclaimed this exclusive statement to an already hostile audience: "There is salvation in no one else; for there is no other name under heaven that has been given among men by which we must be saved" (Acts 4:12).

Only One Mediator

The apostle Paul made this exclusive declaration: "For there is one God, and one mediator also between God and men, the man Christ Jesus" (1 Timothy 2:5).

Only One Way

The Lord Jesus declared, "I am the way, and the truth, and the life; no one comes to the Father but through Me" (John 14:6). He said, "the way is narrow that leads to life, and there are few who find it" (Matthew 7:14).

Only One Source of Eternal Life

The apostle John declared: "God has given us eternal life, and this life is in His Son. He who has the Son has the life; he who does not have the Son of God does not have the life" (1 John 5:11-12). John also said, "He who believes in the Son has eternal life; but he who does not obey the Son will not see life, but the wrath of God abides on him" (John 3:36).

Only One Exemption from Judgment

Jesus satisfied divine justice as the sinless substitute for all believers. "He who believes in Him is not judged; he who does not believe has been judged already, because he has not believed in the name of the only begotten Son of God" (John 3:18).

The Gospel is also exclusive because it is the only message with the divine power and promises to reverse the curse of sin (Rom. 1:16; 8:21). How can Christians communicate the exclusivity of the Gospel effectively in our religiously pluralistic society? We need to understand that the Gospel is offensive to those who are offensive to God. It humbles people under the sovereign hand of God and strips them of their own righteousness. We must tell them they have broken God's law, they are condemned by God's justice, they deserve God's wrath, they need God's mercy, and their only hope is God's Son.

Attacks on the Gospel's Exclusivity

The greatest attacks on the Gospel today are the frequent attempts by evangelicals to make it more inclusive to everyone who has ever been baptized. Many are seeking to broaden the narrow road by embracing and promoting apostate forms of Christianity. Some undiscerning Christians have been seduced by the pope's aggressive ecumenical agenda to reverse the Reformation and unite all professing Christians under the papacy. Part of the pope's strategy is to look for soft targets within the Evangelical Church who will promote Roman Catholicism as a valid expression of Christianity.

Tragically, his strategy has been successful and is gaining a great deal of traction. In recent years, Al Mohler, Carl Truman, Russell Moore and Matt Chandler have recommended a disturbingly popular book written by Rod Dreher, who is a major promoter of Roman Catholicism, ecumenical unity, and contemplative prayer. Dreher is a former Catholic who converted to the Eastern Orthodox religion, not because of Rome's false Gospel, but because of its sexual abuse scandal. His book, *The Benedict Option*, calls people of faith to emulate a sixth-century Catholic monk as an example of how to live in a collapsing culture. Almost all the heroes of *The Benedict Option* are Catholic monks who lived solitary lives in a monastery while participating in the daily sacrifice of a Eucharistic Christ.

Like most proponents of ecumenism, Dreher promotes subjective spiritual experiences over the objective truths of Scripture. He said he never had a problem with praying the rosary as a Catholic, and he now encourages his readers to practice contemplative prayer and mysticism. He said "my life is shaped around liturgy that's been in our church for 1500 years" and "on all kinds of sensual ways that embody the faith." His Eastern Orthodox religion preaches the same works-righteousness salvation as Catholicism and other religions. We are not to affirm or receive "anyone who goes too far and does not abide in the teaching of Christ" (2 John 9-10).

For Evangelical leaders to recommend a book that applauds the heretical people and traditions of Roman Catholicism, especially during the 500th anniversary of the Reformation, is lamentable. The prevailing influence of these leaders, along with their reluctance to guard sound doctrine and reject false Gospels, have left many Christians confused. They do not know if the Roman Catholic Church represents a huge mission field that needs to be evangelized or if it represents a valid expression of Christianity. They need to know that Catholicism has long been a bitter enemy of the Gospel of Christ. The apostate religion has not only condemned those who believe the Gospel, but brutally tortured and killed hundreds of thousands of those who refused to compromise it. Evangelical leaders who are sanctioning ecumenical unity with Catholics must be lovingly confronted in their error with the truth of God's Word.

In a troubling interview with Al Mohler, Dreher said, "the West owes an incalculable debt to those Benedictine monks." Mohler does acknowledge there are differences between their two faiths, but he said evangelicals can learn from people of the Orthodox and Catholic faith, who embrace a different Gospel. The apostle Paul did not encourage Christians to learn from the Judaizers, who were distorting the Gospel and leading them away from Christ (Galatians 1:6-9). Mohler says the book encourages living together in a way that is "truly Christian", yet he never defines what a true Christian is, or the Gospel that a true Christian must believe. Mohler stated, "The book is very important. I want to commend it to every thinking Christian. We ought to read this book, and we ought also to read far beyond the title." Yet, there was a glaring omission both in the book and in the interview by Mohler and Dreher. Neither one referenced the most powerful tools Jesus Christ gave us to fight the cultural wars—His Word and His Gospel (Hebrews 4:12; Romans 1:16).

Evangelicals who endorse a book that obfuscates the lines that once separated biblical Christianity from apostate Christianity are minimizing the powerful effect of error. The accommodation of doctrinal error and falsehood will always be dangerous to the life of the church, which is called to be sanctified by the truth (John 17:17). God's Word warns us to "be on your guard so that you are not carried away by the error of unprincipled men and fall from your own steadfastness" (2 Pet. 3:17). The critical issue in the church today is the purity of the Gospel. It is the rudder that must guide us through stormy waters that have been stirred up by every wind of doctrine (Eph. 4:14). Either we seek the approval of God by protecting the purity of the Gospel, or we seek the approval of men by applauding those who peddle another Gospel. There is no other "option."

As blood-bought Christians, we must contend earnestly for the faith and challenge those who embrace a false Gospel. If we fail to fight the good fight of faith, we leave our own convictions and beliefs open to question. There is so much more at stake than winning cultural wars. We are also fighting the age-old war against truth waged by the powers of darkness. The truth of God's Word is our only hope in a world spinning out of control. We must endeavor to defend the glory and honor of our Lord Jesus Christ, the purity of His Gospel, and the sanctity of His church.

Chapter 5

THE PROMISE OF THE GOSPEL

The glorious Gospel of God is the greatest news anyone could ever hear because it promises eternal life for those who repent and believe it. We can know right here and now, with absolute certainty, that the moment we die, we will enjoy the presence of God forever. Salvation is secured by God's faithfulness and power to all who trust the Lord Jesus Christ alone.

The apostle John, under the inspiration of the Holy Spirit, revealed this wonderful truth as the purpose for one of his letters, "I write these things to you who believe in the name of the Son of God so that you may know that you have eternal life" (1 John 5:13). Anyone who repents from trusting in things that cannot save them (Hebrews 6:1) and puts all their trust in Jesus will never face the condemnation of God's wrath. Jesus said, I tell you the truth, whoever hears my word and believes Him who sent me has eternal life and will not be condemned, he has crossed over from death to life" (John 5:24).

All believers have a special relationship with God. To all who have received Christ, "to those who believed in His name, He gave the right to become children of God—children not born of natural descent, nor of human decision or a husband's will, but born of God" (John 1:12-13). The relationship God the Father has with His children is an eternal relationship (John 8:35). It is permanent. Nothing will ever separate His children from His love (Romans 8:35-39). Our heavenly Father will discipline His children (Hebrews 12:10-11), but He will never condemn them. In a way, it is similar to the unchanging relationship we have with our earthly parents. Nothing we could ever do will change who our parents are.

Over half of professing Christianity denies or rejects the Gospel's promise of eternal life. Roman Catholicism goes so far as to call it a sin to presume that you are assured of eternal life. That's because Catholics are taught they receive salvation through water baptism, but they can lose it in an instant by committing a mortal sin. Only by confessing the sin to a priest and doing penance can they be justified again. This cycle is often repeated hundreds of times in a Catholic's life.

Many people go through life hoping they will go to heaven when they die. They hope, after living a good enough life, they will receive favor from God and a place in His Kingdom. Those who depend on their personal righteousness, performing good works, or adhering to a religious system, can never be assured of salvation. They will never know if they have ever done enough. It seems absurd to put your faith in what you can do instead of what God has done. Those who believe God's Word know that "salvation by grace" means to trust solely in the source of grace—Jesus Christ. When salvation depends on God, there is no chance for failure. A wonderful acronym for grace is:

God's
Riches
At
Christ's
Expense

Whenever man is involved in attaining and preserving salvation, there can be no assurance. We have assurance through the Father. Some believe it is possible to walk away from God or renounce your faith and lose your salvation. Jesus said no one has the power to do so. "I give them eternal life, and they shall never perish . . . My Father, who has given them to Me, is greater than all, no one can snatch them out of my Father's hand" (John 10:28-29). The Father has the power to assure the life Jesus gives is everlasting, not temporal or perishable.

We have assurance through Jesus Christ. Christians are often accused of being self-righteous and boastful because they know for sure they are going to heaven. The accusers fail to understand it is not what man does for God that qualifies him for heaven, but what God has done for man. God made His holy and perfect Son become sin for us, so we could become the righteousness of God in Christ (2 Corinthians 5:21). "We have been made holy through the sacrifice of the body of Jesus Christ, once for all...by one sacrifice he has made perfect forever those who are being made holy" (Hebrews 10:10,14).

The Catholic Church teaches that mortal sin results in the loss of eternal life. John refuted this teaching in his first epistle when he encouraged believers not to sin. "But if anybody does sin, we have one who speaks to the Father in our defense—Jesus Christ, the Righteous One. He is the atoning sacrifice for our sins" (1 John 2:1-2). This comforting truth is also revealed in Hebrews 7:25, "He (Jesus) is able to save completely those who come to God through Him, because He always lives to intercede for them."

We also have assurance through the Holy Spirit. Many skeptics refuse to believe that a repentant sinner can simply believe the Gospel and be assured of eternal life. Yet the Apostle Paul could not make it any clearer,

You also were included in Christ when you heard the word of truth, the Gospel of your salvation. Having believed, you were marked in him with a seal, the promised Holy Spirit, who is a deposit guaranteeing our inheritance (Ephesians 1:13-14).

The moment anyone understands and believes the Gospel, they are sealed and indwelt by the Holy Spirit, who guarantees they will be co-heirs with Christ (Romans 8:17).

We have assurance through God's promises that are upheld by His sovereign power. The gift of salvation is secured forever by the faithfulness of God. He promises never to take back the gifts He has given. "God's gifts and His call are irrevocable" (Romans 11:29). His "promise comes by faith, so that it may be by grace and may be guaranteed" to those who have the faith (Romans 4:16). "And if by grace, then it is no longer by works, if it were, grace would no longer be grace" (Romans 11:6). Paul is making it crystal clear that salvation can only be assured when a repentant sinner receives it as a gift of God's grace. Anyone who believes that salvation can be earned nullifies God's grace.

This may be your first exposure to the great biblical truth of eternal security. If you want to be certain of your salvation, then put aside any teaching, experience or feeling that opposes the Word of God. You will never have the subjective feeling of assurance until you comprehend and believe the objective truth of the Gospel. Once you do, you will be more certain of living eternally in heaven than one more day on earth.

When you read and study God's Word you will know that eternal life is secured by the:

Power of God – 1 Pet. 1:5

Promises of God – John 6:37

Perpetual Intercession of Jesus – Heb. 7:25

Proof of His Unconditional Love – Rom. 8:35

Protection of the Shepherd – John 10:27-30

Permanence of Divine Gifts - Rom. 11:29

Plain Meaning of the word "eternal" – 1 John 5:13

Words have meanings and the word "eternal" means everlasting. Consider all the places the word "eternal" is used to describe everything that is everlasting. Believers in the eternal Gospel have eternal redemption through the eternal Spirit who guarantees an eternal inheritance (Heb. 9:12; Eph. 1:14). Our eternal God's eternal purpose promises eternal life and eternal glory to His children in His eternal kingdom (Rev. 14:6; Rom. 16:26; 1 John 5:13; 1 Pet. 5:10; 2 Pet.1:11).

> If anyone rejects or denies God's promise of eternal life to those He has saved need to consider the following questions:
>
> How can one who has been made complete in Christ, become incomplete? (Col. 2:10).
>
> How can one, who has been born again of incorruptible seed, die again? (1 Pet. 1:23).
>
> How can one who is kept by the power of God ever fall away? (1 Pet. 1:5).
>
> How can one who has been perfected forever be found imperfect? (Heb. 10:14).
>
> How could God break His promise to glorify everyone He justifies? (Rom. 8:30)
>
> How can the Good Shepherd fail to protect and keep His sheep? (John 10:1-30)
>
> How can the proof of God's unconditional love be invalidated? (Rom. 8:31-39)

God accomplishes His eternal purpose because He has sovereign control over all His creation. He is able to do whatever He pleases according to His will. No one can defeat His counsel, thwart His purpose or resist His will. God directs the universe according to His foreordained plan. He said, "I am God, and there is none like me, declaring the end from the beginning ...My counsel shall stand, and I will accomplish all my purpose" (Isa. 46:10).

Chapter 6

THE COMPROMISE OF THE GOSPEL

Following any discussion on maintaining the purity and exclusivity of the Gospel must include a warning to those who are compromising the Gospel for the sake of ecumenical unity. There is an ongoing attempt to reconcile the opposing views of the Gospel among Protestants and Catholics. In recent years, two notable attempts to resolve differences between Evangelicals and Catholics should raise concerns for all who hold to salvation by grace alone, through faith alone in Christ alone.

Unity and harmony between Evangelicals and Roman Catholics were the objectives of the declaration entitled "*Evangelicals and Catholics Together: The Christian Mission in the Third Millennium.*" While it may have united those who endorsed the agreement, it has created lingering discord and controversy in the Evangelical community. Many believe it has blurred the biblical distinctions of the Gospel and set the mission of the church back 500 years. On March 29, 1994, Evangelicals, including Chuck Colson, Bill Bright, Pat Robertson, and J. I. Packer, signed the agreement with Roman Catholics that compromised the eternal truth of the Gospel for the sake of temporal social and political issues.

The document attempted to minimize the ten doctrinal disagreements that exist between Evangelicals and Roman

Catholics, and yet it failed to mention the one most critical—the means of salvation. The biblical plan of salvation by grace alone, through faith alone in Christ alone is not taught in the Catholic Church. Instead, Catholics are taught they must do good works, obey the commandments, be baptized and receive the sacraments to be saved.

In the sixth century, the Vatican created a place called purgatory, where those who do not fulfill these requirements perfectly on earth can be purged after death of their sin. Catholics are also taught "they can attain their own salvation and at the same time cooperate in saving their brothers" through good works (CCC 2010). Obviously this is a different Gospel that produces only false hope.

The Divine Anathema for Compromising the Gospel

Paul declared that anyone who preaches a different Gospel stands condemned (Galatians 1:6-9). There is only one Gospel. Therefore, if there is even the slightest deviation, distortion or perversion of it, it is no longer the Gospel. That is because only the pure Gospel of grace has good news. No other message offers condemned sinners the only way they can become right with God. The Gospel is the greatest news anyone could ever hear because it offers the greatest gift anyone could ever receive. There is no greater gift than the gift of eternal life which is made of available by a sovereign act of God's grace and mercy, through Christ's all-sufficient and completed work of redemption, apart from any works or merits of man.

The Judaizers were promoting a distorted version of the true gospel which does not save anyone, and it condemns those who teach it. By adding works of the law to the Gospel of grace, the Judaizers had nullified the only means by which God saves sinners (Rom. 11:6). They had renounced the free gift of God's grace with a works-righteousness salvation, which cannot save anyone.

Paul emphasized the utter importance of maintaining the purity of the Gospel of grace by calling down a divine curse on anyone who would distort it. Those who distort the Gospel are accursed. The word "accursed" means to be turned over to God for destruction. This means that anyone and everyone who distorts the Gospel is accursed. It does not matter who you are, a pope, a cardinal, a bishop, a priest, or a pastor in a Protestant church. It does not matter how many works you have done in the name of Christ, or how diligently you have served, or how sacrificially you have given, or how fervently you have prayed; if you preach a false gospel you are accursed.

The only other time Paul condemned anyone with an anathema was for not loving God (1 Cor. 16:22). Maintaining the purity of the Gospel and loving God are equally important.

Yet, in spite of this waring from the inspired words of Paul, the ECT document claims all Catholics are brothers and sisters "in Christ". It appears the endorsers of this document overlooked what it means to be "in Christ". In the first chapter of Ephesians, Paul describes those who are "in Christ" as: redeemed by the blood of Christ, forgiven, and sealed with the Holy Spirit guaranteeing their inheritance. Yet any Catholic who believes he is eternally secure in Christ is cursed with an anathema by his church (Canon 30, 6th Session, Council of Trent).

The document also declares conversion to Christianity "is a continuing process so that the whole life of a Christian should be a passage from death to life, from error to truth, from sin to grace" (Section V). Why did Evangelicals sign this document, knowing that conversion occurs the moment a repentant sinner is born again of the Spirit by placing his trust in Christ alone for salvation? It is so disturbing to see the most essential doctrine of Christianity undermined and rejected.

Why did Evangelicals sign an agreement that prohibits them from proselytizing Catholics? It may have developed from threats from high ranking Roman Catholic clergy. At the 31st National Conference of The Bishops of Brazil, Bishop Bohn threatened to declare a holy war against Evangelicals. He said, "The Catholic Church has a ponderous structure, but when we move, we'll smash anyone beneath us." Bishop Bohn stated the only way to avoid an all-out holy war is if Protestants halt their evangelism efforts in Brazil. Must the Great Commission be compromised because of a threat?

If this agreement is sustainable, then its endorsement must declare the Reformation was a terrible mistake and the martyrs who died defending the Gospel, died in vain. Let us pray for the discernment of those involved, that they may realize the severe implications of their actions and annul the agreement. Evangelicals must unite to defend the integrity of the Gospel and boldly contend for the faith that was once entrusted to the saints. Truth, not tolerance, is the only basis for Christian unity.

Another Unity Accord

Three years after the original ECT Document was signed, 19 evangelicals, including Chuck Colson, Bill Bright, and J.I. Packer along with 15 Roman Catholic theologians met to affirm agreement on basic articles of Christian faith, while at the same time acknowledging important differences. They came to the conclusion that their ongoing progress was dependent on a firm agreement on the meaning of salvation or the doctrine of justification. They agreed that "justification is not earned by any good works or merits of our own; it is entirely God's gift." Their six-page document, The Gift of Salvation (GOS), attempts to reconcile their fundamentally different views about the meaning of salvation that began at the Reformation. The new document of compromise marked the first time Evangelicals and Catholics "have publicly agreed to a common understanding of salvation," according to Richard John Neuhaus, a Catholic signer, who also coauthored the Evangelicals and Catholics Together Accord with Chuck Colson.

This is just one of the many strategic moves by the Vatican to bring all religions under the influence and power of the Pope. Other recent ecumenical efforts include: an ongoing dialogue with the Anglican Church; the establishment of diplomatic relations with the sovereign state of Israel, 46 years after its rebirth as a nation; and the welcoming of voodoo worshippers with their pagan practices into the Catholic Church. In order to build a bridge with Islam, Vatican II also included the Muslims, who deny the deity of Christ, in its plan of salvation.

The language employed by the authors to clarify important theological doctrines appears to be deliberately vague so that terms can be affirmed by both sides. Consider this statement, "We understand that what we affirm is in agreement with what the Reformation traditions have meant by justification by faith alone." Are the signers telling us the Reformation debate is now over? This is not the first time Catholics have tried to convince Protestants that sola fide (faith alone) has been the essence of Catholic teaching all along, and that the Reformation was just a misunderstanding of Catholicism.

Rome's First Attempt to Reverse the Reformation

In 1541 at Regensburg, King Charles V invited three Lutheran and three Catholic theologians to search for a compromise to heal the breach in the German church. The six men issued a statement expressing full agreement with the doctrine of sola fide. Their language was also ambiguous so as to allow for opposing views of justification to be harmonized. The Roman Church has always taught that justification is a process that begins at baptism. Through good works and receiving the sacraments, Catholics can then merit for themselves and others, "all the graces needed to attain eternal life". The Reformers, on the other hand, taught that justification is the immediate imputation of Christ's righteousness through faith alone in Christ alone. It is only by having the alien righteousness of Christ that we can ever be acceptable to God. Luther, who was keenly aware of this, immediately rebuked the Regensburg agreement with these words:

> Popish writers pretend that they have always taught, what we now teach, concerning faith and good works, and that they are unjustly accused of the contrary; thus, the wolf puts on the sheep's skin till he gains admission into the fold.[1]

The Creators of the GOS document may want us to believe they are affirming "justification by faith alone." However, they are merely affirming a misrepresentation of what the Reformers meant by "justification by faith alone". The Reformers were never so careless as to limit the definition to "the gift of justification is received through faith", as GOS proposes. The Reformers knew that Catholic theologians could affirm language like that and still miss the Gospel. If we choose to be ambiguous on the doctrine of justification, then we end up with a Gospel that anyone can embrace, a Gospel void of the power of God to save. It is quite strange that leading Roman Catholic priests and theologians would agree to *sola fide*, knowing that it brings condemnation upon them from their church. From the 6th Session of the Council of Trent, Canon 9, we read: "If anyone says that the sinner is justified by faith alone, meaning that nothing else is required to cooperate in order to obtain the grace of justification...let him be anathema."[2] Thus, in doctrine and practice, Rome denies justification by faith alone.

Another statement from the GOS is disturbing: "We have found that, notwithstanding some persistent and serious differences, we can together bear witness to the gift of salvation in Jesus Christ." For the signers to profess they have "some persistent and serious differences" is an admission to professing

---

[1] James Buchanan, *The Doctrine of Justification*, (Grand Rapids, Baker, 1977)
[2] The Catechism of the Catholic Church (San Francisco, Ignatius Press, 1994), 2010.

different Gospels. Paul gave the strongest of warnings to those teaching another Gospel: "But though we, or an angel from heaven, preach any other Gospel unto you than that which we have preached unto you, let him be accursed" (Galatians 1:8).

Another apparent contradiction with Catholic teaching is the GOS statement: "The restoration of communion with God is absolutely dependent upon Jesus Christ, true God and true man, for he is the one mediator between God and men" (1Timothy 2:5). The Catholic Church nullifies this truth in stating that Mary, the Mediatrix, also mediates salvation. "Taken up to heaven she did not lay aside this saving office but by her manifold intercession continues to bring us the gift of eternal salvation".[3]

Many questions arise from the GOS statement: "As believers we are sent into the world and commissioned to be bearers of the good news, to serve one another in love, to do good to all, and to evangelize everyone everywhere." Which Gospel did they agree to proclaim? The essential elements of the Gospel are nowhere to be seen in this document. Where did the authors say how one receives the salvation accomplished by Jesus? Rome's Gospel directly opposes the Gospel of Christ, yet the authors insisted that "Evangelicals must speak the Gospel to Catholics and Catholics to Evangelicals."

The Gift of Salvation concluded with: "...we recognize that there are necessarily interrelated questions that require further and urgent exploration. Among such questions are these: the meaning of baptismal regeneration, the Eucharist, sacramental grace...diverse understandings of merit, reward, purgatory, and indulgences; Marian devotion and the assistance of the saints in the life of salvation; and the possibility of salvation for those who have not been evangelized." If the evangelical signers of this document really wished to

---

[3] Ibid, 969

"urgently" explore these elements which oppose the Biblical Gospel, we wonder what has kept them from doing so. They are all readily available in the 1994 Catechism of the Catholic Church. It is more likely they tried to say something like this: "We must urgently explore language vague enough so that these disagreements can also be affirmed by both sides."

The compromise of the Gospel is made clear with this final statement: "We affirm our unity in the Gospel that we have here professed." The Gospel which they professed is neither the Gospel of grace nor the Gospel of Rome. It is a Gospel of ecumenical unity that will only bring a deeper division within the evangelical church.

Any attempt to merge these two opposing views of the doctrine of justification without radically changing one or the other is futile, and it is a complete dilution and destruction of the true Biblical doctrine of salvation. As of this writing, there have been other and ongoing attempts to reconcile Protestant and Catholic theology.

The Manhattan Declaration Calls for More Unity

On November 20, 2009, a 4,700-word document called the Manhattan Declaration: A Call of Christian Conscience was released (http://manhattandeclaration.org/). A coalition of 150 Catholic, Orthodox and Evangelical leaders, calling themselves "Christians" and "fellow believers", joined together in ecumenical unity to fight against abortion, same-sex marriage and anything that betrays their religious beliefs. The document was drafted by Chuck Colson and Princeton University professor Robert George, a Roman Catholic.

Similar to the impact of the Manhattan Project of the 1940's, the Manhattan Declaration represents an atomic blast on Christian faith. Anytime born-again Christians link arms with unregenerate professing Christians, even for ostensibly moral purposes, they are impeding the Great Commission.

The fallout from Chuck Colson's previous attempts to reverse the Reformation has been devastating to the Evangelical Church. During his life he influenced many evangelical leaders to embrace Roman Catholicism as a valid expression of biblical Christianity. According to the second Evangelicals and Catholics Together Accord (ECT II) that Colson drafted in 1997, the following differences should not divide Catholics and Evangelicals as "brothers and sisters in Christ": baptismal regeneration, the Eucharist, sacramental grace, justification by works, purgatory, indulgences, the role of Mary and the saints in salvation and salvation for those not evangelized.

Many of the signers of Colson's Evangelicals and Catholics Together Accord gave their name to this Declaration as well. Purposefully, the Gospel is never defined, explained or presented in the Manhattan Declaration. This is because the signatories embrace contradictory and opposing views on the Gospel of Jesus Christ. The implication throughout the document is that Roman Catholics, Eastern Orthodox and Protestant Evangelicals share a common faith. There is nothing that could be further from the truth. Evangelicals and Catholics submit to different authorities, read different Bibles, worship a different Jesus, believe a different Gospel, have a different view of sin and are on a different path to eternity. Furthermore, we disagree on the necessity, sufficiency and efficacy of our Lord Jesus Christ in the salvation of sinners. There can never be unity between true Christianity and apostate or counterfeit Christianity. Believers and unbelievers are as distinctively different as light and darkness (2 Corinthians 6:14-18). Have we forgotten the Reformers who were tortured and burned at the stake for refusing to compromise with Rome? The apostle Paul never signed unity accords with people who perverted the Gospel of Jesus Christ; he condemned them with anathema (Galatians 1:6-9). It was Paul's great fear that we would put up with counterfeit Christians who preach another Jesus and another Gospel (2 Corinthians 11:4). He warned us that these false apostles and deceitful workers, who disguise themselves as brothers in Christ, could corrupt our minds and lead us astray (2 Corinthians 11:13). In these times of great deception and compromise, we must heed his warnings. People who preach another Gospel are not Christians; they have betrayed Christ. The true church ought to rise up against such persons and declare that they are not Christians. They are counterfeits who shame the name of Jesus.

Although it is good to unite as co-belligerents with one voice to fight moral and political issues, any accord that attempts to overlook, dismiss, nullify or compromise the Gospel is antithetical to the command for all Christians to earnestly contend for the faith. We can never deny the profound importance of protecting the life of every baby and the sanctity of marriage between one man and one woman. We must earnestly contend against those who seek to destroy both (Psalm 82:3-4; Proverbs 24:11, 31:8-9; Isaiah 1:17; Jude 3). However, we must remember that this is a spiritual battle which can only be won through fervent prayer and the proclamation of the true Gospel, a Gospel that is denied by every Catholic priest when he offers the Eucharistic Christ upon his altar for the forgiveness of sins. If Evangelicals must put their names on accords, why not remain sanctified and set apart by drafting our own accords? We can start by declaring our unity was established when the Holy Spirit baptized us into one Body upon believing the one and only Gospel of grace (1 Corinthians 12:13).

Those Who Oppose the Manhattan Declaration Are Slandered

Eric Teetsel, a graduate of Wheaton College and president of the Manhattan Declaration, gives the following response to anyone who opposes the Manhattan Declaration or tries to remove their names from it. "There are a number of ignorant, angry rabble rousers who regularly lie about us to serve their small, twisted propagandas. Some are filled with hate for those who don't comply with their version of Christianity. These fools harm and hinder the Gospel."

Teetsel has it all reversed because he embraces a compromised Gospel. It is the unity accords between Evangelicals and Catholics that hinder the Gospel from being proclaimed to Catholics.

None of this is new. Throughout the history of the church, Satan has unleashed his fiery darts against the Christian faith. He has been most successful when God's children lack discernment. Charles Spurgeon said, "To pursue union at the expense of truth is treason to the Lord Jesus." Since we have been sanctified by the truth, we must remain separate for God's glory and purpose.

Ecumenical Unity and the Coming One-World Religion

As the church awaits the glorious return of our Lord Jesus Christ, we are witnessing the formation of a global religious system that will one day worship the Beast (Revelation 13:12). Jesus warned that a widespread dynamic deception would be one of the signs of His return to the earth. His Word reveals there will be many false teachers, who will prepare an unsuspecting bride for the Antichrist. This counterfeit religious system will give her allegiance and worship to one who will blaspheme God.

The ongoing dialogue among world religious leaders seeks to find common threads of truth as a basis for unity. As diverse as some religions appear, there are some common bonds of unity. One is the teaching that salvation is attained by what men must do for God, instead of what God has already done for man through His Son. All religions, with the exception of biblical Christianity, arrogantly deny that salvation is by grace, the unmerited favor of God.

Several organizations have been working diligently to unite the people of the world, but none as aggressively as the Roman Catholic Church. The Second Vatican Council made this clear when it stated: The Catholic Church endeavors "to gather all people and all things into Christ, so as to be for all an inseparable sacrament of unity... expressed in the common celebration of the Eucharist."

The Vatican has been building strategic bridges to all Christian denominations and non-Christian religions for the purpose of bringing all people under the papacy. In a 1998 speech to the leaders of Islam, Pope John Paul declared: "Dialogue between our two religions (Islam and Catholicism) is more necessary than ever. There remains a spiritual bond which unites us and which we must strive to recognize and develop." Later, in January of 2002, many of the most influential religious leaders of the world responded to the pope's invitation to gather in Assisi, Italy to discuss unity and peace. The pope, whom Catholics believe is the supreme head of the entire Christian Church, made all the leaders of non-Christian religions feel comfortable by removing all the images, crucifixes and icons of Jesus Christ.

Rome's Strategy for Christian Unity

The Vatican has a well-defined and aggressive strategy for uniting all of Christianity under the papacy and thus promote a one-world religion. Some of the elements of this master plan are outlined below:

1. Promote the opinion that Catholics, Orthodox and Protestants are all brothers-in-Christ and therefore must be reunited. This is why the Vatican is urging all "separated brethren" to come back home to Holy Mother, the Church, to enjoy the "fullness of salvation". Rome believes the salvation of Protestants cannot be complete unless and until they receive the transubstantiated Christ in the Eucharist.

2. Another important part of their strategy is to redefine evangelical terms in vague and ambiguous words, to make them acceptable to both Catholics and Protestants. This strategy has been used effectively in their recent unity accords with Evangelicals and Lutherans. They have also been effective in identifying and seducing highly visible and influential evangelicals to promote Catholicism as a valid expression of Christianity.

3. The Vatican's strategy also involves exploiting post-modernism and the emerging church movement, which has gained widespread popularity. These movements have caused confusion, biblical ignorance and a lack of discernment within Protestant churches. In turn, these have produced fertile soil for seeds of deception and compromise to grow. Many who are uncertain of the true Gospel are easily deceived and willing to embrace the false Gospel of Catholicism.

4. Rome is also encouraging tolerance of all faiths because tolerance unifies and brings peace, while doctrinal truth divides. Whenever doctrinal truth is suppressed, there can be no distinction between believers and unbelievers.

What is the One True Church?

There is, and always will be, only one true church—the one established by the Lord Jesus Christ Himself (Matthew 16:18). Following the resurrection of our Lord and His ascension into heaven, the beginnings of the early church are chronicled in the book of the Acts of the Apostles. Believers must take care to distinguish the one true church from any and all attempts to forge a world religion that is an abomination to our Holy God and Creator.

THE ONE TRUE CHURCH	THE WORLD RELIGION
Receives divine revelation from Scripture alone (2 Peter 1:20)	Receives "divine" revelation from demonic sources (1 Timothy 4:1-4)
Is called by God their Father, saved by Jesus Christ and sealed and sanctified by the Holy Spirit (Colossians 1:9; Eph. 2:8; 1 Cor. 1:3)	Is blinded by their father the devil, deceived by false Christs and bonded by another spirit (2 Corinthians 4:4; John 8:44; Revelation 9:20)
Is saved by God's grace for good works (Ephesians 2:8-10)	Teach they are saved by works, but their works deny God (Titus 1:16)
Is intolerant, believing there is only one way to God (John 14:6)	Is tolerant, believing there are many ways to God
Is baptized by the Holy Spirit into one body (1 Corinthians 12:13)	Is ensnared by another spirit to do his will (2 Timothy 2:24-26)
Is alive in Christ and abides in His Word (Romans 6:11; John 8:31-32)	Is spiritually dead and abides in the world (1 John 2:16)
Contends for the apostles' faith (Jude 3)	Seeks common truth among all faiths
Is the Bride of Christ, united in love for the Savior (Revelation 19:7; John 13:35)	Is the harlot of anti-Christ, united in hatred for the saints (Revelation 17:6)
Will worship and serve the true Christ when He appears in glory (Titus 2:13-15)	Will worship and serve a false Christ when he appears in deceit (Revelation 13:12)
Will rejoice in God's peace (Revelation 21:4)	Will weep in an eternal fire (Matthew 13:42)

Chapter 7

THE OPPOSITION TO THE GOSPEL

——————

From the early days of the church, millions of people have been influenced and led astray by the heretical teaching of false prophets and teachers. During His earthly ministry, Jesus warned His followers often of the destructive teaching of these deceivers:

> Beware of the false prophets, who come to you in sheep's clothing, but inwardly are ravenous wolves. (Matthew 7:15)

> Many false prophets will arise and will mislead many. (Matthew 24:11)

> For false Christs and false prophets will arise and will show great signs and wonders, so as to mislead, if possible, even the elect. (Matthew 24:24)

In 2015, Pope Francis made his first visit to North America, spending time in Cuba, the United States, and also visiting the United Nations. There were several troubling observations in the published itinerary that the Vatican issued to describe his trip: "Apostolic Journey of His Holiness Pope Francis to Cuba and the United States of America, and Visit to the United Nations Organization Headquarters, on the occasion of his participation at the Eighth World Meeting of Families in Philadelphia." Considering his trip as an "Apostolic Journey" erroneously elevates his authority and should be a red flag for all discerning Christians. Unfortunately for many, that was not the case.

As we watched the non-stop coverage of the pope's visit to America, many of the scenes appeared to be apocalyptic. Multitudes of people flocked to get a glimpse of a mortal man who was unknown just three years prior to his visit. The national excitement for this false prophet was overwhelming, as gullible people hung on his every word. It was heartbreaking to see such adoration given to a deceiver, who holds people captive in his false religious system. Warnings from the true Head of the church were ignored. The Lord Jesus said, "Beware of false prophets, who come to you in sheep's clothing but inwardly are ravenous wolves" (Mat. 7:15). Jesus said, "I have come in my Father's name, and you do not receive me. If another comes in his own name, you will receive him" (John 5:43). Clearly, the pope did not come in the Father's name, but he arrogantly wears the title reserved for the one and only "Holy Father" (John 17:11). Tragically, most Catholics do not know the Word of God, and their ignorance makes them easy prey for the worst kind of deception.

Pope Francis did not mention Jesus Christ a single time in his entire address to Congress, yet he claims to be the Vicar of Christ and the Head of Christ's Church. Knowing that the Lord Jesus is the very foundation of the Christian faith, the pope's omission speaks volumes about his worldly agenda. Following his message to Congress, the next day at St. Patrick's Cathedral, the pope did mention Jesus, but in a deceptively misleading way, from his words, it should be clear to all that he is indeed a false teacher. He said, "We need to remember that we are followers of Jesus... and his life, humanly speaking, ended in failure, the failure of the cross."

Where is the outrage among Roman Catholics? When will they awake from their stupor and run from this blasphemer?

The life of Christ was anything but a failure at the cross. His death, which satisfied divine justice for the sins of His people, was according to the predetermined plan of God (Acts 2:23). When the sinless Savior accomplished everything necessary to save His people, He cried out in victory, "It is finished!" (John 19:30). The good shepherd laid down His life for the sheep (John 10:11). No one took the Lord's life; He laid it down on His own accord (John 10:18). How dare the pope say the life of Jesus ended in failure! The pope, and all other false prophets, are described by Jesus as thieves who come to steal and kill and destroy the sheep (John 10:10). The pope knows the difference between success and failure. No one has been more successful than the pope in directing people with his perverted gospel towards the wide road to destruction.

By the authority of God's Word, we know the pope is under divine condemnation for preaching a Gospel contrary to the Gospel of God. The apostle Paul warned us: "There are some who trouble you and want to distort the Gospel of Christ. But even if we or an angel from heaven should preach to you a Gospel contrary to the one we preached to you, let him be accursed" (Gal. 1:6-9). Salvation is by grace alone, through faith alone, in Christ alone, according to Scripture alone, for the glory of God alone. The pope's distorted Gospel deceives people into believing salvation is by baptism, sacraments, good works, law-keeping, and the Mass. Paul warned us:

> For such men are false apostles, deceitful workmen, disguising themselves as apostles of Christ. And no wonder, for even Satan disguises himself as an angel of light. So it is no surprise if his servants, also, disguise themselves as servants of righteousness. Their end will correspond to their deeds. (2 Corinthians 11:13-15)

We know the "father of lies" does his deceptive work through religious leaders, and the pope is the most influential false teacher in the world today. He continues to shut the kingdom of heaven in people's faces and will not allow them to enter because of his false and fatal Gospel (Matthew 23:15). He must be exposed as a pawn of the devil. Some may think I am unloving and harsh for saying this, but the truth must be told for the sake of those who are being deceived. The Lord Jesus pronounced many "woes" on false teachers who lead people to hell (Matthew 23). It was tragic to see such a lack of discernment, as multitudes praised and adored the most influential false prophet in the world.

The counterfeit head of the church also showed his true colors when he did not refer to even one Scripture from God's Word during his hour-long speech before Congress. Instead, he encouraged people to follow the "Golden Rule." The next day, in his message to bishops of the Catholic Church, the pope said, "Our mission as bishops is first and foremost to solidify unity." In other words, the bishops' primary goal is not to proclaim the Gospel, but to unite all people under the power and influence of the papacy. True Christians must contend against Rome's ecumenical agenda and silence the ignorance of foolish people (1 Peter 2:15).

I have great compassion for the precious Catholic souls who are where I was for many years of my life—believing I was in the one true church, when I actually was destined for the eternal fires of hell. The nature of deception is such that people do not know they are deceived until they are confronted with the truth. It is my prayer that Roman Catholics will start abiding in God's Word. Only then will they come to know the truth that will set them free from religious deception (John 8:31-32).

The pope is but one example of a false teacher or false prophet whose influence leads millions of people away from Biblical truth. There are many others. The best preparation for believers to combat the heresies attacking the purity of the Gospel is first to know the fundamentals of the Gospel, as discussed earlier. Second it is important to understand what is at the heart of all false teaching. For the rest of this chapter, we will answer these questions, as well as examine the most common attempts to dilute, taint, compromise or distort the glorious Gospel of grace.

Three Common Errors of False Teachers

Since we are now living in the age of religious tolerance and ecumenical unity, there are some people who will immediately call attempts to claim the Gospel as the only means of eternal life, unloving and divisive. Others will ask, "What right do you have to judge another religion?" The answer is given in Scripture. All God-fearing people are called to make right judgments, judgments that have already been established by the objective principles of God's Word (John 7:24). There may be nothing more important than warning people who are being deceived about their eternal destiny. If we do not lovingly confront them with God's Gospel, they may never know how to escape the eternal fire of God's punishment. Clearly, the most unloving thing we can do is to ignore them and let them continue down the road to destruction. For this reason, I am always willing to offend people with the offense and exclusivity of the Gospel, in the hopes that God may grant some of them repentance leading to a knowledge of the truth (2 Timothy 2: 25). Let us look at three fatal errors of false prophets and learn how to handle them.

False Teachers Usurp the Authority of God

The supreme authority of the Bible is established both by its divine origin and inspiration (2 Peter 1:21). It is the infallible Word of God, and it will accomplish God's purpose (Isaiah 55:11). It is the very foundation upon which all Christian truths rest. For followers of the Lord Jesus Christ, the Bible is the final court of appeal in all matters pertaining to faith and godliness. "All Scripture is God-breathed and is useful for teaching, rebuking, correcting and training in righteousness" (2 Timothy

3:16). The divine authority of Scripture corrects and rebukes all false teaching, because there is no higher authority or infallible source in which to appeal. It is the Word of God, and God cannot lie, cannot break His promise and cannot deceive.

Many modern cults either claim higher authority over Scripture or elevate their own writings to the same level as the Bible. The Church of Latter Day Saints includes *The Book of Mormon*, the *Doctrine and Covenants*, and *The Pearl of Great Price* as writings they consider to be sacred Scripture. The Christian Science Church, which is neither Christian, science, nor a church, gives equal authority to Mary Baker Eddy's *Science and Health with Key to the Scriptures*. Followers of Sun Myung Moon believed he received divinely inspired revelation from God and worshiped him as "Lord of the Second Advent."

People fall into serious error and sin when they exalt their own authority over God's authority, or when they suppress the truth of God's Word to promote their own self-serving agendas. For example, the Roman Catholic religion has done this by establishing its traditions and teachings to be equal in authority with Scripture (Catechism of the Catholic Church [CCC] par. 82). In doing so, it has usurped the supreme authority of our sovereign God, who alone has the right to rule and determine the eternal destinies of men. This fatal error has opened the flood gates to numerous other deadly heresies including: the preaching of another Gospel, the worship of a counterfeit Jesus, the buying and selling of God's grace through indulgences, the creation of a fictitious place called purgatory, the establishment of other mediators, and praying to and for the dead. These errors are fatal, because anyone who is embracing them when they take their last breath will experience eternal death.

Catholics who are being deceived by these fatal errors must be told that the world has known only one infallible teacher. He is the Lord Jesus Christ, who was the personification of truth, and every word He spoke was truth (John 14:6, 17:17). Those who are seeking the truth need to look only to Christ and His Word. The Catholic religion has become corrupt the same way Judaism became corrupt—by following the traditions of men instead of the Word of God (Mark 7:13). The Pharisees taught much truth, but by mixing it with error, they "made the word of God of no effect." We must never forget that the Bible is what God says, and religion is what *man says* God says.

False Teachers Distort the Person of Christ

If you went out on the streets and asked people who they think Jesus is, the answers will range from good man, prophet, religious leader, myth, fictional character, philosopher, or lunatic. Rarely will you hear an accurate description of Jesus Christ— God's perfect man and man's perfect God.

One of the first major indicators of a false teacher or a false religion is their view of our Lord Jesus Christ. Jehovah's Witnesses deny the very deity of Christ and dethrone Him as God's one and only unique Son. In the distorted version of the Bible they use in their teaching, John 1:1 is erroneously translated, "In the beginning was the Word, and the Word was with God, and the Word was 'a' God" (emphasis added). In the most respected Greek manuscripts upon which our translations are based, there is no indefinite article in the sentence, yet the Jehovah's Witnesses' translators inserted the indefinite article "a" to fit their blasphemous theology. They also preach that Jesus was not God but instead claim he was Michael, the archangel.

Paul warned us that some would come preaching another Jesus. They will offer a counterfeit Jesus "whom we [the apostles] have not preached" (2 Corinthians 11:4). The Mormons erroneously teach that Jesus is the brother of Lucifer and was a man who became God. Roman Catholicism preaches a Jesus that was unable to purge all sin and pay the complete penalty for sin. Is the Jesus of the Roman Catholic Church the biblical Jesus? Knowing and believing the real Jesus is critical because

Jesus said, "If you do not believe that I am the one I claim to be, you will indeed die in your sins" (John 8:24). A different Jesus is preached by many deceivers (2 Corinthians 11:3-4) who deny His finished work of redemption.

The True Jesus of the Bible

Jesus Christ is the perfect High Priest who offered Himself—the perfect sacrifice—once for the sins of His people. This one sin offering has perfected for all time those who are being sanctified (Hebrews 10:14). For this reason, there are no more offerings for sin (Hebrews 10:18). The believer's eternal sin debt was paid in full and redemption was secured when God raised Jesus Christ from the dead (Romans 4:25). Would there be false teachers who would deny this and steal away the honor and glory of our Savior?

The Biblical Jesus assures Christians they have been saved from condemnation. "Now that we have been justified by His blood, it is all the more certain that we shall be saved by Him from God's wrath" (Roman 5:9). The one time, perfect and all-sufficient sacrifice of Jesus completely satisfied the wrath of God (1 John 2:2). Roman Catholicism denies this fundamental teaching and deceives its people into believing that the sacrifice of the Mass satisfies God's wrath, not only for the sins of the living but also for the sins of the dead (Canon 3, Council of Trent). Catholics are cursed with anathema by their church if they claim they are saved from God's wrath (Canon 30, Council of Trent). Catholics know Jesus only as a "gate-opener" to heaven. For Catholics to go through the gates of heaven, they must save themselves through the Mass and sacraments.

The Jesus of the Bible expiates sin. "Through His blood, God made Him the means of the expiation for all who believe" (Romans 3:25). Yet the Catholic Church teaches Catholics must expiate their own sins. "This may be done through the sorrows, miseries and trials of this life and, above all, through death. Otherwise the expiation must be made in the next life through fire and torments of purifying punishments" (Vatican Council II).

The Jesus of the Bible is the only mediator between God and man (1 Timothy 2:15), yet the Roman Catholic Church offers Mary as the mediator. Pope Pius IX proclaimed that "God has committed to Mary the treasury of all good things, in order that everyone may know that through her are obtained every hope, every grace, and all salvation. For this is His will: that we obtain everything through Mary."

The Jesus of the Bible claimed He was the only way to the heavenly Father (John 14:6). Vatican II denies this by stating, "the plan of salvation also includes those who acknowledge the Creator, in the first place amongst who are the Muslims."

So why does the Roman Catholic Church hide the real Jesus from its followers? Because the real Jesus sets people free! In contrast, the Roman Catholic Church maintains control of its people through legalistic rituals, sacraments and threats of anathemas. The Biblical Jesus saves believers from the bondage of sin, deception and religion.

Many of today's false teachers are Roman Catholics who preach a "Jesus" who does not save sinners completely and forever. They say Catholics must do their part by expiating and making satisfaction for their own sins through penance (CCC, 1459). In this way, they attain their own salvation through good works (CCC, 1477). The Catholic Jesus offers conditional life, not eternal life (CCC, 1035). This counterfeit Christ is said to return physically to Catholic altars during the Mass, which occurs worldwide over 200,000 times each day, to be a sin offering for the living and the dead (CCC, 1367).

Catholics must be warned of the consequences for not knowing and believing the true Jesus. This was made clear by Jesus when He said: "unless you believe that I am He, you shall die in your sins" (John 8:24). Whenever religion rejects God's authority, it creates "another Jesus" which always leads to "another Gospel." Why? Because whenever the sufficiency of Christ is denied, another Gospel must be concocted to instruct people what they must do to be saved.

False Teachers Pervert the Gospel of Christ

The Gospel is the joyous proclamation of God's redeeming work through Jesus Christ, which saves His people from the punishment, power, and ultimately, the presence of sin. It is the one and only message of redemption and is the same message for every generation (Ephesians 4:4-6, Revelation 14:6). Since the Gospel is about one Savior, it is exclusive and thus declares that all other faiths and religions are false (John 14:6; Matthew 7:13-14). This glorious Gospel declares that salvation is entirely of grace and those who add anything to it stand condemned. The Apostle Paul states this clearly and forcefully:

> I am amazed that you are so quickly deserting Him who called you by the grace of Christ, for a different gospel; which is *really* not another; only there are some who are disturbing you and want to distort the gospel of Christ. But even if we, or an angel from heaven, should preach to you a gospel contrary to what we have preached to you, he is to be accursed! As we have said before, so I say again now, if any man is preaching to you a gospel contrary to what you received, he is to be accursed. (Galatians 1:6-9)

It comes as no surprise that the most popular perversion of the Gospel is the fatal lie that good works or inherent righteousness are necessary to appease a holy God. Every religion in the world perpetrates this lie of the devil. However, Satan's oldest and most deadly lie is "You surely shall not die" (Genesis 3:4). This lie is still spread in Catholicism (CCC, 1863).

Why would any religious leader want to distort the glorious Gospel of grace? The primary reason is to control people by holding them captive in legalistic bondage. It is for this reason the Lord Jesus gave the mark of a true disciple. He said, "If you abide in My word...and you shall know the truth, and the truth shall make you free" (John 8:31-32). People in religious bondage can only be set free when they come to a knowledge of the truth found in Scripture.

Roman Catholicism is not alone in perverting the Gospel of God. There are many cults and Protestant sects which do the same. Catholicism, however, not only deceives its people with a false Gospel, but foolishly condemns those who believe the true Gospel. Over 100 condemnations from the Council of Trent are pronounced on Christians who believe the Lord Jesus is sufficient to save sinners completely and forever. The Catholic "Gospel" emphasizes what man must DO to be saved instead of what Christ has DONE. This would include the necessity of doing good works (CCC, 2016), receiving sacraments (1129), attending meritorious masses (1405), keeping the law (2068), buying indulgences (1498), and purgatory (1030).

False Teachers Must Be Confronted

We must never let doctrinal error go unabated, because it dishonors God and deceives the unsuspecting. It defiles the conscience, corrupts the heart and destroys the soul. According to Scripture, that which flows from the lips of false teachers includes: "strange doctrines," "commandments of men," "doctrines of devils," "damnable heresies," "traditions of men," "lies," "falsehood," "vain deceit" and "deceptive philosophy." Lying lips are an abomination to the Lord at all times and in all cases (Proverbs 12:22). Knowing the fruit of false teachers, we must earnestly contend against them. Peter and Paul said false teachers cause believers to fall from their steadfastness and pure devotion to Christ (2 Peter 3:17; 2 Corinthians 11:3). They disagree with the words of Jesus and bring constant friction within the church (1 Timothy 6:4-5). They give rise to speculation and fruitless discussion which hinder the purposes of God (1 Timothy 1:4-6).

Many who profess Christ are no longer embracing sound doctrine, because they want their ears tickled and are seeking teachers who will do just that (2 Timothy 4:3). Using the Word of God, we must be ready to reprove, rebuke and exhort with great patience and instruction. Those who have been entrusted with the truth must take a stand against those who try to lead men astray. Even when Peter was not straightforward about the truth of the Gospel, Paul withstood him to his face and rebuked him sharply (Galatians 2:11-14). Jude exhorted us to "earnestly contend for the faith once delivered to the saints" (Jude 3). Those who refuse to defend God's truth are demonstrating their lack of passion for the truth. We must love the truth and hate every false way (Psalm 119:104). Let us never be intimidated by false teachers, because "the fear of man brings a snare" (Proverbs 29:25).

False Teachers Offer a False Hope Instead of Divine Forgiveness

Anyone who has read the Bible knows that man's greatest problem is sin. There is a day of judgment coming when God's holy anger will be poured out on unforgiven sinners. Since no one can escape God's justice, man's greatest need is divine forgiveness. Every other human need in this life pales in comparison with our need to be forgiven of the eternal debt for our sins. Without God's forgiveness, we would all be destined for a fiery furnace with absolutely no hope of escape. God created man to exist forever, eternally reconciled to Him in heaven because of His forgiveness through Christ, or eternally separated from Him in hell because of sin. Those who have experienced God's forgiveness are blessed with an everlasting joy and peace that surpasses all understanding. However, there are many who have never been forgiven because they have been deceived about this most important doctrine. The purity of the Gospel is tainted when there is no discussion of the sin of man and the need for repentance. There is no excuse for being deceived because God's Word sets forth the truth plainly for everyone to see. The Scriptures reveal how God graciously forgives sins completely and forever.

Yet, Catholics are required to confess specific mortal sins to priests and then make satisfaction for them before they can be forgiven (CCC 1459). In many ways, the Roman Catholic religion is an extension of Judaism under the Old Covenant. Jews were required to confess specific sins and bring guilt offerings to the Lord for them (Lev. 5:5-6). They depended upon a sacrificial priesthood for the forgiveness of sins. Catholics have the same dependence upon their priesthood. "Only priests can forgive sins in the name of Christ" (CCC, 1495).

Under the Old Covenant, sins were covered by the sacrifice of animals, but the sacrifices could never make the Jews perfect. In the same way, the Sacrifice of the Mass can never make Catholics perfect, which is why the Mass must be repeated every day. However, under the New Covenant of Christ's blood, His one sacrifice has made perfect forever those who are being sanctified (Hebrews 10:14).

Profile of a Wolf in Sheep's Clothing

The Lord Jesus Christ warned His followers, "Beware of the false prophets, who come to you in sheep's clothing, but inwardly are ravenous wolves" (Matthew 7:15). The warning was important, because Jesus later said to them: "Behold, I send you out as sheep in the midst of wolves; therefore be shrewd as serpents, and innocent as doves" (Matthew 10:16). The apostle Paul, with tears and a deeply troubled spirit, penned a similar warning: "I know that after my departure savage wolves will come in among you, not sparing the flock" (Acts 20:29). Throughout church history, these warnings have seldom been taken seriously. Christians continue to be deceived because they cannot discern truth from error.

According to Webster's Dictionary, "deceive" means "to lead astray or to cause to accept as true or valid what is false or invalid." Could it be the church has not only lost its ability to discern truth from error but also to discern wolves from sheep?

Consider Brennan Manning, an inactive Roman Catholic priest, who has some obvious characteristics of a "wolf," yet goes mostly undetected. Prior to his death in 2013, he was a popular speaker in many "evangelical" churches. Manning was ordained to the Franciscan priesthood after graduating from St. Francis Seminary in 1963. Later, he was theology instructor at the University of Steubenville (a Catholic seminary, and catalyst for Mary to be named co-redeemer). After being treated for alcoholism and leaving the Franciscan Order in 1982, he married Roslyn Ann Walker. The marriage ended in divorce, but his popularity as a writer and speaker continued to grow despite his proclamation of "another" Gospel.

The teachings of Manning were charming, seductive, cunning and dangerous as he took advantage of his undiscerning audiences. He taught that you can overcome fear, guilt and psychological hang-ups, even alcoholism, through meditation. His meditation techniques were drawn from a mixture of eastern mysticism, psychology, the New Age Movement and Catholicism. Manning gave the impression that he had a very intimate relationship with God and reported to have had many visions, encounters and conversations with Him. He assured his audiences that if they applied his teachings, they too would become more intimate with God.

I first met Manning at the *Christian Booksellers Association* in New Orleans. As he was signing autographs for his book, *The Ragamuffin Gospel*, widely read by many evangelical Christians, I asked him if his "ragamuffin Gospel" followed the Catholic plan of salvation or the biblical plan of salvation. He responded, "Read it and find out for yourself." Still trying to gain insight into his theology, I gave him a tract I had written, called *Roman Catholicism: Scripture vs. Tradition*, and asked for his comments. After looking at it for a couple of minutes, he tore it into pieces and threw it in the trash.

The next time I saw Manning was a few years later at Hill-crest Church, a congregation of over 5,000 members in north Dallas. Manning's message was about our need for a second conversion, a conversion that can only take place when one overcomes self-rejection and gains esteem through self-acceptance. After the service, I asked two elders of Hillcrest Church how they could allow a Roman Catholic priest speak to their congregation. Their response was, "we welcome everyone who loves God." This was indeed a fulfillment of Paul's prophetic words: "For the time will come when they will not endure sound doctrine; but wanting to have their ears tickled, they will accumulate for themselves teachers in accordance to their own desires; and will turn away their ears from the truth, and will turn aside to myths" (2 Timothy 4:3-4).

Is All Mankind Redeemed?

As with many such teachers who gain popularity by tickling ears, Manning overemphasized the love and grace of God, while ignoring His attributes of justice, righteousness and holiness. He taught that Jesus redeemed all of mankind. His "good news" was that everyone is already saved. Among those Manning believed he would see in heaven is "the sexually abused teen molested by his father and now selling his body on the street, who, as he falls asleep each night after his last 'trick,' whispers the name of the unknown God."[1] Manning's theology opposes God's Word again and again: "those who practice such things shall not inherit the kingdom of God" (Galatians 5:21). "He who believes in the Son has eternal life; but he who does not obey the Son shall not see life, but the wrath of God abides on him" (John 3:36). Accordingly, Manning thought that sinners are forgiven if they "trust the love of God."

This is a major theme of *The Ragamuffin Gospel*, "trusting the love of God," because God loves you no matter what you do.

[1] Brennan Manning, *The Ragamuffin Gospel*, Portland, OR: Multnomah Press, 1990, page 33.

There is no call to sanctification or holiness. Instead, Manning excused sin as human weakness that God will tolerate regardless of whether the sinner is repentant or not. In saying this, Manning turned "the grace of our God into licentiousness" (Jude 4). He wrote: "False gods—the gods of human understanding—despise sinners, but the Father of Jesus loves all, no matter what they do. But, of course, this is almost too incredible for us to accept."[2] Yes, too incredible, because it violates God's Word: "Thou dost hate all who do iniquity" (Psalm 5:5).

Should We Stop Thinking About God?

In *The Signature of Jesus*, another one of Manning's books, he taught his readers how to pray, using an eight-word mantra.[3] He said, "the first step in faith is to stop thinking about God at the time of prayer" (p. 212). The second step is "without moving your lips, repeat the sacred word [or phrase] inwardly, slowly, and often." If distractions come, "simply return to listening to your sacred word" (p. 218). He also encouraged his readers to "celebrate the darkness" because "the ego has to break; and this breaking is like entering into a great darkness" (p. 145). Jesus said, "He who follows me shall not walk in the darkness" (John 8:12).

The Spirit of Antichrist

Manning often cited Catholic saints, humanist philosophers, heretics, monks and medieval mystics. Some of the monks he quoted maintained that salvation is really a transformation of consciousness to be awakened to the oneness of all creation. Possibly Manning's most dangerous practice and teaching was his New Age mind-emptying method of meditation. This was an open invitation to satanic activity. Many of the expressions and techniques Manning employed in *The Signature of Jesus* are not found in the Scriptures, such as: centering prayer, paschal

---

[2] Ibid, page 22.
[3] Brennan Manning, *The Signature of Jesus*, Sisters, OR: Multnomah Books, 1996, pp. 94, 219.

spirituality, the discipline of the secret, contemplative spirituality, mineralization, practicing the presence, inner integration, yielding to the Center, notional knowledge, contemporary spiritual masters and masters of the interior life. Extra-biblical spiritual practices can only produce confusion. They originate from the "father of lies" in whom there is no truth. What a contrast Manning is to the way Paul described the first century teachers. He said: "We have renounced secret and shameful ways; we do not use deception, nor do we distort the word of God. On the contrary, by setting forth the truth plainly we commend ourselves to every man's conscience in the sight of God." (2 Corinthians 4:2)

Manning rarely used Scripture, and he showed his disdain for those who did and for those who believed "The Word was God" (John 1:1). He wrote: "I am deeply distressed by what I only can call in our Christian culture the idolatry of the Scriptures. For many Christians, the Bible is not a pointer to God but God himself. In a word—bibliolatry.... I develop a nasty rash around people who speak as if mere scrutiny of its pages will reveal precisely how God thinks and precisely what God wants" (p. 188). He criticizes several churches he has visited, where "religiosity has pushed Jesus to the margins of real life and plunged people into preoccupation with their own personal salvation" (p. 193). Although Manning believed he taught the life, death, and resurrection of Christ, *The Signature of Jesus* is not a guide to follow Jesus, but to follow "the masters of the interior life." Paul wrote, "For such men are slaves, not of our Lord Christ but of their own appetites; and by their smooth and flattering speech they deceive the hearts of the unsuspecting" (Romans 16:18).

Manning reinterpreted some of the most essential biblical truths in the light of psychological healing. He looked upon "human nature as fallen but redeemed, flawed but in essence good" (p. 125). His instruction to meditate on nothingness instead of God's Word was an exercise of modern occultism. This practice invites demonic influence and contact with the spirit world. Manning's Catholic mysticism has no place in the true church of Jesus Christ.

Christian leaders should warn others about Manning and all "deceitful workers who masquerade as apostles of Christ" (2 Corinthians 11:13). They must be exposed (Ephesians 5:11). We all live in days of great deception. May God give His church the gift of discernment as we take Paul's warning seriously: "See to it that no one takes you captive through philosophy and empty deception, according to the tradition of men, according to the elementary principles of the world, rather than according to Christ" (Colossians 2:8).

Opposition in the Form of Religious Pride and Indoctrination

The greatest obstacle to learning the truth is to believe that you already know it. Some religious people have a dogged determination to never change their position on doctrinal issues. Even when opposing views are presented from God's authoritative Word, they refuse to consider the possibility that they could be wrong.

Religious indoctrination is one of the most powerful tools Satan uses to blind people from the light of the Gospel (2 Corinthians 4:4). Many former Catholics have said they were indoctrinated at an early age with a set of religious beliefs that they were never to question. When I was being catechized as a young boy, I was strictly forbidden to think independently of the church's authority. Looking back, I can see that I was pressured to submit my mind, intellect and will to the "infallible" teachings of the "one true church."

All religions, apart from Christianity, teach that salvation is dependent upon what man does for God instead of what God has done for man through His only begotten Son. This is why the Gospel is offensive to those who are offensive to God. It strips man of all his "good works" and his feeble efforts to gain salvation, while calling those works filthy rags in the sight of God (Isaiah 64:6). Man deceives himself into believing he is good enough when he is not (Galatians 6:3; Romans 3:23).

Religious pride is powerful tool Satan uses to hold people captive to do his will (2 Timothy 2:24-26). Religious pride usually takes the form of spiritual arrogance or a fierce, unbending loyalty to an institution. Many Roman Catholics refuse to engage in spiritual conversations with non-Catholics, because they are so proud of their religion. They are indoctrinated with the false and fatal belief that the Catholic Church is the one true church and necessary for salvation. We were also brainwashed with the fear that we would forfeit our salvation if we ever left the Catholic Church. According to the *Catechism of the Catholic Church*, we read: "Basing itself on Scripture and Tradition, the Council teaches that the Church, a pilgrim now on earth, is necessary for salvation...Hence they could not be saved who, knowing that the Catholic Church was founded as necessary by God through Christ, would refuse either to enter it or to remain in it" (paragraph 846).

We should not be surprised that God's adversary uses pride as a means to keep sinners ignorant of the Gospel. The deceiver gives man something to do to appease God, so he can boast. The spiritually blind sinner does not know that any attempt to merit salvation actually nullifies God's grace—the only means by which God saves sinners (Romans 11:6). The only thing a repentant sinner can bring to the cross is his sin. He must leave everything else behind (Ephesians 2:8-9).

I witnessed this religious pride in my uncle, a Catholic priest of 61 years. He spent 30 years in southeast Asia leading Hindus and Buddhists to his religion, but not to Jesus Christ. After he returned to America, I was delighted to share God's Gospel with him every time we got together. However, each time he rebuked me with a condescending attitude for daring to question his priestly position of authority. Blinded by religious pride, he belittled my references to the Gospel of grace because of his stubborn confidence in his priestly rituals and sacraments. Clearly, religious pride is one of the greatest obstacles to genuine saving faith. Many Catholics have an unbending loyalty to earthly priests, who offer the same daily sacrifices which can never take away sin (Hebrews 10:11).

Satan does a masterful job of using man's religions to conceal God's glorious Gospel of grace. He and his pawns, who disguise themselves as servants of righteousness, deceive the unwary through a variety of false religious systems (2 Corinthians 11:14-15). To be deceived about one's relationship with God is the most dangerous and perilous position. To leave this earth embracing a false Gospel will result in the most horrifying existence that man could ever experience. Those who die in such a state have no recourse, no escape, and no second chance. May God give us all humble and teachable spirits and a desire to know the truth of His Word!

Those who reject the Gospel usually do so because of their pride. It is interesting that the middle letter in both pride and sin is "I." Self-centeredness is at the heart of all sin, including the sin of unbelief. For out of the heart of men comes, among other sins, the sin of pride (Mark 7:21-23). We have heard the proclamations of prideful unregenerate men. "I am my own authority. I am in control. I am good enough. I don't need the Bible. I can live independent of God. I am happy just the way I am." Whenever "I" is on the throne, it causes men to reject God's Word and His sovereignty.

We know from God's Word that pride is followed by shame, debasement, wrath and destruction. It not only produces self-deception, but it also leads to a persecuting and brazenly contentious spirit. It is demonstrated by the devil, false teachers, the unregenerate and those with unteachable spirits. For many people, the greatest obstacle to learning the truth is their prideful insistence that they already know it. Such were the religious leaders of the first century. The Lord Jesus rebuked them soundly, saying, "They do all their deeds to be noticed by men...they love the place of honor at banquets, and the chief seats in the synagogues, and respectful greetings in the market places" (Matthew 23:5-7). They sought the approval of men over the favor of God. In doing so, they "shut off the kingdom of heaven from men" (Matthew 23:13).

Those who have truly been saved by the precious blood of Jesus will boast in the Lord (1 Corinthians 1:31). "Let him who boasts boast of this: that he understands and knows Me, that I am the Lord who exercises loving kindness, justice, and righteousness on earth" declares the Lord (Jeremiah 9:24). It is time for the proud to humble themselves under the mighty hand of God and seek His forgiveness. For God will look favorably upon "him who is humble and contrite of spirit, and who trembles at My word" (Isaiah 66:2).

God Opposes the Proud but Gives Grace to the Humble

In a Christian's life, there are many paradoxes that the unbelieving world cannot comprehend. We must humble ourselves to be exalted; we must lose our life to find it; we must be the least to become the greatest; and we must die to self to live for Christ (Mat. 16:25, 18:4; 23:12, Rom. 8:13). Of all these paradoxes, the Bible probably gives more vivid contrasts between pride and humility than any other. That is because God hates pride and arrogance while favoring those who are humble (Prov. 8:13).

Pride is a condition of the heart that exchanges the rightful rule of God for self-rule. Instead of depending on God, a proud heart seeks its own glory and purpose. It was pride that led Adam and Eve to disobey God in order to become like God. Our sovereign Lord has never been pleased with the proud, who seek glory for themselves rather than for God. Instead of loving others with kindness and compassion, the proud man harbors criticism and bitterness towards others. Scripture warns us that the proud will ultimately fall but can also be forgiven if and when they are humbled under the sovereign hand of almighty God.

Following are 10 revelations about pride and humility from Scripture which heightens the urgency of the message of the Gospel calling for all people to fall before a holy God in humble submission.

1. **The proud man stands in opposition to God.** The humble man receives God's grace. "God is opposed to the proud, but gives grace to the humble" (James 4:6).

2. **The proud does not acknowledge his weakness.** The humble is content in his weakness for Christ's sake. "I am well content with weaknesses, with insults, with distresses, with persecutions, with difficulties, for Christ's sake; for when I am weak, then I am strong" (2 Corinthians 12:10).

3. **The proud demands his rights.** The humble yields his rights to God. "Have this attitude in yourselves which was also in Christ Jesus...He humbled Himself by becoming obedient to the point of death, even death on a cross" (Philippians 2:5-8).

4. **The proud seeks self-vindication and revenge.** The humble overlooks offenses and waits on God's vindication. "Humble yourselves, therefore, under the mighty hand of God, that He may exalt you at the proper time" (1 Peter 5:6). "A man's discretion makes him slow to anger, And it is his glory to overlook a transgression" (Proverbs 19:11).

5. **The proud is obsessed with praising himself.** The humble lets praise and recognition come from others. "Let another praise you, and not your own mouth" (Proverbs 27:2). "It is not the one who commends himself who is approved, but the one whom the Lord commends" (2 Corinthians 10:18).

6. **The proud is bold to compare himself with others.** The humble avoids comparisons. "We are not bold to class or compare ourselves with some of those who commend themselves; but when they measure themselves by themselves and compare themselves with themselves, they are without understanding" (2 Corinthians 10:12).

7. **The proud exalts himself, bringing dishonor.** The humble is wise to wait for God's exaltation. "For whoever exalts himself will be humbled, and whoever humbles himself will be exalted" (Matthew 23:12). "When pride comes, then comes dishonor, but with the humble is wisdom" (Proverbs 11:2).

8. **The proud seeks the approval of men.** The humble desires the approval of God. "For am I now seeking the favor of men, or of God? Or am I striving to please men? If I were still trying to please men, I would not be a bond-servant of Christ" (Galatians 1:10).

9. **The proud finds greatness in exercising authority over others.** The humble finds greatness through serving others. Jesus said, "You know that the rulers of the Gentiles lord it over them, and their great men exercise authority over them. It is not so among you, but whoever wishes to become great among you shall be your servant" (Matthew 20:25-26).

10. **The proud perceives humility as a weakness.** The humble perceives humility as a strength. "Whoever then humbles himself as this child, he is the greatest in the kingdom of heaven" (Matthew 18:4).

Needless to say, these are profound observations to consider when pride and humility are contrasted. Of the two traits, humility is much more attractive. People are turned off by those who are proud and condescending, because they see pride as a form of self-worship. Humble people are not afraid to seek counsel and take constructive criticism. Prideful people think they know it all and rarely seek the counsel of others or admit they are ever wrong.

Humble people understand their utter dependence on God and yield to Him and His will. Proud people are self-serving, self-centered, and self-dependent on their own strength and wisdom.

Humble people don't have to constantly prove or defend themselves; a stark contrast to prideful people, who are obsessed with proving they are always right. Humble people seek to correct those who are in opposition with gentleness and kindness (2 Timothy 2:25). Proud people sit above God's Word and seek glory for themselves. Humble people submit to God and seek to glorify Him with their lives (1 Corinthians 10:31).

God said the one He favors is "the one who is humble and contrite of spirit, and who trembles at My word" (Isaiah 66:2). What better example do we have than Christ Jesus. He was meek and lowly in heart and "humbled Himself by becoming obedient to the point of death, even death on a cross" (Philippians 2:8).

L.R. Shelton gave an appropriate warning concerning pride. He said, "The Scriptures not only abound with references which show the Lord's hatred of this sin, but they also describe a proud, haughty, conceited, vain, boastful man as being a child of the devil. Why? Because when Satan was in heaven as the highest created being, his heart was lifted up in pride and he fell to become the deceiver. Yes, ever since that moment of haughtiness when Satan's heart was lifted up with pride, he has sought to blight angels and men with the same form of iniquity." Dr. John Ogilvie said, "Pride demands the false worship of ourself. It is the original sin, wanting to be our own gods and run our own lives."

God said the one He favors is "the one who is humble and contrite of spirit, and who trembles at My word" (Isaiah 66:2).

What better example do we have than Christ Jesus. He was meek and lowly in heart and "humbled Himself by becoming obedient to the point of death, even death on a cross" (Philippians 2:8).

We must encourage others to humble themselves under the sovereign hand of almighty God, because He hates pride and arrogance (Proverbs 8:13). Every proud person must be brought down. "The proud look of man will be abased, and the loftiness of man will be humbled, and the Lord alone will be exalted in that day. For the Lord of hosts will have a day of reckoning against everyone who is proud and lofty" (Isaiah 2:11-12). God will not endure anyone "who has a haughty look and an arrogant heart" (Psalm 101:5).

Rome's Opposition to God's Word

As with so many other Catholic doctrines, Rome's teachings on confession and forgiveness stand in opposition to the Word of God. The following fallacious teachings are found in the Catechism of the Catholic Church, paragraphs 1423 to 1498. Through the sacrament of Penance, Catholics make "the first step in returning to the Father from whom one has strayed by sin." The Catechism claims Christ instituted the sacrament of Penance for all sinful members of his Church who, since Baptism, have fallen into grave sin, and have thus lost their baptismal grace. The sacrament of Penance offers a new possibility to convert and to recover the grace of justification. This sacrament is the second plank of salvation after the shipwreck which is the loss of grace. This second conversion is necessary because sin is a rupture of communion with God. Penance, they say, is the only ordinary means of reconciliation with God and with the Church. They believe the authority of priests is expressed in Christ's solemn words to Simon Peter: "I will give you the keys of the kingdom of heaven, and whatever you bind on earth shall be bound in heaven, and whatever you loose on earth shall be loosed in heaven" (Mat. 16:19). "Bind and loose" means whomever you exclude from your communion, will be excluded from communion with God; whomever you receive anew into your communion, God will welcome back into his.

Rome's Denial of God's Promise of Forgiveness

In those few Catholic teachings, we see many denials of God's promises. His Word reveals that those who have been born of God through faith in Jesus Christ will never be separated from the love of God (Rom. 8:33-39). At the cross, God forgave all the sins of all believers. They are all gone, completely forgiven and forever forgotten: the sins against God, against man, against the body, against the law, the sins of commission and the sins of omission, the sins in the past and the sins in the future (Col. 2:13-14). All are removed as far as the east is from the west (Psalm 103:12). This forgiveness is given freely to those who repent and believe the Gospel (Luke 24:47; Acts 10:43). Once sinners have been reconciled to God, future sins can never cause death or separation, because God no longer counts their sins against them (2 Corinthians 5:19). The Bible never speaks of falling in and out of fellowship with God. It never speaks of "a new possibility to convert and recover the grace of justification." Justification is eternal, and conversion is a work of the Holy Spirit, who, along with Christ, guarantees the relationship will never be broken (Hebrews 10:14,13:5; Ephesians 1:13-14).

Who Makes Satisfaction For Sins?

Rome's proclamation that sinners can make satisfaction for their sins is both erroneous and foolish speculation. The sin debt is eternal; no finite man could ever cancel the infinite sin debt. The redemption of his soul is costly, and he should cease trying forever (Psalm 49:8). Nowhere does the Bible say "Penance is the only ordinary means of reconciliation with God." What the Bible does make clear is that the only ground for forgiveness and reconciliation is the precious blood of Jesus Christ (Colossians 1:20; Ephesians 1:7; 1 Peter 1:19). At Calvary, the very thorns God used to curse the earth were worn by the One who became a curse for us. God's righteous wrath, which had been stored up for over 4000 years of man's sin, exploded upon the spotless, innocent Lamb. In an instant, God's eternal wrath was poured out on His only Son. Two Persons of the Trinity, who had and have been eternally joined together were temporarily torn apart (Matthew 27:46). Divine holiness caused the Father to forsake His Son as the bearer of human sin. The all-sufficient Savior made complete satisfaction for sin. To teach otherwise is to blaspheme God and rob Christ of His glory and honor.

Who Does the Binding and Loosing?

Nowhere in the New Testament do we see divine power to bind and loose given to a sacrificial priesthood. Nowhere do we see the need to confess sins to a man in order to be forgiven. The keys which were given to Peter in Matthew 16:19 represent the authority (not the power) to make pronouncements concerning sin. This authority is given to everyone who has received the Spirit, as we see in John 20:22-23. Jesus said to them, "Receive the Holy Spirit. If you forgive the sins of any, their sins have been forgiven them; if you retain the sins of any, they have been retained." Every believer can use the authority of God's Word to say to those who believe the Gospel: "Your sins are forgiven." Likewise, believers can say to those who reject the Gospel: "Your sins are retained." During my 37 years in the Roman Catholic Church, no priest ever asked me if I believed the Gospel. Tragically, I left the confessional box hundreds of times with a false hope, believing I was forgiven, but still carrying the eternal debt for sin.

The Origin of Penance

The Catechism gives the following history of how the ungodly practice of penance originated.

During the first centuries the reconciliation of Christians who had committed particularly grave sins after their Baptism, (for example, idolatry, murder, or adultery) was tied to a very rigorous discipline. Accordingly, penitents had to do public penance for their sins, often for years, before receiving reconciliation. During the seventh century, Irish missionaries took to Europe the "private" practice of penance, which does not require public and prolonged completion of penitential works before reconciliation with the Church. From that time on, the sacrament has been performed in secret between penitent and priest. This new practice envisioned the possibility of repetition and so opened the way to a regular frequenting of this sacrament. It allowed the forgiveness of grave sins and venial sins to be integrated into one sacramental celebration (CCC, 1447).

Chapter 8

THE DEPARTURE FROM THE GOSPEL

———

The Gospel is simple biblical truth coming out of the infinite wisdom of God that brings glory to Him and all of His awesome attributes. It is the great divide that separates the human race into two groups for all eternity.

Tragically, the Gospel of God has been undermined by religion, apostate churches and the seeker sensitive, church growth movement. It has been replaced by a seductive message that makes unbelievers feel comfortable instead of convicted. Churches everywhere are filled with the tares that have been planted with another Gospel. The professing church has invited the world into its assemblies and no longer contends for the faith. It has substituted:

- God's Gospel for synthetic gospels
- Christ for the culture
- worship for entertainment
- repentance for recovery
- enduring hope for instant gratification.

Several years ago a jury awarded $2.2 billion to a cancer patient because her pharmacist had watered down her chemotherapy drugs to make a bigger profit. The hero in the case was the pharmaceutical salesman who blew the whistle after one of his patients died of cancer. He exposed the pharmacist for diluting a drug that was produced to save the lives of cancer victims. It is truly hard to imagine a more deadly form of betrayal. But there is a much more tragic deception going on in many churches.

The Gospel is being diluted of its divine power. The watered down version is no longer a cure for the deadly disease of sin. It has been compromised so much that it has no power to save souls. Many who think they have been saved have been dreadfully deceived. Paradoxically, those discerning Christians who blow the whistle on these compromisers of the Gospel are not considered heroes. Instead, we are called trouble makers, who are divisive, unloving, intolerant and narrow minded. But, we must continue to expose these synthetic gospels for the glory of our Savior and the eternal destiny of those being deceived.

Compromise and capitulation with the enemies of the Gospel are common place. Satan's strategy to attack, misrepresent and pervert the Christian faith has continued unabated throughout the last 2000 years. Organized religion has long been an enemy of the Gospel of Jesus Christ. It is the duty and responsibility of all Christians to contend earnestly for the faith and to expose all forms of deception. We must also warn those who continue to depart from the eternal Gospel of Jesus Christ.

I have compassion for those who are committed to a religion without any real understanding of how the religion may oppose the Word of God. For example, to be "committed to Roman Catholicism" simply because a person was born into a Catholic family is foolish. To be loyal to a religion without investigating its core doctrines, its lifeblood, is ignorance masquerading as faithfulness. It is the sin of religious pride that is usually accompanied by an unteachable spirit.

I also have compassion for "religious" people, who mechanically live out their "faith" because they've been told it's the right thing to do. People who blindly follow religious leaders and rituals are too proud to admit their lives are empty...too paralyzed by deceit to investigate the Truth. They do not know why they believe what they do. They have blindly inherited someone else's tradition. Their religion determines their identity, and they will defend it even if they are not actively involved in it. Their faith is so "personal" that they dare not speak of it to others. They swallow every false teaching as Truth, without question.

Each individual has a right to embrace God's truth or reject it. But don't expect me or others like me to cheer them on as they stomp proudly toward hell's gates. Expect us to be bitterly angry, savagely grieved, and desperately fighting. We are angry at a very real enemy (the master deceiver) for being such a devious and convincing liar. We are grieved at the destiny others have chosen. We are fighting and praying for their very souls.

And it is a battle we are determined to continue to fight—not for ourselves, but for those who continue in their blindness. If we step on their toes in the process, forgive us. But don't expect us to give up the fight simply because it becomes uncomfortable for them. If our roles were reversed, I hope they would do as much for me. "Pride goes before a fall" (Proverbs 16:18). How grievous for the countless millions with religious pride that their fall is into the pit of everlasting torment.

Satan's Assaults on the Christian Faith

Some evangelical leaders have been joyfully announcing that there is a great spiritual revival taking place in our country. However, a closer and more discerning look reveals there is actually a massive infiltration of countless deceivers, masquerading as messengers of Christ, who are counterfeiting the Christian faith and distorting the Gospel. "And no wonder, for even Satan disguises himself as an angel of light." (2 Corinthians 11:14-15). These legions of liars are all part of Satan's insidious assault on the only true faith. Satan's ultimate goal is to thwart

God's harvest of lost souls by holding them captive with his fatal lies. His relentless attacks are strategically aimed at six targets.

The Supremacy of God's Word

Satan's all-out assault on the Word of God began in the Garden of Eden. Disguised as a charming serpent, he persuaded Eve to dismiss God's Word and believe his lie. First, he created doubt by asking: "Has God indeed said, 'You shall not eat from any tree of the garden?'" (Genesis 3:1). Then Satan convinced Eve that God's Word was not true and could not be trusted. He said: "You surely shall not die!" (Genesis 3:4).

The "father of lies" uses this same strategy to deceive the world through all of his religions. He uses religious leaders to ask: "Has God indeed said, 'The wages of sin is death?'" (Romans 6:23). Then speaking through the Roman Catholic Church, he says: "You surely shall not die" - venial sins do not bring death. It impedes the soul's progress in the exercise of the virtues and the practice of the moral good; it merits temporal punishment. (CCC 1863).

Satan's attack on the Word of God is understandable, because it is the supreme authority for the Christian faith and brings forth eternal life to those who believe it (1 Pet. 1:23). Nothing else possesses its divine character. Scripture is absolutely trustworthy because it is true and is given by the inspiration of God (2 Timothy 3:16; John 17:17). The Bible is also the only book that foretells the future, and it does so with great precision and detail. It is sacred and never to be altered (Proverbs 30:6). In fact, God gave a strong rebuke to those who would pervert the Word of God with the words of men (Jeremiah 23:36).

Yet, Roman Catholic bishops have chosen to do just that. They dare to say their traditions, which they have foolishly added to Scripture, make up one single deposit of the Word of God (CCC 97). By doing this, the bishops have elevated their tradition to the same authority as Scripture and, to their advantage, have become the supreme authority for the Catholic faith (CCC 85). Whenever the supreme authority of God is replaced by the authority of men, the perversion of biblical doctrines runs rampant.

The Sufficiency of God's Word

The adversary's attack on God's Son is skillful, because Jesus is the Author and Perfecter of the Christian faith. Christ alone is able and sufficient to save sinners completely from sin (Hebrews 7:25). His one offering for sin makes believers perfect forever (Hebrews 10:14). His blood is sufficient to purify every believer from every sin (1 John 1:7). His death was sufficient to cancel the eternal sin debt of every believer (Colossians 2:14). Paul described the sufficiency of Jesus when he wrote: "In Him you have been made complete" (Colossians 2:10). Every spiritual blessing that anyone could ever desire or need is found in Christ Jesus.

For these reasons, Satan attacks the sufficiency of Christ with a vengeance. The prince of this world has convinced many that they need Christ plus psychology, or Christ plus rituals and sacraments, or Christ plus purgatory and indulgences, or Christ plus law-keeping and good works. His agents deny Christ's work of redemption is finished. They foolishly believe they have the power to call the Lord Jesus back down from heaven to offer Him again and again on their altars. These slanderous assaults on the sufficiency of Christ not only rob the true Jesus of His glory, but also point the lost to another Jesus who is unable to save them without help from others (2 Corinthians 11:4). Satan offers other mediators, but God has given us only One (1 Timothy 2:5). Satan offers other saviors, but God has given only one Name (Acts 4:12). Ministers of the devil who deny the sufficiency of God's Son must preach another Gospel to instruct people what they must do to be saved. Another Jesus always produces another Gospel.

The Singularity of God's Gospel

You would think Paul's undisputed condemnation of the Judaizers for perverting the Gospel would keep the Gospel pure within the professing church. However, the Gospel of Rome is a much greater distortion. It requires Catholics to receive sacraments, keep the law, attend weekly sacrifices and do works of mercy for their salvation (CCC, para. 815; 1032; 1129; 2068). Satan's relentless assaults against the Gospel continue to come from two distinct enemies - legalism, which is most prominent in Roman Catholicism, and antinomianism, which is most noticeable throughout liberal Protestantism. Those who teach antinomianism distort the Gospel by declaring any person who has been justified by faith in Christ is no longer obligated to obey the moral law. The apostle Paul corrected this ungodly doctrine in 1 Corinthians 5-6.

Whenever the "father of lies" enters the pulpit, he does not deny the Gospel but perverts it with additions or subtractions. Any perversion of the Gospel is ultimately the devil's delusion, which keeps his captives in bondage. With so many perversions in the church today, there is a desperate need for the preaching of the pure Gospel of God. It alone has the power to save sinners from the punishment, power and, ultimately, the presence of sin (Romans 1:16).

The Sovereignty of God's Grace

One of the strongest expressions of God's sovereign grace is given by Paul: "He chose us in Him before the foundation of the world... In love He predestined us to adoption as sons through Jesus Christ to Himself, according to the kind intention of His will, to the praise of the glory of His grace, which He freely bestowed on us in the Beloved" (Ephesians 1:4-6).

Clearly it is the will of God, not man's will, that determines who will be graciously adopted into The Father's eternal family (John 1:12-13). Yet the Roman Catholic Church rejects God's sovereignty and teaches it is the will of man that determines who becomes a child of God. Consider the teachings of Rome: "Baptism... makes the neophyte a new creature, an adopted son of God ... and co-heir with Him" (CCC, 1265). "The church and the parents, would deny a child the priceless grace of becoming a child of God, were they not to confer Baptism shortly after birth" (CCC, 1250).

Sovereign grace is the only means by which our merciful God saves sinners (Ephesians 2:8-9). Satan, being fully aware of this, created a false way of salvation which nullifies or suspends God's saving grace. His system of works-righteousness is found in all the religions of the world. From Buddhism to Zoroastrianism, the devil's influence is found in teachings that say you must do good works to merit God's favor or appease His justice.

The Security of God's Children

The Prince of Darkness knows he can never kidnap the children of God, who have been delivered into the glorious light of the Son, but he can make their walk ineffective. His most effective tool is deception. He uses false teachers to lie about the power and promises of God, which are explicitly revealed in the Gospel of grace. The very promise of the Gospel is eternal life, backed up by the power of Almighty God to keep those He has saved. This divine gift of everlasting life can never be lost, revoked or rejected once received (John 10:28; Rom. 11:29). Christians who are uncertain about the eternal duration of their salvation are often paralyzed in their walk with Christ. They stumble in doubt and feel defenseless against the attacks of Satan.

The Sanctity of God's Church

As the master counterfeiter, Satan depreciates the sanctity of the church by planting tares among the wheat (Matthew 13:25-30). These tares may never realize they are pawns of the devil, but they infect the church and bring much shame to the name of Jesus Christ. No assembly is immune from these demonic infiltrators, who cause turmoil and division with their doctrinal error and habitual sin. Paul wrote: "I know that after my departure savage wolves will come in among you, not sparing the flock; and from among your own selves men will arise, speaking perverse things, to draw away the disciples after them" (Acts 20:29-30). We know the primary commission of the church is to equip and encourage believers to go into the world and make disciples for the Lord Jesus Christ. In order to counter this objective, Satan brings the world into the church to distract it from its purpose. Rather than feeding the sheep, the church starts entertaining the goats.

How Must Believers Respond

As spiritual darkness overcomes the diminishing light of the Gospel, believers must be of sober spirit and be on the alert (1 Peter 5:8). Those who belong to the Lord Jesus must put on the full armor of God each day and be prepared for spiritual warfare (Ephesians 6:10-18). Satan will continue taking advantage of those who are ignorant of his schemes (2 Corinthians 2:11). His sustained attacks on the Christian faith will become more and more fierce as we approach the day when Jesus Christ returns triumphantly for His church. Until that glorious appearing of our Savior, deceiving spirits will continue to influence the great apostasy from the faith. "The falling away" is taking place everywhere, as apostates turn from the truth to follow doctrines of demons (1 Timothy 4:1).

How can believers brace for the storm that we know will cause shipwreck to the faith of apostates? Paul exhorts us: "Be strong in the Lord and in the power of His might" (Ephesians 6:10). "Be steadfast, immovable, always abounding in the work of the Lord" (1 Corinthians 15:58). In the epistle of Jude, which is often called the Acts of the Apostates, we are exhorted "to contend earnestly for the faith which was once and for all delivered to the saints" (Jude 3).

Apostasy from the Faith

One of the greatest mysteries in life is how anyone could come to a knowledge of the Lord Jesus Christ and then depart from Him. Judas is the classic example of an apostate—one who abandons the faith he once held. Judas walked and lived with the Son of God for over three years, a royal privilege granted to only 11 other men. Yet after witnessing the Messiah's sinless life, seeing His miracles, experiencing His divine power and hearing His profound wisdom, Judas betrayed Him. It was during the celebration of the Passover meal that Judas deliberately defected from the faith of the apostles and sealed his eternal destiny in the lake of fire (Matthew 26:24-25).

Many others have departed from the faith since that fateful night. The apostle John wrote about apostates who "went out from us" because "they were not really of us; for if they had been of us, they would have remained with us" (1 John 2:19). Most apostates never reject the Christian faith completely; they fall away to a counterfeit form of Christianity. It is for this reason we have seen two streams of Christianity operating side-by-side for 2000 years.

The Apostolic Church

One stream is the apostolic church, founded by the Lord Jesus, who is the Master Builder. It includes only the few who have entered through the narrow gate (Matthew 7:13). They have been born of the Spirit and sanctified by the truth. This Spirit of Promise seals and indwells each member, thus guaranteeing their eternal inheritance (Ephesians 1:13-14). This church will be persecuted, hated and despised, but will continue holding to apostolic faith until Jesus returns to take it to heaven as His bride. The gates of hell shall not prevail against this church (Matthew 16:18).

The Apostate Church

The other stream is an apostate church made up of those who profess Christ but are spiritually dead. They believe a distorted Gospel, follow another spirit and reject the faith of the apostles (1 Timothy 4:1). This church is being built by men who ignore the Master Builder's blueprint and instead follow their own methods and movements. Maligning the way of truth, they seduce many with their sensuality (2 Peter 2:2). Apostates will increase in number and grow worse and worse, deceiving and being deceived, until the Day of our Lord (2 Timothy 3:13). These "professing" Christians will not endure sound doctrine. Instead they will turn away from the truth and turn to teachers who tickle their ears with messages of self-esteem (2 Timothy 4:3-4). Paul called these teachers "grievous wolves", who enter the church, speaking perverse things to draw away disciples after them (Acts 20:29-30). It is important to note that all apostates are unbelievers but not all unbelievers are apostates.

The Primary Cause of Apostasy

The major cause of apostasy can be traced to various spiritual influences that include demonic deceptions and divine judgments. The "father of lies" has been seducing the visible church into an ecumenical spirituality in an attempt to unite the religions of the world. Driven by his desire to be worshipped as god, he will continue to attack God's Word with an unrestrained determination. Post-modern philosophy is currently his most effective tool. Church leaders who are caught up in this movement are saying we cannot know absolute truth. And since we cannot know absolute truth, we cannot be dogmatic about doctrine or moral standards. They say dogmatic preaching must give way to dialogue between people of all faiths in order to seek unity for common goals.

Divine judgment is also a cause for apostasy. Those who refuse to love and believe the truth for salvation will be sent a deluding influence, so they might believe what is false and be judged (2 Thessalonians 2:9-12). A divine judgment in the form of moral apostasy is also given to those who suppress the truth in unrighteousness. By refusing to acknowledge God any longer, He gives them over to depraved minds and degrading passions for people of the same sex (Romans 1:18-32).

The Step-by-Step Drift into Apostasy

Step One

God's Word is rejected as the supreme authority for faith and practice. This creates uncertainty over whether to follow Jesus and His Word or the traditions and movements of men. Traditions and movements of men cause confusion and divided loyalties. Man's words and wisdom become as important as God's Word. People start following "Christian" personalities instead of the Word of God. Pastors discard the Lord's blue print for building His church and create their own strategy. Pastors win the approval of men for the size of their church, rather than their faithfulness and fidelity to God's Word. Churches give people what they want instead of what they need. The power of the Gospel is weakened by compromise and made more inclusive to gain a larger following. Biblical evangelism is replaced by man's methods of conversion, "easy-believism," or sacramental salvation.

Scripture is cited only for selfish ambition, resulting in little or no discernment. Their spurious faith is exposed when trials and temptations arise. The pursuit of sanctification is neglected. Biblical warnings to expose false teachers are ignored. A little leaven in the form of heresy is allowed to circulate. Contenders for the faith are labeled as divisive and intolerant. Women are allowed to teach and have functional authority over men.

Step Two

Scripture is twisted and distorted to gain power, control and riches. Truth is determined by subjective personal experiences rather than the objective Word of God. Biblical ignorance provides fertile ground for false teachers. "Infallible" bishops claim to be successors of the apostles. The Gospel becomes more inclusive to attract more people. Expository preaching is replaced by topical messages. Biblical ignorance in the pew provides fertile ground for false teachers to prosper. Trials and persecution expose dead and spurious faith. The exhortation to contend earnestly for the faith is ignored. Ungodly men creep in and turn the grace of our God into licentiousness. Doctrinal error and sin are tolerated by pastors who neglect their responsibility to protect the sheep. Worldliness and ungodly influences are present. Hearts are unresponsive to the Holy Spirit. God is honored with lips but hearts are far from Him. Love for God grows cold. Those who contend for the faith are asked to leave. Satan sows his tares in the church with little or no resistance.

Step Three

Entertainment, idolatry, liturgy and rituals replace the Lord Jesus as the central focus of worship. Programs and entertainment have forced Jesus out of the church. Pastors are more interested in entertaining the goats than feeding the sheep. Ear-tickling messages give people what they want instead of what they need. Pop psychology or politically correct viewpoints become the starting point for Sunday's message rather than the text of Scripture. Sound doctrine and truth are suppressed for the sake of ecumenical unity. Hearts become hardened and love for God grows cold. Doctrinal error flourishes and is embraced with stubborn pride. There is no love for the truth and no discernment. People stand for nothing and fall for everything. A form of godliness exists, but it is void of power. Blatantly immoral lifestyles and sin are present and accepted. Idolatry is practiced and encouraged. Women are ordained as pastors. A stubborn refusal to accept correction is present. The devil is no longer resisted.

God's Gospel is totally rejected and Jesus has been removed from the church. Deception is full-blown. Lying signs and wonders, including apparitions, are embraced as messages from God or Mary. Idolatry and prayers to the dead are encouraged. Those who embrace truth are called "anathema" and asked to leave. Grace is turned into a license to sin. The holy things of God are mocked. Doctrines of demons are followed. The church's lamp stand has been removed and a certain terrifying judgment is now unavoidable.

Perhaps you are in a church or denomination that is drifting into apostasy. Will Jesus Christ use you to contend earnestly for the faith and protect the sanctity of His church? In these last days of growing apostasy and deception, we all need to heed the warning of Peter and encourage others to do the same: "Therefore, dear friends, since you have been forewarned, be on your guard so that you may not be carried away by the error of the lawless and fall from your secure position" (2 Peter 3:17). Will you defend the glory and honor of our great God and Savior and protect the purity of His Gospel? May God's Word exhort and encourage us to fight the good fight of faith!

Past and Future Apostasy

Biblical history confirms there have always been apostate churches like the one at Laodicea (Revelation 3:14-22), as well as individual apostates (Hebrews 10:26-31). However, "the apostasy" will reach its prophetic peak just prior to the Day of our Lord (2 Thessalonians 2:3). Paul's use of the definite article suggests that the downward spiral into apostasy will be culminated by one identifiable act. It will occur when the "man of lawlessness is revealed". This "son of destruction, who opposes and exalts himself above every so called god or object of worship...takes his seat in the temple of God, displaying himself as being God (2 Thessalonians 3:3-4). This apostasy will be a blasphemous act of unprecedented magnitude by a demonically influenced world leader. This "second Judas" will desecrate the temple which will be rebuilt in Jerusalem at that time, by declaring himself to be God, thus committing the abomination of desolation. The "first Judas" desecrated the temple with the money he received by betraying the Son of God (Matthew 27:5).

The Lord Jesus warned us the end times would be marked by great deception, such that the world has never known (Matthew 24). The spiritual deception which covers the earth will be so prevalent that Jesus asked the question: "When the Son of Man comes, will He find faith on the earth?" (Luke 18:8). This fatal deception will cause more churches, denominations, seminaries and individuals to drift into apostasy unless biblical warnings are heeded. Each professing Christian's faith will be constantly tested, as more seducing spirits invade the church.

What Are Believers to Do?

1. Pray that we will be strong in the Lord as we put on the full armor of God. Recognize we are in an intense battle for truth against the schemes of the devil and the wicked forces of darkness (Ephesians 6:10-12).

2. Earnestly contend for the faith. When anyone in our circle of influence is deceiving or being deceived, we must lovingly confront and correct them using Scripture (2 Timothy 3:16).

3. We must abide in God's Word to discern truth from error (John 8:31-32). Do not be swept away by every wind of doctrine. Every few years a new fad hits the church. These movements divert people away from the sure Word of God. We must guard against the craftiness and trickery of men (Ephesians 4:14).

4. Pray for your church leaders and hold them accountable to the Word of God. We must be like the Bereans, who

examined the Scriptures daily to test the veracity of the Apostle Paul's teaching (Acts 17:11).

5. Identify and avoid false teachers so others will not be deceived (Rom. 16:17-18).

May our love for Jesus Christ compel us to be His light in an ever-darkening world. Be encouraged! Jesus said these things must take place before He comes for His church. Keep looking up, our redemption is near. Born again Christians must embrace hope!

Two Streams of Christianity

BORN AGAIN CHRISTIANS	APOSTATES
Contend for the God-given faith of the apostles (Jude 3)	Have deliberately departed from the apostles' faith (1 John 2:19)
Exalt Jesus Christ as the only Master, Lord and Head of the Church (Ephesians 1:22)	Deny Jesus Christ as the only Master, Lord and Head of the Church (Jude 4)
Possessors of Christ, made alive by the Spirit (Romans 8:10-11)	Professors of Christ, twice dead (Matthew 7:22; Jude 12)
Are devoted to apostolic teaching and sound doctrine (Acts 2:42)	Introduce destructive heresies and do not endure sound doctrine (2 Timothy 4:3; 2 Peter 2:1)
Proclaim salvation by grace alone through what God has done in Christ (Romans 3:24-26; 11:6)	Deceive people with a "salvation" by grace plus what man must do for God (Galatians 1:6-9)
Receive grace and turn from ungodliness and worldly desires (Titus 2:11-12)	Turn the grace of our God into licentious-ness (Jude 4)
Children of God called out of the world and enrolled in heaven (2 Timothy 3:12; Hebrews 12:23)	Godless people blinded by the prince of the world and condemned (2 Corinthians 4:4; Jude 4)
Know God and do good works prepared by Him (Ephesians 2:10)	Profess to know God, but deny Him by their deeds (Titus 1:16)

People May Never Know They Are Deceived

If I were to insult you, you'd feel the sting immediately. If I were to embarrass you, you'd be the first to know. But if I were to deceive you...you might never know it! As painful as being insulted or embarrassed can be, at least you're aware of what's taking place. But deception can be deadly, because you don't realize you are being betrayed, misled, seduced or ensnared. It's much more than a clever sleight of hand. Deceived people are not even aware they are being misled unless they are confronted with the truth. Tragically, many go to their graves deceived about their relationship with God.

The Starting Point: Your Source for Truth

Needless to say, no one wants to be victim of deception. The key is to be anchored in the truth. To be firmly rooted and guarded from deception, one must answer the question Pontus Pilate asked when responding to Jesus: "What is truth?" (John 18:38). How would you answer that question? What is your source for truth? Is it trustworthy? Will it protect you from the schemes and lies of the master deceiver, Satan?

The biblical prophet Jeremiah gave wise counsel for choosing who to trust. He said if you put your trust in man, you will be cursed like a withered bush in a barren desert. However, if your ultimate trust is in God, Jeremiah said you will flourish like a tree planted by the water (Jeremiah 17:5-8). If our trust is in God, we also trust His Word, which is eternally true (John 3:33-34, 17:17; 2 Samuel 7:28; Psalm 119:160).

Still many people today disregard Jeremiah's advice and these assertions in Scripture. In their search for truth, they put their trust in man and religious leaders—instead of God and His Word.

Whom Will You Trust?

Catholics, for example, believe that the pope and the Roman Catholic Church teach exactly what Jesus and the Bible teach. But how do we know if the pope's teachings or the dogmas of the Roman Catholic Church are true? The only way we can be 100 percent sure is to do what the church of Berea did in New Testament times. They examined the Scriptures to see if what the Apostle Paul taught them was true (Acts 17:11). We must use the same scriptural standard for the teachings of all religious leaders. Disregarding the objective truth of God's Word in favor of the subjective teachings of men can be a tragic mistake.

The Danger of Deception

Many religious teachings today and throughout history go against what the Bible clearly teaches. Why is this such a critical concern? Because your eternal destiny depends on how you respond to what God has said, not man.

For example, as we have seen in many places throughout this book, here is how Catholic doctrine misleads people about God's plan of salvation:

- All graces needed to attain eternal life can be merited (Catechism of the Catholic Church (CCC), 2027).
- Catholics are reborn as sons of God and freed from sin through water baptism (CCC 1213).
- Purgatory is a cleansing fire that achieves the holiness necessary for heaven (CCC 1030-31).
- Jesus is offered daily as a sacrificial victim on Catholic altars (CCC 1367).
- Venial sins are not deserving of hell (CCC 1863).
- By performing acts of penance, Catholics can expiate their own sins (CCC 1459,1477).

The Bible says man is saved by believing God's truth (Ephesians 1:13-14; Romans 10:17). God can never deceive anyone (Titus 1:1-2). But man remains condemned if he continues in deception. Without the Scriptures as the final authority and basis for truth, there is no way to counter or refute what the Roman Catholic Church says—or any religious institution for that matter.

False religious systems hold people in bondage to deception by perverting God's truth and grace. Any religion that teaches its followers that salvation is obtained through human effort and merit is nullifying the grace of God. Yet grace is the only means by which God saves sinners! The Bible says "if by grace, it is no longer because of works; otherwise grace would no longer be grace" (Romans 11:6). Moreover, any religion that deviates from God's eternal Word is a perversion of the truth and a grand deception that subtly or overtly draws people away onto a path that leads to destruction.

Misplaced Faith

Some people blindly put their faith in religious leaders, assuming that their leaders would never seduce anyone with a false plan of salvation. Yet the Apostle Paul warned that "from your own group, men will come forward perverting the truth to draw the disciples away after them" (Acts 20:30). Other people simply choose not to respond or conform their lives to truth. Instead, they turn away to listen to teachers who say what they want to hear (2 Timothy 4:3-4). Then there are people who have a zeal for God, but not in line with the truth. Many people have been indoctrinated with false teaching and have difficulty believing the truth. They fail because they refuse to let go of unbiblical beliefs or don't know how to discern the difference.

It was disobedience to God, a lack of faith in His purpose, plan, and Word, that separated Adam and Eve from Him. Instead, they chose to put their faith in the deceiver, which brought spiritual and physical death to us all. Adam fell prey to Satan's distortion of God's Word rather than evaluate what Satan said in comparison to the accuracy of God's command. We must know the Scriptures so we are not deceived and led astray by man's misrepresentation of what God has said for all eternity.

Two Spiritual Fathers

God has revealed that trusting in anything other than Christ and His Word is evidence of deception. Those who choose to follow the traditions, opinions, and philosophies of men will be condemned. Jesus said "Whoever rejects Me and does not accept My words has something to judge him: the word that I spoke, it will condemn him on the last day" (John 12:48). By contrast, how wonderful are the words, "to those who did accept Him He gave power to become children of God to those who believe in His name" (John 1:12). "Whoever believes in Him [Jesus Christ] will not be condemned, but whoever does not believe has already been condemned, because he has not believed in the name of the only Son of God" (John 3:18).

When it comes to the Gospel, are you basing your life and eternal destiny on the eternal truths of God's Word or on the Catholic traditions added to God's truth? How will you respond to God's truth? All people fall into one of two categories:

We are either children of the devil (John 8:43–45)	— OR —	children of God (John 1:12).
We live as slaves to sin	— OR —	as slaves to righteousness (Romans 6:16–18).
We will spend eternity under the wrath of God	— OR —	in His loving presence.

The safeguard against deception is to be able to discern truth from error by abiding in God's Word. Jesus was saying to those Jews who had believed Him, "If you continue in My word, *then* you are truly disciples of Mine; and you will know the truth, and the truth will make you free." John 8:31-32

When we drift from God's Word, the truth, we become easily deceived and lack discernment. Sadly, the lack of discernment is the reason so many churches around the world are drifting into apostasy or dying.

The Death of Discernment in The Church

Have you considered the spiritual health of your church in these days of tolerance and compromise? Is the leadership earnestly contending for the faith against the current wave of ecumenism? A. W. Tozer used the illustration of circulating blood to describe the health of a church. "The red corpuscles are like faith: they carry the life giving oxygen to every part of the body. The white cells are like discernment: they pounce upon dead and toxic matter and carry it out to the drain. In a healthy heart there must be provision for keeping dead and poisonous matter out of the life stream."

Using Tozer's analogy, churches that are dead or dying are the churches that no longer have the ability or the desire to discern truth from error. If they cannot identify toxic doctrinal error, the poison can never be removed from the body. And if it is not removed, it will continue to circulate, bringing confusion to believers and false hope to "seekers."

Based on the reports we hear from people all over the world, there are many churches on the edge of apostasy. Many are subscribing to the latest post-modern fad called "the Emerging Church" which attempts to reach the emerging generation with a new way of "doing church." If you key "Emerging Church" in your favorite search engine, you will see numerous entries declaring that worship should now be a mystical and holistic experience using images, candles, stained glass windows and even darkness to enhance spirituality. One of the leaders of the movement is Brian McLaren, pastor and author of the controversial and award winning book, *A New Kind of Christian*. The book expressly argues that the Bible should not be regarded as infallible or authoritative. McLaren seeks unity between Catholics and Evangelicals and applauds Chuck Colson for leading this unbiblical movement.

The Emerging Church places more importance on mystical and sensual worship experiences that unite rather than essential biblical doctrines that divide. Churches that move from a Word-driven message to an image-driven message only contribute to the "dumbing down" of professing Christians. Few will be able to discern the difference between the true Gospel and a counterfeit Gospel. The end result will be unsanctified churches which tolerate, embrace and encourage unbelievers instead of edifying and equipping a new generation of believers.

Those Who Stand for Nothing Will Fall for Anything

Irving Bible Church, located in Texas between Dallas and Ft. Worth, has emerged into a church without discernment. The pastor, Andy McQuitty, has publicly stated that both John Paul II and Mother Teresa are most assuredly in heaven. In the May issue of the church's monthly magazine, *Chatter*, he featured an 11 x 14 picture of these two influential Catholics, who deceived the world with another Gospel. McQuitty called the differences between Catholics and Protestants "theological pettiness." He said, "it is just plain silly to write each other off as far as true Christianity is concerned. We'll have plenty of time in heaven to figure out who was right about purgatory and Mary." McQuitty can't see why both faiths can't cooperate "in building the Kingdom of our common Lord Jesus Christ." He described John Paul as "a Man of God, not a man of this world, who became popular by testifying to the unpopular truths of Jesus Christ." According to McQuitty, the pope was "a great man whom all Christians should admire, thank and emulate." Finally, he wrote, "I confess as a protestant pastor that my spiritual life and faith has been enriched by this Catholic pope who taught me that being a hero isn't about success or power."

Evidently Irving Bible Church (IBC) has a few discerning souls, whose concerns prompted McQuitty to send out this public e-mail. "A few of you have raised concerns, most of which can be boiled down to this question: 'Is IBC becoming Roman Catholic?' To which the answer is, 'No way, Jose.'" He wrote: "I understand where the question comes from, though. The introduction at IBC of certain elements such as candles and liturgies and communion wafers and the reference to communion as the "Eucharist", combined with the recent death of Pope John Paul II and the attendant recognition that his life received here, has caused some (particularly those who were raised Catholic and had a less than happy experience) to bristle."

McQuitty sounds like many Catholics who think we left the Roman Catholic Church because we "had a less than happy experience." No, we left when our Sovereign Lord opened our eyes to see the true Gospel as He revealed it in His supremely authoritative Word. As with other born-again former Catholics, we all left because we could no longer stay in a false religion that deceives its people on life's most critical issue: "What must I do to be saved?" We all left in obedience to God's Word, to worship Him in Spirit and Truth (John 4:24). If we were members of Irving Bible Church, we would have to leave that church as well, because the pastor has demonstrated no discernment and an unwillingness to be corrected by Scripture. A pastor without spiritual discernment cannot protect his congregation from Satan's continuous attacks on the Gospel of Jesus Christ.

Some will say that I am being judgmental and that I have no right to do so. But how can Christians contend earnestly for the faith unless they make judgments on what "the faith" is? How can Christians defend and proclaim the Gospel without discerning what "the Gospel" is? We see a biblical example of one brother judging another when Paul publicly corrected Peter, who was not being "straightforward about the truth of the Gospel" (Galatians 2:11-14). A. W. Tozer said: "Among the gifts of the Spirit, scarcely is one of greater practical usefulness than the gift of discernment. This gift should be highly valued and frankly sought as being almost indispensable in these critical times. This gift will enable us to distinguish the chaff from the wheat and to divide the manifestations of the flesh from the operations of the Spirit."

Christians Are Exhorted to Judge

Many Christians are unaware of their responsibility to judge and test all things. Paul exhorted: "I pray that your love may abound still more and more in real knowledge and all discernment, so that you may approve the things that are excellent, in order to be sincere and blameless until the day of Christ" (Philippians 1:9-10). Christians need to take discernment and judgment seriously in this life because of the great responsibility that awaits us in the future. Paul reminds us: "Do you not know that the saints will judge the world? Do you not know that we shall judge angels? How much more, matters of this life?" (1 Corinthians 6:2-3). Paul even commended the Bereans for rightfully judging his teaching. "They received the word with great eagerness, examining the Scriptures daily, to see whether these things were so" (Acts 17:11). The apostle John warned and exhorted Christians: "Beloved, do not believe every spirit, but test the spirits to see whether they are from God; because many false prophets have gone out into the world" (1 John 4:1). Clearly, all Christians are called to judge righteously by using the Word of God as the plumb line for discerning truth from error.

Discernment Is A Discipline

New babes in Christ must discipline themselves to go beyond the "milk" of the Gospel and begin chewing on "solid food" by studying the whole counsel of God. "For everyone who partakes only of milk is unskilled in the word of righteousness, for he is a babe. But solid food belongs to those who are of full age, that is, those who by reason of use have their senses exercised to discern both good and evil." (Hebrews 5:13-14). Spiritual discernment is a discipline and a privilege that only Christians can exercise. Paul wrote: "But the natural man does not receive the things of the Spirit of God, for they are foolishness to him; nor can he know them, because they are spiritually discerned. But he who is spiritual judges all things." (1 Corinthians 2:14-16).

How Are We to Judge?

John wrote: "Do not judge according to appearance, but judge with righteous judgment" (John 7:24). Jesus said: "For in the way you judge, you will be judged; and by your standard of measure, it will be measured to you" (Matthew 7:1-5). The instruction Jesus gives for judging others is to make sure you are not guilty of the same error or sin! Paul echoed these words when he wrote: "Do you suppose this, O man, when you pass judgment upon those who practice such things and do the same yourself, that you will escape the judgment of God?" (Romans 2:3). When we judge, we must judge righteously and with pure hearts!

The Goal of Discernment

As we practice the gift of discernment, let us question our motives. Is our objective to be obedient to God's Word for the purpose of helping, healing, correcting, warning and sharing in the spirit of love? Does our discernment lead people towards truth and righteous living? Are we concerned for the purity of the body of Christ? Have we come to acknowledge that when the gift of discernment is not exercised, the church cannot be purged of error and sin and the name of Jesus Christ cannot be fully glorified and honored as the Holy Head of the Church?

The critical issue in the church today is the purity of the Gospel. That alone is the rudder that must guide the church through stormy waters that have been stirred up by every wind of doctrine. Take away the ability to discern objective truth and churches turn into cafeterias serving whatever junk food people want instead of the disciplined diet they need for spiritual life and health. Without a steady diet of the whole counsel of God, churches become entertainment centers for goats instead of sanctuaries for the Shepherd's sheep (Matthew 25:32). Unregenerate people, who are never exhorted to examine their faith, will continue attending church to enjoy the music, entertainment and "feel good" messages. Unless these people are confronted with their sin, their need for a Savior and the eternal consequences of a spurious faith, they are destined to hear these terrifying words from Jesus: "I never knew you; depart from Me" (Matthew 7:23). May God help us all to be part of the solution and not part of the problem.

The Consequences of Deception and Lack of Discernment

A record number of Evangelicals and Protestants are departing from the faith of the apostles to the apostate religion of Roman Catholicism. We must wonder if they are departing because they were never part of us. If they had been part of us, they would have remained with us (1 John 2:19). Only God knows their hearts, but it is difficult to understand how anyone can join a false religion after being born again of the Spirit of Truth. True converts to Christ are instantly sealed with the Holy Spirit, who is a deposit guaranteeing their eternal inheritance (Ephesians 1:13-14). False converts are prone to apostasy because they do not have a Divine Shepherd protecting them from thieves who seek to steal, kill and destroy them (John 10). This growing number of apostates is a tragic fulfillment of end-time prophecy. Jesus warned that during the last days many will be deceived by many false prophets in His Name (Matthew 24:4-24).

When people are prone to deception, due to Scriptural ignorance and lack of discernment, they can be led down virtually any destructive path through lies, distortions or exaggerations of the truth, or any other selfishly motivated purposes. Ultimately, all such defections or deceptions have their root in a perversion of Scriptural authority.

I believe one of the catalysts for the mass exodus of Evangelicals to Rome is the push to reverse the Reformation. As more Evangelical leaders sign unity accords with Roman Catholics, we will see more defections. Every Evangelical leader who signs a document stating he shares a common faith in the Gospel with Roman Catholics has, knowingly or unknowingly, endorsed Catholicism as a valid expression of true Christianity. But there is another catalyst I would like to address, with a hope that we can be better prepared in our witness for Christ.

The Question of Authority

At one point during my ministry, I corresponded with two former Dallas Seminary students, who left to join the Roman Catholic religion. Their departures were over the issue of authority. Both contended that the Catholic Church gave birth to the Bible, established the canon, and, therefore, was the only infallible interpreter of Scripture. However, history reveals a different story on the development of the canon. Long before a church council formally recognized the canon, the books were received and recognized as being the inspired Word of God. They were functioning with supreme and complete authority in matters of faith and doctrine. To separate the inspired writings from other spurious writings, and place them into one volume, was the task given to Christians who were already converted to Christ through the Word (1 Peter 1:23). Therefore, it was the Bible that gave birth to the church, not the church that gave birth to the Bible.

Two Competing Authorities

Roman Catholics argue that the reason there are over 25,000 Protestant denominations is because there is no infallible Protestant interpreter to teach the Bible correctly. They contend that there is no unity, only divisions, among the churches and denominations that submit to "Sola Scriptura." We need to correct this misunderstanding with the truth. The denominations that submit to "Sola Scriptura" are much more unified than religious institutions and cults that submit to the "Bible plus an infallible interpreter." Mormons and Catholics, who both use the "Bible plus an infallible interpreter" system, do not refer to one another as brothers-in-Christ, but exclude one another as heretics. On the other hand, most denominations in the "Sola Scriptura" camp would definitely refer to one another as brothers. In fact, if we were to randomly select five denominations that submit to "Sola Scriptura" and compare them with five that submit to the "Bible plus and infallible interpreter" as the rule of faith, the former group would be much more unified than the latter. True unity is found whenever it is centered on the true Gospel.

Are "Infallible" Interpreters Trustworthy?

Roman Catholics claim that anyone who studies church history and the early church will be led to the "one true church" of Rome. However, for anyone to rely on their own interpretation to come to any such conclusion goes against the very teaching of Roman Catholicism. According to Rome, we cannot trust our own ability to understand and interpret Matthew 16:18 and church history. So, if this is true, how can anyone be sure that God's infallible interpreter is Roman Catholicism? In other words, how can a Catholic know his religion is infallible when he must rely on his fallible interpretation to arrive at that conclusion? Every "infallible interpreter" claims you cannot understand Scripture and church history without their help. Eastern Orthodox, Mormons and Jehovah's Witnesses all make the same claim. Therefore, if we were to choose one of the "infallible interpreters" over the others, how can we possibly know we have made the right choice? Furthermore, if we make the wrong choice, we risk eternal damnation for trusting an "infallible interpreter" rather than our own judgment of what the infallible Word of God says.

Rome Forbids Private Interpretation

Some Catholics may argue that their religion does not forbid private interpretation of Scripture. However, when the truth of God's Word began setting thousands of people free from the bondage of religious deception, Rome tried to prevent access to the truth. The 16th Century Council of Trent gathered the Bishops of the Catholic Church together to counter the Reformation. The Bishops not only placed the Bible on the list of forbidden books, but also outlawed private interpretation of Scripture. From the 4th Session of the Council we read, "In order to restrain petulant spirits, it decrees, that no one, relying on his own skill, shall, in matters of faith, and of morals pertaining to the edification of Christian doctrine, wresting the sacred Scripture to his own senses, presume to interpret the said sacred Scripture contrary to that sense which holy mother Church, whose it is to judge of the true sense and interpretation of the holy Scriptures." The Second Vatican Council restated the dogma this way: "The task of authentically interpreting the word of God, whether written or handed on, has been entrusted exclusively to the living teaching office of the Church." The Council went on to pronounce: "The way of interpreting Scripture is subject finally to the judgment of the Church, which carries out the divine commission and ministry of guarding and interpreting the word of God" (Dei Verbum, II, 10 and III,12).

Paul Encouraged Private Interpretation

The apostle Paul, who wrote more than half the New Testament, understood Scripture to be the final and supreme authority in matters of faith. In his letter to the churches of Galatia, he encourages every believer to use private judgment in discerning truth from error. He warns readers not to believe anyone who comes preaching a Gospel that is different from the one already delivered by the apostles (Galatians 1:6-9). Since the original Gospel is completely contained in Scripture, it must be every Christian's standard for making private judgments (1 Corinthians 15:1-4). Paul includes himself and even angels from heaven as "religious authorities" that must be tested for veracity. Every man's teaching, whether it be popes, bishops, pastors, evangelists or faith healers, must conform to the written Word of God. If it does not conform, it must be rejected. We know that the books of the New Testament were not addressed to bishops but, in most cases, to individual saints. Paul said, "by the manifestation of truth we commend ourselves to every man's conscience in the sight of God" (2 Corinthians 4:2). If we take Paul seriously, we will engage in private judgment and interpretation of God's Word to test the authenticity of any religious teachers (Acts 17:11). Those who do not heed his exhortation risk the fatal mistake of following false teachers and turning from Jesus.

Principles of Interpretation

Christians must become serious students of the Bible to avoid being deceived by religious teachers. In doing so, we need to follow some important principles of interpretation. Always approach the study of God's Word with a teachable spirit and a desire to be taught by the Holy Spirit, our most trustworthy teacher (1 John 2:27). We must interpret passages literally unless they were written in a figurative or allegorical sense. It is important to observe the context for each verse and seek to understand the writer's intent as well as the historical and cultural setting in which the events took place. It is always wise to compare Scripture with Scripture and interpret each passage consistent with God's complete revelation. Difficult passages can be cleared up by comparing other passages that relate to the same subject. By studying word meanings and grammar carefully and consulting the original languages, we can gain a deeper understanding of a passage.

One Infallible Authority

There is no higher authority than almighty God who speaks only the truth and cannot lie (Titus 1:2). He inspired the Scriptures to reveal Himself to mankind through Jesus Christ as Creator, Lord and Savior. Since Jesus Christ is the personification of truth and His Word is truth (John 14:6, 17:17), why would anyone choose to look anywhere else for truth? Scripture must be the supreme and infallible authority in all that it reveals.

Application for Christians

The prevailing tendency in the church today is to avoid confrontation and just be "positive". This is no way to contend against "infallible interpreters" who masquerade as ministers of righteousness (2 Cor. 11:14-15). Their clever counterfeit Gospels appear genuine to the undiscerning and are deceiving millions. It is the duty of every Christian to know, proclaim, guard, defend and pass on the truth of God's Word to the next generation (1 Timothy 6:20-21). To allow error to go unabated is to be unmoved by the truth. Christians who simply proclaim truth without confronting error could be endorsing errors that are covered with a veneer of truth. Subtle errors give birth to fatal errors unless they are exposed and confronted. As false teachers become subtler in their propagation of error, truth must be proclaimed with greater clarity!

We know God does not try to confuse anyone about life's most critical issue: "What must I do to be saved?" However, to avoid being confused or deceived by religious teachers, we must put away any Catholic or Protestant tradition or teaching that opposes His inspired authoritative Word!

Should "Infallible Interpreters" Be Trusted?

When confronting or engaging someone or some group that claims to be an infallible interpreter, remember these key points and verses of Scripture:

- "Infallible interpreters" rule with unchallenged authority in every cult.

- Let God be true and every man a liar (Romans 3:4).

- It is better to take refuge in the Lord than to trust in man (Psalm 118:8).

- Do not trust in princes, in mortal man, in whom there is no salvation (Psalm 146:3).

- Cursed is the man who trusts in mankind...and whose heart turns away from the Lord (Jeremiah 17:5).

- From among your own selves men will arise, speaking perverse things, to draw away the disciples after them. Therefore, be on the alert (Acts 20:30).

- If anyone advocates a different doctrine and does not agree with sound words, those of our Lord Jesus Christ...he is conceited and understands nothing (1 Timothy 6:3-4).

The Consequences of Departing from the Faith

We may have a tendency to think that only the weak or uninformed are subject to deception and apostasy. But as we have seen, departures from the faith begin when the authority of God's Word is questioned or improper methods of interpretation are applied. All are subject to deception, unless there is a consistent clinging to God's Word as the final authority with an unceasing commitment to understand clearly and accurately what He has declared in the pages of Scripture.

Hank Hanegraaff, known as the *Bible Answer Man*, was chrismated into the Orthodox Church on Palm Sunday, 9 April 2017. According to Orthodox teachings, Chrismation is the mystery by which a person is granted the gift of the Holy Spirit through the anointing of Holy Chrism. How could a man who spent so many years helping Christians identify various counterfeits now make the most foolish decision to join a counterfeit form of Christianity? Like its former protagonist, the Roman Catholic Church, the Orthodox also teach a false and fatal Gospel of salvation by sacraments and works. They are both to be accursed for teaching a Gospel contrary to the Gospel of Christ (Galatians 1:6-9).

How could the *Bible Answer Man* disregard the Bible when making a decision that has eternal consequences? Hanegraaff said, "I've been impacted by Eastern Orthodox people who have a very keen sense of Church history and have absolute fidelity to the essentials of the historic Christian faith." It is hard to believe that someone who claims to know the Bible so well can say the Orthodox religion has "absolute fidelity to the essentials of the historic Christian faith." Does Hanegraaff not know that the primary essential of the Christian faith is the non-negotiable Gospel of Christ? (1 Corinthians 15:1-4).

The Orthodox people do not believe or proclaim the one-time, all-sufficient, unrepeatable sacrifice of the Lord Jesus Christ for the finished work of redemption. Instead, their priests continue to offer what they believe is the physical body and blood of Jesus Christ every day on an altar. This Eucharistic sin-offering not only blasphemes Christ, but also rejects His victory cry, "It is finished" (John 19:30). By continuing their sacerdotal priesthood, the Orthodox also reject Jesus as the one mediator between God and man (1 Timothy 2:5). In the Orthodox Church, forgiveness of sin and salvation can only come through its priests and its sacraments.

One of the immediate consequences of Hanegraaff's conversion to the Orthodox Church was having his radio program booted from the Bott Radio Network. We applaud the network's decision to discontinue the *Bible Answer Man* program after carrying it since the 1980's. Hanegraaff's perplexing decision to join an apostate church, that long ago departed from the faith of the apostles, also may have eternal consequences. The Orthodox religion holds its people captive through an utter dependence on a superfluous priesthood for salvation, along with the idolatrous worship of icons, necromantic prayers and worship for the dead. Unlike Paul, who did not yield in submission to the Judaizers so that the truth of the Gospel might be preserved, Hanegraaff has submitted to a much more corrupt religion (Galatians 2:5).

Throughout the New Testament, we are warned that there will be false converts, false teachers, and apostates in the church. We cannot judge anyone's heart, but we must be fruit inspectors (Mat. 7:15-20). Only God knows if Hanegraaff is a true or a false convert. However, it is inconceivable that a true Christian would exchange a *relationship* with the One Mediator for a *religion* that offers ungodly mediators. Hanegraaff's departure is not unprecedented. "They went out from us, but they were not really of us; for if they had been of us, they would have remained with us; but they went out, so that it would be shown that they all are not of us" (1 John 2:19).

We need to remember that the last days will be marked by widespread deception and growing apostasy. "The Spirit explicitly says that in later times some will fall away from the faith, paying attention to deceitful spirits and doctrines of demons" (1 Tim. 4:1). Paul exhorts the church to be on the alert. He wrote: "I know that after my departure savage wolves will come in among you, not sparing the flock; and from among your own selves men will arise, speaking perverse things, to draw away the disciples after them" (Acts 20:28-30). Only time will tell how many undiscerning people will follow Hanegraaff on the wide road to destruction.

We are living in a church age where many people are choosing to follow persuasive personalities rather than the Lord Jesus Christ and His Word. These undiscerning people need to be warned that there are eternal consequences for those who follow the teachings of men without testing them with the supreme authority of God's Word. The only way false teachers can succeed is when professing Christians put up with them (2 Corinthians 11:4). May God give us the courage and boldness to contend earnestly for the faith that was signed, sealed, and delivered 2000 years ago (Jude 3).

The State of the Evangelical Church

Many professing Christians now think it doesn't really matter what you believe, as long as you label it "Christianity." Their only test for becoming a Christian is a simple acceptance of Jesus as a historical figure. In our post-modern church, doctrine is out and tolerance is in. We are told that, for the sake of unity, doctrine should not be tested or contested. We are not supposed to draw any definitive lines or declare any absolutes. Doctrinal and moral issues which were once painted black and white, are now seen as gray. The state of the church is now in a state of confusion.

Paul forewarned us that this would happen when he wrote:

The time will come when they [*the people in the church*] will not endure [*tolerate*] sound doctrine; but wanting to have their ears tickled, they will accumulate for themselves teachers in accordance to their own desires; and will turn away their ears from the truth, and will turn aside to myths. 2 Timothy 4:3-4 (*Emphasis added*)

When "Christians" turn to popular teachers who tickle their ears with messages on self-esteem and self-improvement, they are also turning away from God's Word. Without a steady diet of Scripture, they will not hear sound doctrine and therefore will be unable to discern truth from error. Ultimately, they will not know if they are following Jesus Christ or his adversary.

Without discernment, the 21st century church is headed for serious trouble, because the enemies of the Gospel are more shrewd and cunning than we are. What the Body of Christ needs now are soldiers of the Lord who are committed to battle for truth! Let us look at some of the cause for the lack of discernment in the Evangelical Church.

Decline of Biblical Preaching

What has happened to pastors who preach the whole counsel of God? Churches that once taught the Bible verse-by-verse are on the endangered species list. We receive letters from all over the world from believers who cannot find them. We have also witnessed this first hand as we listen to sermons on church web sites. It appears pastors today are more concerned with popularity, church growth, methodology, psychology and meeting felt needs than biblical doctrine. Pastors are teaching less and less from the Bible, which ultimately calls people to trust in the words of men instead of the Word of God.

Three Kinds of Preachers

In one category are teachers who faithfully preach the whole counsel of God. They exhort in sound doctrine and refute those who contradict (2 Timothy 4:2; Titus 1:9). These men are devoted to seeking the approval of God over the approval of men (Galatians 1:10).

In the second category are teachers who cater to desires of men (2 Timothy 4:3). These teachers are dangerous, not because of what they say, but for what they don't say. They purposefully avoid the offense of the Gospel for fear it will make people uncomfortable. Whenever preachers avoid the Word of God, believers don't get discernment and "seekers" don't get saved. We see an example of this type of preacher in Joel Osteen, the pastor of one of America's largest churches, located in Houston, Texas. In an interview on Larry King Live, he was asked if atheists go to heaven. He replied, "I'm going to let God be the judge of who goes to heaven and hell." When asked where Jews or Muslims go without trusting Jesus, he replied, "I'm very careful about saying who would and wouldn't go to heaven; I don't know." Rather than unashamedly respond with the power and exclusivity of the Gospel, Osteen chose to remain silent so that no one would be offended.

The third category is made up of false teachers, who secretly introduce destructive heresies and malign the way of the truth (2 Peter 2:1-2). These teachers deceive the hearts of the unsuspecting and the undiscerning (Romans 16:18). Without discernment, listeners will not be able to distinguish between who has been sent by Christ and who is a mouthpiece for Satan.

Wooing the World into The Church

Proponents of the church growth movement have developed attractive gimmicks and techniques to invite the world into our churches. Their thinking is this: "If we can get the world to like us, maybe they will like our Savior." Their approach to post-modern ecclesiology has been labeled "seeker-friendly" or, more profoundly, "sinner-friendly." Jesus is being disguised to make Him and His Gospel "less offensive" to seekers. Their goal is to make sinners feel comfortable by giving them what they want instead of what they need. Their strategy is to throw soft balls at non-Christians rather than challenge and confront their unbelief with convicting truths from Scripture. As the goats are being entertained with this nonsense, the sheep of the Shepherd are being deprived of His Word.

We must ask: Where does God's Word tell us to woo the world? Did not Jesus say, "The world ... hates Me because I testify that its deeds are evil" (John 7:7)? James wrote: "Whoever wishes to be a friend of the world makes himself an enemy of God" (James 4:4). Church history confirms this, and we should learn from the past. The churches and denominations which made friends with the world began a downward slide into apostasy. By trying to woo the world, they had to compromise their preaching, tolerate sin and immorality and abandon nearly every doctrinal position they once held.

Those who remain faithful to the Gospel will be an offense to the world, because the Gospel is inherently offensive. Christ Himself is offensive to all who reject the truth. He is "a stone of stumbling and a rock of offense" (1 Peter 2:8). The message of the cross is also a stumbling block and foolishness to those who are perishing (1 Corinthians 1:18; Galatians 5:11). Tragically, there are multitudes who profess Christ but cannot articulate the Gospel's basic elements. What is left for the church if it can't communicate the only message that brings forth life?

The decline of doctrine (and ultimately the ability to discern) occurs in our churches when any one of three things take place. First, when drama and entertainment become more important than preaching the Word. Secondly, when the pastor's goal becomes "making people happy instead of holy." You know this is taking place when he shifts his sermons from "this is what God says" to "this is what I think people want to hear." Thirdly, when the pastor spends more time addressing "felt needs" over "spiritual needs." Eventually these churches become filled with gullible people who believe their lovable pastor is speaking for God. Might they consider a quote from A. W. Tozer, who said: "Gullibility is not synonymous with spirituality. Faith keeps its heart open to whatever is of God, and rejects everything that is not of God."

Tolerance Has Replaced Absolute Truth

Some Christian leaders are calling for the church to adapt to the new generation by eliminating all absolutes. They are saying that we can no longer proclaim absolute truth. Truth is now said to be subjective and in the eye of the beholder. Needless to say, this is producing a Christian faith void of doctrine but full of confusion. Tolerance and acceptance of other faiths is now firmly established within Christianity. We are called to be tolerant of everything except absolute truth. This tolerance is being used as a platform for unity with the Roman Catholic Church. Some evangelicals would rather have a counterfeit unity based on tolerance than authentic spiritual unity based on truth. Anyone who stands in their way is labeled divisive or troublesome.

Warnings Are Being Ignored

There are numerous warnings in Scripture that tell us the church will be bombarded with perverse teachings, empty philosophy, vain deceit, speculations, lying spirits, worldly fables, false knowledge, doctrines of demons, destructive heresies, myths, falsehoods, traditions of men and worldly wisdom. Jesus and Paul warned of false prophets who would come in as wolves in sheep's clothing not sparing the flock (Matthew 7:15; Acts 20:29). We must do as Jesus and the apostles did and warn Christians of these destructive influences, which are weakening the church and bringing shame to the precious name of our Savior!

Spiritual Immaturity

When sound doctrine is replaced with shallow teaching made up of humorous stories and opinions, you will find spiritual ignorance and biblical illiteracy in the pew. New babes in Christ will have difficulty growing in the grace and knowledge of their Savior when pastors do not preach the whole counsel of God. When the Word of God is not being faithfully taught, people will not hear truth. And if they don't hear truth, they will be unable to discern God's way from man's way, truth from error and right from wrong. We must all become more and more discerning, because no man is infallible and no preacher is beyond the possibility of doctrinal error. We must always be ready to reject what is false and hold fast to what is true. As disciples of Jesus, we must be known for what we're for as well as what we're against.

We must recognize that all truth sets itself against error. Sound doctrine divides and confronts, it judges and separates, it reproves and rebukes and it exposes and refutes error. It leads us from the broad way to the narrow way (Matthew 7:13-14). It commands us to submit to God and resist the devil (James 4:7). It exhorts us to discern between the spirit of truth and the spirit of error (1 John 4:6). It demands that we turn away from evil and do good (1 Peter 3:11). It tells us that our ways are not God's ways, nor are our thoughts His thoughts (Isaiah 55:8). It warns us against exchanging the truth of God for a lie (Romans 1:25). It guarantees that the righteous shall be blessed and the wicked shall perish.

True Christians cannot continue to tolerate or ignore Satan's wicked schemes to weaken the church. We must stand firmly on sound doctrine, heed the biblical warnings and live passionately for the truth, so that Jesus Christ will be glorified and His church will grow in holiness and strength.

Does the Contemporary Christian Church Need to be Evangelized?

In the previous chapter, we saw distinguishing marks of some of the current contemporary churches. This raises the question: Does the contemporary church need to be evangelized? The contemporary Christian church is no longer a sanctuary for the people of God. Instead, it has become a huge mission field that needs to be evangelized. Churches are now filled with professing Christians, who say they have faith but have never been born of God. This should not surprise us because of the parable Jesus gave in Matthew 13:25-43, describing the last days. He spoke of a landowner who sowed good seed [sons of the kingdom] in his field, but while his men were sleeping, the enemy came and sowed tares [sons of the devil]. Jesus said the landowner is the Son of Man and the enemy is the devil.

Today we have many tares in our churches because church leaders are not protecting the fields. Many have been growing their churches man's way instead of God's way. This self-serving strategy has produced some tragic consequences, the most serious of which is the false hope it gives to the unconverted tares. Some of the tares are victims of unbiblical methods of evangelism; others are victims of counterfeit Gospels. These victims cannot tell you the essential elements of the Gospel or what God requires for entrance into heaven. The biblical call to the Gospel, "Repent and believe in the Gospel," has been replaced with vague, sentimental, and false invitations such as "Say yes to Jesus," or "Are you ready to make Jesus your forever friend?" There may be some who know their eternal sin debt must be forgiven, but very few know they also need the righteousness of Jesus and to be born again of the Spirit.

The Necessity of the New Birth

Jesus told Nicodemus, "Truly, truly, I say to you, unless one is born again, he cannot see the kingdom of God." Only the triune God can bring forth life. Jesus said: "just as the Father raises the dead and gives them life, even so the Son also gives life to whom He wishes" (John 5:21). "It is the Spirit that gives life" (John 6:63). God calls the spiritually dead to life through His Word. "In the exercise of His will He brought us forth by the word of truth" (James 1:18). God's children are "born again not of seed which is perishable but imperishable, that is, through the living and abiding word of God" (1 Peter 1:23).

Saving faith comes from hearing the Word of Christ. From it we learn the essential doctrines of salvation: the attributes of God, the Gospel of grace and the redemptive work of Jesus Christ. When people hear the Word of God, enabled by the Spirit of God, to trust the Son of God, they become a child of God, all for the glory of God.

Just as man could not initiate his physical birth, he is unable to cause his spiritual birth. Before any of us were born, we could not have pleaded with our parents to conceive us. We did not exist! The same is true in the spiritual realm (John 1:12-13). Children of God are not born of blood (spiritual life is not inherited genetically), nor of the will of the flesh (physical life cannot produce spiritual life; flesh can only produce flesh), nor of the will of man (spiritual life cannot be initiated by the desires of men).

So, how do we help the unconverted tares see they have been misled or deceived? As believers, we should encourage everyone to test their faith for their own good as well as for the glory of Christ. Paul wrote: "Examine yourselves to see whether you are in the faith; test yourselves. Do you not realize that Christ Jesus is in you—unless, of course, you fail the test" (2 Corinthians 13:5). Peter exhorted us: "Be all the more eager to make your calling and election sure" (2 Peter 1:10).

I always love to hear testimonies of how our Sovereign Lord calls lost sinners to Himself. So, whenever I meet Christians, I often ask them to describe the events surrounding their conversion. A red flag goes up if they say they became a Christian at the moment they were: baptized, came forward in an altar call, repeated a prayer, signed a commitment card, joined a local church, or were born to Christian parents. Speaking the truth in love, I explain to them that no one can become a Christian without repentance and faith in the Lord Jesus Christ (Acts 20:21).

Many Believe A Counterfeit Gospel

What about those who say they have faith in Jesus but show no evidence of a changed life. All of them may believe in the historical Jesus who lived 2000 years ago, but few believe what He taught, what He promises, what He commands, what He accomplished and what He is doing now. They may be victims of a counterfeit Gospel, a watered-down version that is offered by a generic god of love. This Gospel offers "fire insurance" with no call to repentance (Luke 24:47). It is a Gospel of cheap grace which fails to instruct people to say "no" to ungodliness and worldly passions (Titus 2:12).

The other counterfeit Gospel which deceives people is the grace-killing Gospel of works. First introduced by the Judaizers, this Gospel nullifies God's grace by adding requirements for salvation such as circumcision, baptism, sacraments, good works, law keeping, penance or indulgences (Galatians 1:6-9).

If we do not lovingly confront victims of unbiblical evangelism and counterfeit Gospels, they may one day hear the most terrifying words anyone could ever hear, when Jesus says: "I never knew you; depart from Me." These horrifying words will be heard by many professing Christians on the last day (Matthew 7:22-23).

Two Ways to Test Faith

Those who want to test their faith now, before it is too late, can do so in two ways: objectively and subjectively. The objective test is this: Have you believed the objective truths of God's Word? Paul wrote: "after listening to the message of truth, the Gospel of your salvation, having also believed, you were sealed in Him with the Holy Spirit" (Ephesians 1:13). The Word of God is our supreme authority for knowing objective truth. We must believe the eternal Gospel as it is revealed in Scripture. It is the same Gospel today as it was 6000 years ago.

The subjective test asks the question: Is there evidence of saving faith? Genuine faith results in good works, but a faith without works is dead (Ephesians 2:10; James 2:17). This second test is subjective because there are different levels of maturity and growth as believers walk with Christ. New babes in Christ may not show as much evidence as those who have walked with Him for many years. When we are first born into God's family, we look nothing like His Son. But as we grow in the grace and knowledge of God, through the power of the Holy Spirit, we are conformed into the image of Christ. We also see this in the physical realm. When a baby is born, he may look nothing like his parents. But as he grows, he begins to take on the physical characteristics of his parents.

The Apostle John gives us a portrait in his first epistle of what God's children look like.

- They who are born of God are adopted into His eternal family to walk in the light (1 John 1:6-7).

- They keep His commandments (1 John 2:3-5).

- They do not love the world system (1 John 2:15).

- They yearn for the return of Christ so they can be like Him (1 John 3:2-3).

- They live to please Him and avoid sin (1 John 3:7-8).

- They love His other children (1 John 3:14).

- They use apostolic doctrine for discernment (1 John 4:6).

Each of us must determine if this picture of God's children resembles the way we look.

Two Kinds of Faith

The test of one's faith is vital, because the Bible speaks of two kinds of faith: a "God-given, supernatural, saving faith" and a "dead" faith that is found in the unconverted natural man. Paul wrote of people who believed in vain because they did not hold to apostolic teaching (1 Corinthians 15:2). Jesus spoke of others who believed for the wrong reasons (John 2:23-25).

Dead faith is limited to what the natural man can comprehend without divine help, because he has been blinded by Satan and cannot see the light of the Gospel (2 Corinthians 4:4). That is why Paul wrote: "your faith should not rest on the wisdom of men, but on the power of God" (1 Corinthians 2:5). One must rely on the Word of God. Jesus is the Author and Perfecter of this faith, which is the assurance of things hoped for and the conviction of things not seen (Hebrews 11:1, 12:2).

Those with God-given faith enter the narrow gate bringing nothing but their sins to the cross (Matthew 7:13). Those with dead faith enter through the wide gate bringing their filthy rags of self-righteousness (Matthew 7:13).

Those with God-given faith prove it by bearing much fruit to the glory of God (John 15:8). Those with dead faith prove it by bearing bad fruit for the glory of self (Matthew 7:15-17).

Those with God-given faith desire to test and prove their faith with Scripture alone (2 Corinthians 13:5). Those with dead faith prove their faith by denominational teachings and man's traditions (John 12:42-43; Acts 15:5-10).

Those with God-given faith will not habitually hear or follow a false teacher (John 10:5,8). Those with dead faith will not habitually follow a true teacher (John 10:19, 2 Tim. 4:3).

God-given faith is initiated in the will of God and is a gift granted from the Father above (Philippians 1:29; James 1:17). It will be perfected by the Son of God, who alone has the power to protect and keep believers (1 Peter 1:5). Those with dead faith trust their own power to keep them from falling away.

Dead faith touches only the intellect. God-given faith involves the whole person. The mind understands, the heart desires, and the will acts upon the Word of God.

There are several probing questions we can ask those who desire to test their faith:

- Have you renounced every false way that opposes the Gospel of grace?

- Do you live in thanksgiving and praise for being chosen and adopted into God's eternal family?

- Do you prove to be Christ's disciple by abiding in His Word?

- Do you discipline yourself for godliness?

- Do your friends, neighbors and co-workers know that Jesus Christ is your Lord and Savior?

- Do you have a desire to share Jesus Christ with others, or are you ashamed of His Gospel?

God's children will know they belong to Him because "The Spirit Himself bears witness with our spirit that we are children of God" (Romans 8:16). The Spirit does this through the Scriptures that He inspired. All of God's children take Him at His Word!

The Emerging Church Submerges Truth

There is a series of three books which herald the testimonies of former Protestant pastors who have found the broad way to Rome more enticing and fulfilling. What is causing this growing apostasy? Who is behind this reversal of the Reformation? Why are so many Protestants being seduced by the piety of this false religion? In earlier chapters, we have seen many prominent evangelical leaders who are leading the charge to reach an unbiblical compromise with the Roman Catholic Church. Others who are less informed are puzzled and are searching for answers. Although it is disheartening and discouraging, we should not be surprised because: "the Spirit explicitly says that in later times some will fall away from the faith, paying attention to deceitful spirits and doctrines of demons" (1 Timothy 4:1).

Does Christianity Need to Be Reinvented?

One of the major influences that is paving the road back to Roman Catholicism is The Emerging Church movement. Proponents say it's time for Christianity to be reinvented for a new generation. It must become more relevant to a postmodern generation. They say the best way to reinvent Christianity for the present generation is to reintroduce ideas and experiences from the past. Emergent leaders say God's Word no longer holds the answers to life's questions. Experience must become the key factor to encounter spiritual reality. The experiential attractions which are being promoted by the Emerging Church include: statues, prayer stations, incense, liturgy, candles, icons, the sacraments and calling communion the Eucharist. It is easy to see how this movement complements and encourages the Vatican's "new evangelization program" to win the "separated brethren" back to the "true church".

A New Kind of Christian

The most influential leader in the Emergent Church movement has been Brian McLaren, a pastor and author from Maryland who wrote the controversial book, *A New Kind of Christian*. *Time* Magazine named McLaren one of the 25 most influential evangelical leaders in the world (2/7/2005). In another one of his books, *A Generous Orthodoxy*, McLaren describes himself as the new kind of Christian, with labels such as: Catholic, Evangelical, post/protestant, liberal/conservative, mystical/poetic, biblical, fundamentalist/Calvinist, Anabaptist/Anglican and Methodist. How can he hold to all these labels at the same time? It is because he rejects the Word of God as the objective authority for truth. McLaren writes: "How do you know something is true? First you engage in spiritual practices like prayer, Bible reading, forgiveness and service. Then you see what happens; you remain open to experience. Finally, you report your experience to others in the field of spirituality for their discernment to see if they confirm your findings or not."

Mystical Feelings Replace Doctrine

It is appalling to see what McLaren and other leaders of the Emergent Church are really promoting. In *A Generous Orthodoxy*, McLaren writes that he "is consistently over-sympathetic to Roman Catholics." Other leaders tell us we need to emulate Roman Catholicism to become more mystical in our reverence of God. Chuck Smith Jr., in his book, *There is a Season* (foreword by Brian McLaren), provides insight into this mystical experience. He writes: "What would happen if we allowed people to "feel" what we cannot explain, to know with the heart and not with the brain? We would open the door of faith to a wider audience than if we continued to insist on a rational belief in the facts as the only legitimate starting point of the Christian faith." Unfortunately, the wider audience Smith will reach are people without discernment, who uphold "truth" that is subjective and believe a Gospel that is compromised. These are people who have no biblical roots and will constantly be blown away by every wind of doctrine. Some will be fatally duped into believing there are no eternal consequences if or when they convert to Roman Catholicism.

The Alluring Power of the Eucharist

Another leader of the Emerging Church has been Dr. Robert Webber, who is recognized by many as the authority on "worship renewal". He taught at Wheaton College for 32 years as Professor of Theology and has authored over 40 books. Dr. Webber had a "life changing experience" at a Catholic conference center, when he decided to receive the Eucharist. His testimony is recorded in a book entitled *Signs of Wonder*. Following is part of his experience in his own words:

> Closing my eyes, I allowed my life in the church to pass before me. My prejudices rose up within me: What are you doing here? You never worshiped in a Catholic setting, let alone received the bread and the wine from a Catholic priest! Then I heard my Catholic friends speak of their love for Christ, pray with fervency, and express a real desire to know the Scriptures and live by its authority. Those memories said, 'Go ahead. After all, there is only one Lord, one church, one faith, one baptism, one Holy Communion.' In that moment, God broke through the walls I had allowed to separate me from my brothers and sisters of different denominations. I am convinced the prejudices we hold and the

walls we build between ourselves and other communities of Christians actually block our experience of God's presence in our lives. Our biases cut us off from the spiritual communion of the fullness of the body of Christ. God dwells in his church, and to reject a part of God's church is to reject him. Furthermore, rejecting a part of God's church keeps us from experiencing what the creed calls "the communion of the Saints." When God broke down my walls, he brought me into richer fellowship with the body of Christ throughout the world. You might say I was surprised by joy! I had never had an experience like that in my life. In that Catholic chapel, a new worship experience had bumped up against that old prejudice of mine, and a new attitude was born. I had taken into myself the experience of another tradition, I had been in dialogue with another worship tradition, and I was surely the richer for it.

Subjective Experiences vs. Objective Truth

Webber's words are echoed by other Protestants who have experimented with the Eucharist and then converted to Catholicism because of their "joyful experience." It comes as no surprise that these apostates, who have converted to a false religion, have been influenced by subjective experiences. Probably the best known Protestant convert to Catholicism is Scott Hahn. His subjective experience was participating in the ungodly pagan practice of praying the rosary (Matthew 6:7). Hahn was convinced "Mary" performed a miracle after he prayed the rosary. By contrast, those who have been gloriously converted to the Lord Jesus Christ have believed the objective truth of His Word (Ephesians 1:13-14; Rom. 10:17). Now sealed with the Holy Spirit, they can never again be ensnared by the deceitful schemes of the devil's religion (2 Timothy 2:24-26).

A common characteristic of Protestants who have converted to Romanism has been a dissatisfaction with their former

Christian experience. One convert cited several things that drove him away from his Evangelical Church: live bands playing loud music consisting of praise choruses repeated over and over again, no place for quiet reverence and prayer, theological shallowness, and movie clips, drama and plays. He said, "After a few years of the kids raving about how much fun they had and not learning anything, we tried the Catholic Church across the street and immediately enjoyed the formal liturgy, the religious rituals and a reverence for God." What a tragedy for this family. They left a shallow worship experience and replaced it with an idolatrous worship experience. There is an instructive lesson here for evangelical pastors: churches which emphasize entertainment over the preaching of God's Word will always have people looking for a more satisfying experience. Whatever you win then "with" is what you win them "to."

What Can We Do?

Let our voices be heard! Expose the evil deeds of darkness with the glorious light of God's Word. Lovingly confront those who are compromising the Gospel and embracing Roman Catholicism as a valid expression of Christianity. Call Roman Catholicism what it is: a false religious system that is holding over 1 billion people in bondage to deception.

To those who have committed themselves to Satan's lies and his evil religious system, we must have a sense of urgency. There is no time for beating around the bush. God doesn't promise anyone tomorrow. Jude wrote: "save others [with the Gospel], snatching them out of the fire" (Jude 23). We need to be prepared to offend them with the truth, knowing that the Gospel will offend those who are offensive to God.

Finally, don't be deceived. Hold onto our supreme and objective authority for truth—the Word of God! It, along with the Holy Spirit, is the only security we have in these days of great deception and compromise.

Chapter 9

THE CATHOLIC CHURCH AND THE GOSPEL

—◦◦◦—

O ctober 31, 1517 was a watershed moment in the history of the church. On that day, Martin Luther nailed his nine-ty-five theses to the door of the Castle Church in Wittenberg exposing indulgences as a wicked method to extort money as a device of Satan to destroy the souls of the deceived. His act of protest against the church ignited a theological firestorm that would burn throughout Europe.

As a Roman Catholic monk, Luther's greatest desire was to become right with God, yet his religion offered no peace or as-surance. This led him to begin a diligent study of God's Word and it was there that he discovered the only way a condemned sinner could be justified by a holy and righteous God. Luther's study of Scripture revealed the glorious doctrine of justification that had been concealed and corrupted by religious traditions for over 1000 years. The Doctrine of Justification soon became the defining doctrine which divided Roman Catholics and the Reformers, and it began a movement that would set thousands of captives free from the bondage of religious deception.

Catholicism had so blatantly corrupted the Gospel that the Reformers sought to reestablish the message of salvation ac-cording to the Word of God with the "five solas." God saves sinners by grace alone, through faith alone, in Christ alone, according to Scripture alone, for the glory of God alone. The

Roman Catholic Church defended its position of "justification by faith plus works" with a counter-reformation at the Council of Trent. It was there that Rome officially condemned the Protestant doctrine of justification by faith on the basis of the imputed righteousness of Christ. In its place, Rome taught an infused righteousness initiated by water baptism and continued through the sacraments. Many Christians are unaware of how the Catholic Church has twisted and distorted the biblical doctrine of Justification and condemned those who believe it. At the Council of Trent, they pronounced 33 anathemas on anyone who believes that they are justified by grace alone, through faith alone, in Christ alone.

The Bible declares that the justification of sinners can only be accomplished by a divine exchange—the imputing of man's sins to Christ, and the imputing of Christ's righteousness to sinners (2 Corinthians 5:21). The only way condemned sinners can be justified is through the sin-bearing, substitutionary death of Christ, who satisfied divine justice.

The doctrine of Justification is said to be the hinge upon which the gates of heaven open and close. Those who get justification wrong also get the Gospel wrong, and those who die embracing a false Gospel will pay for that mistake forever. The doctrine of Justification declares the inflexible righteousness of God as a Judge who must punish every sin, that has ever been committed, by everyone who has ever lived. It also declares His love, mercy, and grace in providing His only Son to be crucified as a substitute for sinners.

Today, there are many evangelicals who think the Reformation was a mistake or unnecessary, and believe we now need to tear down the walls of separation and seek unity with Catholics. These evangelicals have been seduced by Rome's strategy to reverse the Reformation and bring "separated brethren" back home to the "holy mother", the church.

In addition to the Doctrine of Justification, there are many areas where the teachings of the Roman Catholic Church have distorted or departed from Apostolic teaching. To avoid being led astray by a counterfeit faith, Christians must study and know the true teaching of the inspired and infallible Word of God in contrast to the many erroneous doctrines of Rome.

Biblical Doctrine of Justification vs. Roman Catholic Teaching

The doctrine of justification has eternal consequences, so it is imperative that the Word of God is rightly divided and understood in contrast to the distorted teachings of the Roman Catholic Church. The numbers in parenthesis are paragraph numbers from the Catechism of the Catholic Church.

1. Justification is **by faith** in what God accomplished in Christ (Rom. 5:1). Rome says initial justification is **by water baptism** (1992).

2. Justification **changes one's legal status** before God, whereby a condemned sinner has been acquitted and declared righteous (Rom. 5:12-21). Rome says justification **changes the inner man**, not his legal status (2019).

3. Justification is an **instantaneous act** of God, which immediately declares a sinner righteous (Rom. 4:3). Rome says justification is an **ongoing process**, the ongoing renewal of the interior man (2019).

4. Justification is **permanent** and is never lost by sin. The legal status of a justified man is as unchangeable as the righteousness of Christ (Heb. 10:14). Rome says justification is **temporal**. It is lost by sin and regained through the sacrament of penance and through good works (1446, 1861).

5. Justification is by **grace apart from works** (Titus 3:7; Rom. 11:6). God justifies those who do not work (Rom. 4:5; Gal. 2:16). Those justified receive the gracious gift of Christ's righteousness (Rom. 5:17). Rome says justification **must include good works** (2010). "If anyone says that the sinner is justified by faith alone, let him be anathema" (Trent, Canon 9). Rome says re-justification must be merited by making satisfaction for sins through works of mercy, prayer, service to neighbors, etc. (1459, 1460, 2027).

6. Justification is by **imputation**, or crediting of Christ's completed righteousness, to the one justified (2 Cor. 5:21; Rom. 4:5). Rome says justification is by **infusion** of God's righteousness which renews the interior man (1989).

7. God justifies **the ungodly** (Rom. 4:5). Rome teaches final justification is only for those who **have become righteousness** (2016, 2020).

8. After justification, all **sins are no longer taken into account or punished** (Rom. 4:5; 2 Cor. 5:19-21). Rome says that sins committed after justification **will be punished** either in purgatory or in hell (1030, 1861).

9. God promises to glorify everyone He justifies, because those justified can **never be condemned** (Rom. 8:1, 8:30). Rome says that God **will condemn to hell** anyone who was justified (by water baptism) but who dies in mortal sin (1861).

10. Justification **precedes sanctification** (Rom. 6-8). Rome says justification is an integral **part of sanctification** (1995).

The righteousness that justifies the ungodly sinner is an alien righteousness that was accomplished outside of and apart from man. It is the completed righteousness of Jesus Christ and is given as a gift from God apart from any merit or work of man. His perfect righteousness is imputed at the moment the redeemed sinner is united with Christ by faith. The righteousness of Christ is our passport into heaven! No one will enter into glory without it (2 Peter 3:13).

Is a "Catholic Christian" an Oxymoron?

With the continuing effort to reverse the Reformation and bring the church worldwide back under the authority of the Catholic Church, the essential question must be answered: If one embraces the teaching and doctrines of the Roman Catholic Church, is he or she a Christian? Hence the question raised in this section: Is a Catholic Christian an oxymoron?

Webster's dictionary defines an oxymoron as "a combination of contradictory words," such as jumbo shrimp, tight slacks and pretty ugly. Would you put Catholic Christian into this category? Some would say "no", because they believe Roman Catholicism is a Christian denomination. Others, who know the official teachings of the Catholic Church contradict the essentials of the Gospel, would say "yes." I propose that a Catholic Christian is indeed an oxymoron for two reasons:

- Who we are is based on what we believe, and

- It is impossible for anyone to believe two opposing views simultaneously.

There may be some Christians attending the Catholic Church, but if they have believed the Gospel as taught in the Bible, they are no longer Catholics. Consider the contradictory beliefs of Catholics and Christians. By definition, I propose that a Christian is one who believes the Gospel as taught in the Scriptures alone, while a Catholic is one who believes the official teachings and traditions of his church (presented by paragraph number from the *Catechism of the Catholic Church*).

A Different Authority

Roman Catholics reject the supreme authority of Scripture by elevating their tradition to the same level of authority. They defend their position by quoting St. Paul who wrote: "Stand firm and hold to the traditions which you were taught, whether by word of mouth or by letter from us" (2 Thessalonians 2:15). But we must make a distinction between traditions which had already been taught by the apostles in the first century and the traditions established by men over the last 1900 years (2 Corinthians 11:3; 2 Thessalonians 3:6).

Clearly there are certain apostolic traditions recorded in Scripture that Christians must embrace, but not all traditions are biblical. Paul encouraged us to make this distinction. He wrote: "See to it that no one takes you captive through philosophy and empty deception, according to the tradition of men, according to the elementary principles of the world, rather than according to Christ" (Colossians 2:8). Paul is warning us that we can become ensnared by the traditions of men when they do not conform to Christ and His Word. Tradition must always be subservient to Scripture because God's Word is divinely inspired while tradition is not.

A Christian believes Scripture has authority over the church. All Scripture is God-breathed and is useful for teaching, rebuking, correcting and training in righteousness (2 Timothy 3:16). By setting forth the truth plainly we commend ourselves to every man's conscience (2 Corinthians 4:2). A Catholic believes the church has authority over the Scripture. Rome teaches that the manner of interpreting Scripture is ultimately subject to the judgment of the church which exercises the divinely conferred commission and ministry of watching over and interpreting the Word of God (CCC 119).

Roman Catholics elevate "infallible" bishops to be equal in authority with the Scriptures and that "bishops have, by divine institution, taken the place of the apostles as pastors of the Church, in such wise that whoever listens to them is listening to Christ and whoever despises them despises Christ" (CCC 862). In practice, the bishops actually sit above Scripture by declaring no one else can give an authentic interpretation of the Word of God (CCC, 85). However, according to God's Word, they are not qualified to be successors of the original twelve apostles. They have not met any of the necessary qualifications listed in Acts 1:21-22. Therefore, they must be identified as "false apostles [and] deceitful workers, [who are] transforming themselves into the apostles of Christ" (2 Corinthians 11:13-14). We know there have only been two successors of the apostles; their names are Matthias and Paul.

The Apostle Paul commended the Bereans (who were not bishops) for interpreting the Scriptures to verify the truthfulness of his teaching. "Now the Bereans ... received the message with great eagerness and examined the Scriptures every day to see if what Paul said was true" (Acts 17:11). It is quite clear that the apostle, who penned over half the New Testament, encouraged his listeners to submit to the supreme authority of the Hebrew Scriptures. The veracity of every man's message must be tested with the same Scriptural authority.

Satanic assaults on the Word of God have been increasing for 6000 years, because it is the imperishable seed that brings forth life (1 Peter 1:23). For this reason, we are exhorted to maintain its purity and warned against adding to God's words, "lest He rebuke you, and you be found a liar" (Proverbs 30:5-6). Yet, the Vatican brazenly ignores this warning by corrupting the Word of God with its religious traditions. Rome then foolishly declares that together Scripture and Tradition "make up a single sacred deposit of the Word of God" (CCC 97). In making this ungodly pronouncement, Rome has established its traditions to be equal in authority to God's infallible and inerrant Word (CCC 95).

Catholics Are Utterly Dependency Upon the Priesthood

One of the most controlling elements of the Roman Catholic religion is its indoctrination concerning the priesthood. Catholics are taught that their salvation is utterly dependent upon the ministry of their priests. According to the unbiblical teachings of Rome, it is the Catholic priest who baptizes infants for their justification and spiritual birth, the priest who hears confession and demands penance as the satisfaction for sin, the priest who dispenses Jesus in the Eucharist, the priest who imparts the Holy Spirit in the sacrament of Confirmation, the priest who gives Last Rites, and the priest who offers the sacrifice of the Mass for souls suffering in purgatory. What a fatal deception!

There is no longer a need for priests offering sacrifices for sin, because by one offering Jesus Christ has perfected for all time those who are sanctified (Hebrews 10:14). At the very moment our Lord Jesus gave up His Spirit on Calvary's cross, the veil of the temple was torn in two from top to bottom (Matthew 27:51). The veil that separated sinful man from the Holy of Holies was ripped open, and now, anyone washed by the blood of Christ can come boldly into the presence of God. When Jesus, our High Priest, offered Himself once for all sin for all time, He made the sacrificial priesthood obsolete. Every believer in Jesus Christ has been sanctified through the offering of the body of Jesus Christ once for all (Hebrews 10:10).

The illegitimacy and obsolescence of the Roman Catholic priesthood is also expressly noted by the sovereign and exclusive work of the triune God in saving sinners. It is God the Father who chooses, calls and draws the lost to His Son (John 6:44; James 2:5). The Holy Spirit convicts them of their sin and the coming judgment (John 16:8-11). Jesus Christ is proclaimed through His Word as the only way of salvation (John 14:6). God gives life to those dead in sin and grants the sinner repentance and faith (Romans 4:17; Ephesians 2:8-9; 2 Timothy 2:25). Jesus exchanges His righteousness for the sins of the believer (2 Corinthians 5:21). The Holy Spirit seals, indwells and empowers the justified believer (Ephesians 1:13-14, Romans 8). The Father adopts, secures and glorifies His children (John 1:12; Romans 8:30). Clearly, God alone is deserving of all glory (Romans 11:36). He alone is worthy to be praised!

Peter expressed the bondage that enslaves religious leaders who exchange the truth of God for the fatal errors of men. He wrote:

> Speaking out arrogant words of vanity they entice by fleshly desires, by sensuality, those who barely escape from the ones who live in error, promising them freedom while they themselves are slaves of corruption; for by what a man is overcome, by this he is enslaved. (2 Peter 2:18-19)

Justification

A Christian is justified once by faith, because justification is a permanent declaration by God (Romans 8:30). To the man who does not work but trusts God who justifies the wicked, his faith is credited as righteousness (Romans 4:5). A Catholic believes one is justified repeatedly by sacraments and works because he loses the grace of justification each time a mortal sin is committed. The sacrament of Penance is said to offer a new possibility to convert and to recover the grace of justification (CCC 1446).

Catholicism perpetuates the first lie of Satan by declaring "you will not surely die" if you sin against God (Genesis 3:4). Catholics are taught that they will not die when they commit "venial" sins (CCC 1861-63). Instead, they are misled into believing they will receive only temporal punishment.

Once the supreme authority of Scripture has been communicated to Catholics, who are enslaved to another authority, the Gospel of God can be heralded. It is wise to present God's Gospel in contrast to Rome's plan of salvation, so Catholics can discern the difference. The distinction between the two Gospels can best be described as the difference between divine accomplishment and human achievement. The true Gospel describes what God has done through Jesus Christ to save sinners, while the Gospel of Rome describes what man must do for God. Paul defines the Gospel according to Scripture alone (1 Corinthians 15:1-4). The glorious Gospel of grace is what one Perfect Man did 2000 years ago to reconcile sinful men to God. It has nothing to do with what any imperfect man has done since or is doing now. This eliminates all the requirements Roman Catholics have added to the finished work of Jesus Christ. It also eliminates Catholic priests making daily sin offerings on their altars.

Regeneration

A Christian believes he is regenerated at the baptism of the Spirit. For we were all baptized by one Spirit into one body (1 Corinthians 12:13). From the beginning God chose you to be saved through the sanctifying work of the Spirit and through belief in the truth (2 Thessalonians 2:13). In contrast, a Catholic believes baptism of water imparts divine life, the water of Baptism truly signifies our birth into the divine life (CCC 694).

Salvation

A Christian is saved by God's unmerited grace. For it is by grace you have been saved, through faith—and this not from yourselves, it is the gift of God, not by works, so that no one can boast (Ephesians 2:8-9). A Catholic believes one is saved by meriting the graces needed for salvation. We can merit for ourselves and for others the graces needed for the attainment of eternal life (CCC 2010).

Satan's primary attack on Christianity is on the Gospel of grace, because it alone has the power to save sinners completely and forever. Any religious teaching or tradition that adds to or takes away from God's revealed truth is a distortion of the

Gospel and a perversion of the nature and work of Jesus Christ. That is why the apostle Paul, under the inspiration of the Holy Spirit, wrote: "If we, or an angel from heaven, should preach to you a Gospel contrary to what we have preached to you, he is to be accursed!" (Galatians 1:8). The apostles preached a Gospel of pure grace declaring that Jesus Christ, the perfect High Priest, offered Himself, the perfect sacrifice, once for all sin for all time. The work of redemption was finished, perfect and sufficient to save believers from their sin (John 19:30; 1 Peter 3:18). Three days later, Jesus was raised from the dead for the justification of all believers (Romans 4:25).

Rome's way of salvation is not only another Gospel, but, is also the antithesis of the Gospel Paul preached. It focuses not on what Jesus has done to save sinners, but on what Catholics must do to be saved. Their list of requirements for salvation include: be baptized (CCC 1256), receive sacraments (CCC 1129), go to purgatory for the purification of sins (CCC 1030), do good works (CCC 2016), keep the law (CCC 2068) and participate in the weekly sacrifice of the Mass (CCC 1405). Rome's false Gospel, that shuts the gates of heaven to those trying to enter, should be enough of a warning, but there is much more.

A Christian is saved *for* good works. For we are God's workmanship, created in Christ Jesus to do good works, which God prepared in advance for us to do (Ephesians 2:10). A Catholic believes one is saved *by* good works. The sacraments of the New Covenant are necessary for salvation (CCC 1129).

A Christian is saved for all eternity. And you also were included in Christ when you heard the word of truth, the Gospel of your salvation. Having believed, you were marked in him with a seal, the promised Holy Spirit, who is a deposit guaranteeing our inheritance (Ephesians 1:13-14). A Catholic believes one is saved until a mortal sin is committed. Those who die in a state of mortal sin descend into hell (CCC 1035).

The promise of God that is revealed in the Gospel is eternal, everlasting life with our Savior (1 John 2:25). Yet this divine promise is flatly denied by Roman Catholicism. In fact, Catholics believe they commit the sin of presumption if they believe this promise of God (CCC 2092). They are said to be presuming on God's mercy because no one can know how much merit is required to achieve eternal life (CCC 2027). This doctrine keeps Catholics in bondage to their false religion. Only by knowing and believing God's truth can they ever be set free (John 8:31-32).

A Christian believes salvation is offered to those outside the church. "We are therefore Christ's ambassadors as though God were making His appeal through us" (2 Corinthians 5:20). A Catholic believes salvation is offered only through the church. Basing itself on Scripture and tradition, the Council teaches that the church, a pilgrim now on earth, is necessary for salvation. Anyone refusing to enter it or remain in it cannot be saved (CCC 846).

A Christian is purified by the blood of Jesus. The blood of Jesus...purifies us from all sin (1 John 1:7). A Catholic believes one is purified by the fires of purgatory. They undergo purification in purgatory, so as to achieve the holiness necessary to enter the joy of heaven (CCC 1030-31).

Saints and Priests

A Christian becomes a saint when the Spirit baptizes him into the body of Christ. And He gave some...for the equipping of the saints...the body of Christ (Ephesians 4:11-12). A Catholic becomes a saint only if the Pope canonizes them. This occurs when he solemnly proclaims that they practiced a heroic virtue and lived in fidelity to God's grace (CCC 828).

A Christian is a priest. But you are a chosen people, a royal priesthood, a holy nation, a people belonging to God (1 Peter 2:9). A Catholic believes one needs a priest. Catholic priests are said to be apostolic successors and guarantee that Christ is acting in the sacraments to dispense divine life (CCC 1120-1131).

Every Roman Catholic priest is said to have the task of not only "representing Christ, before the assembly of the faithful, but also of acting in the name of the whole Church when presenting to God the prayer of the Church, and above all when offering the Eucharistic sacrifice" (CCC 1552). In this way, Catholics are totally dependent upon priests for their salvation. It is the priest who is said to cause regeneration and justification in baptism (CCC 1992, 1213); absolve mortal sin in the confessional; dispense the body and blood of Jesus in the Eucharist; impart the Holy Spirit in the sacrament of Confirmation; and offer the sacrifice of the Mass for souls suffering in purgatory. It is no wonder why Catholics trust their religion and their priests as mediators to usher them into heaven. Yet, the truth must be told: "There is one God, and one mediator also between God and men, the man Christ Jesus" (1 Timothy 2:5). By faith in the shed blood of Jesus, the High Priest, believers can go boldly into God's presence without an earthly priest (Hebrews 10:19-20). Since the resurrection of the one Mediator, there is no longer a need for a mediating priesthood.

Catholic priests are said to be able to do what only God can do, and that is, bring those who are dead in sin to life in Christ. As the priest sprinkles the water of baptism, the baptized is said to be reborn as a new creature, adopted as of son of God, purified of all sin and justified (CCC 1263-66). This false teaching violates the sovereign regenerating work of God. Those who become sons of God are born again, "not of blood, nor of the will of the flesh, nor of the will of man, but of God" (John 1:13). They are saved on the basis of God's purpose and grace (2 Tim. 1:8-9).

The Lord's Supper

A Christian believes what the Bible teaches: the Lord's Supper is a memorial. "Do this in remembrance of me" (1 Cor. 11:24-25). A Catholic believes the Lord's Supper is a sacrifice. The sacrifice of Christ and the sacrifice of the Eucharist are one single sacrifice...the same Christ who offered Himself once in a bloody manner on the altar of the cross is contained and offered in an unbloody manner (CCC 1367).

A Christian receives Jesus once, spiritually, in the heart. Yet to all who received him, to those who believed in his name, he gave the right to become children of God (John 1:12). God... put his Spirit in our hearts as a guarantee (2 Corinthians 1:22). A Catholic believes he receives Jesus physically, frequently, in the stomach. The body, blood...soul and divinity of our Lord Jesus Christ...is truly, really and substantially contained in the Eucharist (CCC 1374-78).

Who Is Condemning Whom?

A Christian is condemned by the Roman Catholic Church. Over 100 anathemas have been pronounced against Christians by the Roman Catholic Councils of Trent and Vatican II. These condemnations are still in effect today and can only be lifted if a Christian returns in submission to the authority of the pope. Yet, a Catholic is condemned by the Word of God. There is a judge for the one who rejects me and does not accept my words; that very word which I spoke will condemn him at the last day (John 12:48). If we or an angel from heaven should preach a Gospel other than the one we preached to you, let him be eternally condemned (Galatians 1:6-9).

These thirteen teachings and traditions of Roman Catholicism demonstrate that a Catholic Christian is indeed an oxymoron. They also affirm how man-made traditions nullify the Word of God (Mark 7:7-13). There are many Evangelicals and Roman Catholics who are unaware of how diametrically opposed Catholic dogmas are to the Word of God. The truth must be told. Catholics who believe they are Christians must be lovingly confronted with the truth. Evangelicals must be educated so they can proclaim the true Gospel to Catholics, instead of uniting with them under a compromised and diluted Gospel.

God's truth coupled with Satan's lies always produces an oxymoron. Yet the "father of lies" continues to seduce many by mixing a little error with truth. In the final analysis, truth mixed with error never hurts the error, it only contaminates the truth. The veneer of truth covering the false Gospel of Rome is deceiving not only Catholics, but many Protestants as well. Let us persuade Catholics to turn from the errors of man's teachings to the truth of God's Word!

God defines truth with His Word (John 17:17). It is objective, authoritative and sufficient! We must use it to expose the evil deeds of darkness, to set captives free from the bondage of deception and to protect God's children from being deceived.

There are, of course, apostate Protestant churches, denominations and cults which also deceive many people. For this reason, we encourage Christians everywhere to examine their faith in light of God's holy Word (2 Corinthians 13:5). It is our prayer that evangelicals will cease from embracing Catholicism as a valid expression of Christianity and expose their fatal flaws (Ephesians 5:11). We must also exhort all Christians to avoid being unequally yoked with unbelievers (2 Corinthians 6:14-18; Proverbs 13:20).

Only God Can Condemn and Save

In the wake of the Reformation, The Catholic Church attempted to thwart the mass exodus of its people by condemning anyone who left the church. During the Counter Reformation, the Council of Trent threatened hostile action on Catholics and former Catholics who would not remain loyal to their religion. They attempted to control people with the threat of over 100 anathemas including 33 specifically related to justification.

One of the anathemas forced people to believe the dogma of indulgences, which Luther had soundly rebuked with his 95 Theses. The Council "condemns with anathema those who say that indulgences are useless or that the Church does not have the power to grant them." An indulgence is "a remission before God of the temporal punishment due to sins whose guilt has already been forgiven, which the faithful Christian...gains under certain defined conditions." They can be applied to the dead by way of prayer, the Rosary, or the sacrifice of the Mass.

When the pope pronounces an anathema, he uses a formula which ends with these words: "We deprive [him/her] of the Communion of the Body and Blood of Our Lord, we separate him from the society of all Christians, we exclude him from the bosom of our Holy Mother the Church in Heaven and on earth, we declare him excommunicated and anathematized, and we judge him condemned to eternal fire with Satan and his angels and all the reprobate, so long as he will not burst the fetters of the demon, do penance, and satisfy the Church; we deliver him to Satan to mortify his body, that his soul may be saved on the day of judgment."

Anathemas are said to condemn former Catholics to the torments of everlasting hell unless they do penance and return home to Rome. They also condemn current Catholics if they do not believe every infallible dogma of their church.

Former Catholics who are now born-again Christians need not worry! "If God is for us, who can be against us? He who did not spare his own Son but gave him up for us all, how will he not also with him graciously give us all things? Who shall bring any charge against God's elect? It is God who justifies. Who is to condemn? Christ Jesus is the one who died, more than that, who was raised, who is at the right hand of God, who indeed is interceding for us" (Rom. 8:31-34). Only God has the power to save and condemn.

More than ever, Bible believing Christians must contend earnestly for the faith and resist the growing pressure to unite with the Roman Catholic Church as a valid expression of Christianity. Evangelicals need to know that we can never have unity with a religion that condemned the Reformers for believing that sinners are saved by grace alone, through faith alone, in Christ alone, according to Scripture alone, for the glory of God alone. Let us all endeavor to defend the glory and honor of our Lord Jesus Christ, the sanctity of His church, and the purity of His Gospel.

The Danger of Following "Infallible" Men

At the end of the Apostle Paul's ministry, he gave us this sober warning:

> I know that after my departure fierce wolves will come in among you, not sparing the flock; and from among your own selves will arise men speaking twisted things, to draw away the disciples after them. Therefore be alert, remembering that for three years I did not cease night or day to admonish every one with tears. Acts 20:29-31

This grim and prophetic warning concerning false teachers went unheeded, and it continues to be ignored in many churches today.

The Roman Catholic Church, as well as many Protestant churches, have drifted into apostasy because they put aside the authority of God's Word and began following the twisted teachings of men. Two of the most preposterous "twisted things" the Catholic Church concocted are the dogma of "infallibility" for its popes and bishops, and the pope as the supreme leader of the Roman Catholic Church.

The dogma of "infallibility" declares that the Catholic Church cannot err in her objective definitive teaching regarding faith and morals. According to the *Catechism of the Catholic Church*: *"In order to preserve the Church in the purity of the faith handed on by the apostles, Christ who is the Truth willed to confer on her a share in his own infallibility."* This is not only a twisted teaching, it is an outrageous scandal! "Infallibility" is just one of several divine attributes the papacy has hijacked from Almighty God. The pope also has the audacity to wear titles given only to the triune God—Holy Father, Head of the Church, and Vicar of Christ. With such clever and swaggering deception, it is no wonder popes have been able to "draw away the disciples after them."

How could any man do something so wicked and sinful as to exalt himself to the point of wearing titles reserved for God alone? (John 14:16, 17:11; Eph. 5:23). These stolen titles must have a deluding effect, because the pope believes he "has full, supreme and universal power over the whole Church, a power which he can always exercise unhindered" (CCC 882).

It is not only Roman Catholics who are being woefully deceived by these "twisted things." There are some Protestants who are leaving their churches to follow "infallible" popes and bishops. Over the years, I have counseled some of them and warned them of the dire consequences for anyone who departs from the faith. Not one of them ever joined the Roman Catholic Church because of biblical doctrine. Instead, they became apostates after reading some of the early church fathers, who had also departed from the faith of the apostles. Tragically, these former Protestants chose to submit to the fallible teachings of men rather than the infallible Word of God.

We can all learn a vitally important principle from the Jews who sat under the Apostle Paul's preaching in the synagogue of Berea. "They received the word with all eagerness, examining the Scriptures daily to see if these things were so" (Acts 17:11). The Scriptures are what God gave us to test the veracity of every man's teaching. Since an apostle, who wrote over half of the New Testament, came under the scrutiny of Scripture, the same scrutiny must be given to every pope, bishop, priest, pastor and religious leader. There is no higher authority than our Almighty God and Creator, whose Name and Word are exalted above all things (Psalm 138:2). The Word of God exposes and refutes error and can be used as a sword to slay the lies of the devil and his minions, who disguise themselves as servants of righteousness (2 Cor. 11:15).

Pope John Paul's Disputable Influence on Christianity

Without question, Catholic popes exert tremendous influence over the members of the Catholic Church. Believing him to be the "Vicar of Christ", followers blindly revere and accept without question anything this mere man says or does. What impact does this religious leader have on those outside the Catholic Church? Consider the legacy of John Paul II.

In the wake of his death, many evangelicals praised the late John Paul II for being a great spiritual leader. But why do they give such honor to the former head of an apostate church, which keeps over a billion people in spiritual darkness?

Back in 2005 on the *Larry King Live* show, Billy Graham praised John Paul as "the greatest moral and spiritual leader of the last 100 years." Graham said: "He's traveled the whole world, giving his version of the Gospel and spreading the Catholic faith." Later that year, after the pope's death, Graham told Larry King that there is no question John Paul II is now with the Lord. Jack Van Impe, an American televangelist, also assured his TV audience that the pope is now in heaven. Rob Moll, the online assistant editor for Christianity Today wrote: "The pope stood for truth, as revealed in God's Word and his creation."

Although John Paul II never claimed to be God, he took pleasure in being addressed with titles reserved for God alone. Like all other popes, he usurped the titles "Holy Father" from God the Father, "The Head of the Church" from the Lord Jesus Christ and "The Vicar of Christ" from the Holy Spirit, whom Jesus promised to send in His place. John Paul often sat in pompous arrogance on his royal throne as his loyal subjects knelt before him. Never did he refuse worship as Peter did when men fell at his feet. Peter, knowing that only God deserved such reverence, immediately ordered: "Stand up; I too am just a man" (Acts 10:26).

Who knew that Pope John Paul II would have greater success in deceiving the world after his death than during his 26-year pontificate? For those who recall the unbridled homage given to him following his death, who knew the global media would become his willing partner in spreading his perverted theology? Through non-stop television coverage, the pope's church became the world's stage. All eyes were focused on the St. Peter's Basilica, the very church that was financed with the filthy lucre obtained from the sale of God's forgiveness through indulgences. Its princes enjoyed the media spotlight as they piously masqueraded in their purple and scarlet robes as "ministers of righteousness." They successfully cast a spell over the TV audience with the splendor or their rituals and the pomp and pageantry of their pagan traditions. The magnificence and grandeur of this corrupt religion bewitched much of the gullible world into believing this is what Christianity is all about. Thousands of hopelessly deceived people stood in long lines for as long as 18 hours to venerate a dead man with a rosary in his hands and a twisted crucifix by his side. The idolatrous veneration and adoration of Pope John Paul II was unprecedented. His elaborate and theatrical funeral was said to be the largest in human history.

The death of Pope John Paul II provided a glimpse of where "Christianity" is headed in the future. Postmodern church leaders have replaced truth and discernment with pluralism and tolerance. Evangelicals and Catholics together have publicly praised John Paul as a godly and holy spiritual leader.

Year after year, he was the most loved and admired man in the world. This should not surprise us. Jesus said "the world would love its own" but hate those whom He chose out of the world (John 15:19). He also warned, "Woe to you when all men speak well of you" (Luke 6:26). The gullible world responded in the same fashion it will when the man of lawlessness is revealed. "God will send upon them a deluding influence so that they might believe what is false, in order that they all may be judged who did not believe the truth" (2 Thessalonians 2:11-12).

Judging the Pope's Gospel

Only God can judge John Paul's heart, but all Christians are all called to judge every man's teachings. The apostle John warned us: "Do not believe every spirit, but test the spirits to see whether they are from God; because many false prophets have gone out into the world" (1 John 4:1). John Paul's false teachings are clearly exposed by the new *Catechism of the Catholic Church* which he endorsed in 1994. His damning Gospel was diametrically opposed to the Gospel of Jesus Christ. Paul warned that anyone (including himself or the pope) would be condemned if they were to preach another Gospel. He wrote, if "we or an angel from heaven should preach to you a Gospel contrary to that which we have preached to you, let him be accursed" (Gal. 1:6). If apostles and angels were to be accursed for preaching another Gospel, how can the pope possibly escape? Clearly the pope condemned himself by perverting God's Gospel of grace with additional requirements for salvation, as can be seen when comparing Scripture to doctrinal positions in the Catechism.

If the Philippian jailer could have asked a pope what he must do to be saved (Acts 16:30), he would have heard a false and fatal gospel: "You must have faith plus baptism (CCC 1256), receive the sacraments (CCC 1129), do good works (CCC 2016), consume the Eucharist (CCC 1405), keep the law (CCC 2068), belong to the Catholic Church (CCC 846) and have your sins purged in purgatory" (CCC 1030). What a contrast to Paul's clear response: "Believe on the Lord Jesus Christ and you will be saved" (Acts 16:31). Paul made it clear there is only one Gospel and anyone who believes another Gospel has believed in vain (1 Cor. 15:1-4). Therefore, either the pope was right and is in heaven, as many evangelicals are claiming, and Christians are wrong and destined for the eternal lake of fire, or the pope is wrong, and those who believe the Gospel are forever saved and destined for heaven.

Few evangelicals have had the courage to expose the pope's false Gospel that shuts the kingdom of heaven to those wanting to enter. Clearly, there is no greater evil than deceiving people about the eternal salvation of their souls.

Eternal Truths Are Confirmed

As with anyone who passes into eternity, the pope now knows the truth. He knows he was never infallible, or holy, or the Vicar of Christ. He knows there is no such place as purgatory. He now knows the Gospel he preached is leading over a billion people down the wide road to destruction. John Paul may now be experiencing what the rich man in Luke 16 endured. Both of them once dressed in purple and fine linen and lived in splendor every day. When the rich man died and found himself tormented in the flames of Hades, he begged the Father to send someone to tell others the truth so they would repent and not end up in the same place. The pope may now be making the same request. What would he tell Catholics if he could return? I believe he would urge them to trust Christ and His Word over the teachings and traditions of men. He would admit that he was terribly wrong about entrusting the church to Mary's protection. John Paul would tell his flock that Jesus indeed finished the work of redemption 2000 years ago and His one offering is necessary and sufficient to save sinners completely and forever.

Whom Did John Paul Represent?

John Paul said he represented Jesus Christ, yet he lived in stark contrast to the Savior, who had no place to lay His head. On several occasions he denied that Jesus was the only way to the Father. He foolishly proclaimed: "If God is the one true God, He must save all people" (Vatican Info Service, 4/21/1999). A year later he pronounced: "All who seek God with a sincere heart, including those who do not know Christ and His church, contribute to the building of His kingdom" (Vatican Info Service, 12/6/2000). He also denied the sufficiency of Christ's sacrifice by declaring punishment for sin could be remitted "by abstaining from unnecessary consumption (of tobacco or alcohol) and donating a proportionate sum of money to the poor" (VIS, 9/29/1999). His perverted theology was also reflected in this pronouncement: "Hell is not a punishment imposed by God…, but the condition resulting from attitudes and actions which people adopt in this life" (Detroit News 7/28/1999). When he addressed Muslim leaders in 1998, he said there is "a common spiritual bond that unites us."

John Paul has also been acclaimed as a great moral leader, yet he failed to discipline American Bishops for tolerating the detestable sexual abuse of children by their depraved priests. After Cardinal Bernard Law of the Boston Archdiocese magnified the scandal by protecting the guilty priests, John Paul appointed him to a prestigious position in the Vatican. Law's cover-up of the abuse of over 600 children, which cost the Boston archdiocese more than $90 million in settlements, outraged many Catholics but not the pope.

Even long after the passing of John Paul II, Christians have a tremendous opportunity to talk about spiritual issues and make the most of every opportunity to speak the truth in love and proclaim the Gospel with clarity and completeness! Let us all seek the approval of the One who purchased us with His precious blood! We must also earnestly contend for the faith against everything that stands opposed to God's Word. May God help us to be faithful in these times of great deception and compromise!

Pope Attempts to Change God's Laws

Whenever a person is elevated to a position of authority equal to Scripture, such as the Catholic pope, all manner of compromise and usurpation of God's holy Word is possible. This has been the history of the role of the pope and continues on into our present day.

The Synod of Bishops, on the *Pastoral Challenges of the Family*, which ran from October 5-19, 2015 created heated discussions on the new direction that the Roman Catholic Church was taking. The primary topics of the Synod included softening the church's position on homosexuals and birth control, streamlining the annulment process and improving pastoral care of divorced and remarried Catholics. It is appalling that there is any discussion on issues where God's authoritative Word has already established His position. No church or pope has the right to ratify a moral position that is inconsistent with God's Divine Law. Marriage was established and clearly defined by God, and no one has the right to pervert what He ordained.

Pope Francis urged the participating bishops to speak their minds clearly and fearlessly. He didn't want to censor the conversation and thereby prevent "the truth" from emerging. One highly controversial proposal suggested that homosexuals have gifts and qualities to offer to the Christian community, and the church should provide for these people and guarantee them a place of fellowship. They said that the question of homosexuality requires serious reflection on how to devise realistic approaches to growth and maturation in the Gospel.

Roman Catholic gay rights groups around the world hailed the report as a breakthrough, but church conservatives called it a betrayal of traditional family values. While the text did not signal any change in the church's condemnation of homosexual acts or gay marriage, it used less judgmental and more compassionate language than seen in statements prior to the election of Pope Francis.

Pope Francis is suggesting a "pastoral approach" to members of the gay community, making it easier or more comfortable for them to either stay in the Catholic Church or come back to it. At this Synod, he said, "the church must become more compassionate toward homosexuals." "If a person is gay and seeks God and has good will, who am I to judge?" It is never his role to judge another person. That is the responsibility of God and His infallible role, which, concerning the sin of homosexuality, He has done (Romans 1:26-28; 1 Corinthians 6:9-11; 1 Timothy 1:8-10). It's not his role to judge, but to proclaim God's Word that condemns sin, including the sin of homosexuality.

The Synod also expressed the need to make annulment cases more accessible for divorced and separated people to allow them to partake of the Eucharist. An annulment is a legal procedure for declaring a marriage null and void. Unlike divorce, it is retroactive, meaning that an annulled marriage is invalid from the beginning as if it had never happened.

Not only has Pope Francis challenged many of the historic positions of the Catholic Church on family values, he has even opened the church up to atheists, stating that, "they can follow their own conscience into heaven." As the first Jesuit pope, he is trying accomplish what the Counter-Reformation set out to do following Martin Luther's protest against the church—keep Catholics in the church and bring all wayward followers back under the domain of the Roman Catholic Church. This is his attempt to be all things to all people to bring everyone under his power and influence. His conflicting views with the traditional teachings of Catholicism has created much confusion within the church. So much so, Catholics don't know who to trust. Jesus Christ is the personification of truth. His Word is truth. He came to testify to the truth, so why look anywhere else? This presents tremendous opportunities for Bible-believing Christians to hold meaningful conversations about the true Gospel of Jesus Christ, which finds its sole authority in the pages of Scripture and never changes.

In his closing address of the Synod, Pope Francis questioned the temptation of "traditionalists" with their "hostile inflexibility" and their failure to allow themselves to be "surprised by God." This is an attempt by Pope Francis to establish himself in the middle between what he views as "hostile inflexibility", and as he says, "the temptation to a destructive tendency to goodness," which he referred to as a characteristic of progressives and liberals.

Since Pope Francis was elected as the current pope, he has sparked controversies and divisions within the hierarchy of the Catholic Church. In response to the many liberal reforms Pope Francis is urging, some cardinals have been quoted to say that the Synod was "working from a position that is virtually irredeemable." Another stated that the document risks "dancing to the world's music" and succumbing to secular influences. "The world truly does not need a counterfeit gospel."

I find that last statement sadly ironic. As I have stated in this book and throughout my ministry, the Catholic Church has, since it departed from the teachings of Jesus and His apostles, preached a counterfeit Gospel. Now, members within the Catholic Church are calling out Pope Francis for promoting a counterfeit to the counterfeit Gospel!

There may be no better time in the history of the Catholic Church for Bible-believing Christians to hold conversations with the deceived members of the apostate church. Catholics need to hear the true Gospel, and allow the power of God's Word to convict, correct, and bring these lost souls to repentance and faith.

A Response to Pope Francis' Attack on Justification

Pope Francis has made frequent allusions to "Satan" which may be part of his effort to cast out the presence of evil and bring back healing and harmony to the Catholic Church, and to parts of the Vatican. He has addressed the sin of calumny in religion, which is defined as "false and malicious statements, or slander, meant to hurt someone's reputation." The pope said, "Calumny aims to destroy the work of God, and calumny comes from a very evil thing: it is born of hatred. And hate is the work of Satan. Calumny destroys the work of God in people, in their souls. Calumny uses lies to get ahead. Be in no doubt, where there is calumny, there is Satan himself."

It appears commendable of Francis to try to clean house both inside and outside of the Vatican, where there is much dissent. However, it is ironic that Francis heads an organization with a long history of calumny against Protestant Christianity. In fact, the reformer John Calvin, in his *Institutes of the Christian Religion*, wrote a whole chapter (chapter 16) to refute the calumnies that were waged by the "papists" against the doctrine of justification.

The following are my responses to each of the four calumnies waged against the Christian faith by Rome:

"Faith Alone" destroys good works and encourages sin

Good works are present in the life of a true Christian. Good works don't save, but they will follow as the fruit of a justified believer (Ephesians 2:10; Titus 3:8). A guilty person has nothing to offer God. In the same way, one who is on trial for murder will not reverse or lighten his sentence by promising to do good works. Without saving faith it is impossible to please God (Hebrews 11:6).

Martin Luther coined the phrase, "We are saved by faith alone, but faith that saves is never alone." Scripture is clear that works don't save (Romans 3:20; Galatians 2:16; Ephesians 2:8-9; 2 Timothy 1:9; Titus 3:5), and in fact, they nullify justifying grace (Romans 11:6). This, however, doesn't mean that works are not present in the believer's life. The true believer evidences good works in their life (John 15:5; Titus 2:14) and strives to obey the teachings of Christ. Roman Catholics have confused justification with sanctification. While both are distinctly different, they are similar in that they are both by the grace of God and both involve human responsibility. Justification means to make righteous and is imputed to the believer, granted by God's grace and received solely by faith (Romans 4:9; Galatians 3:6) and repentance (turning from what opposes the truth). Rome denies the imputed nature of justification and has long taught that it is infused, a continual process as man strives to become righteous. The problem with this view is that the basis of one's right standing before God is no longer on the basis of Christ's blood, but on man's works. The biblical view is simply that a man is made right before God by faith in Christ's blood shed for him. He is restored to God and enabled by grace to thrive in a progressive sanctifying relationship with God. He does good works with joy as a result of the work done in him. The process of sanctification accompanies all who are justified (1 Corinthians 1:30; Romans 6:22).

A husband's generosity to get flowers for his wife does not contribute to his love for her; the flowers are a demonstration of the love he already has for her. Likewise, the good fruit on a tree is not the source of the tree's goodness; it is the evidence that the tree is healthy (Luke 6:43-44). Good works do not cause or contribute to salvation, but rather they are the evidence (Romans 2:10).

"Faith Alone" destroys merit, which dissuades men from doing well

It is misguided to believe that man's only motivation to do well is in light of a promised reward. All false religions function with the same driving force, that man must strive to earn favor with God. Biblical Christianity stands distinctly apart in that it declares that our enablement and motivation are in light of what has already been done by God and received by true believers (1 John 4:19). The justified believer is set free from their slavery to sin (Romans 6:17), is given a new heart (Ezekiel 36:26) and is a new creation in Christ (2 Corinthians 5:17), imputed with the righteousness of God (Romans 6:18). They do good works out of the overflow of joy, love, and gratitude for what has been done for them. This is analogous to two children, one who obeys his parents to try to win favor with them and another who obeys his parents simply because he loves them and desires to please them. The child who tries to win favor is focused on himself and his position before his parents, which he believes he can increase. In contrast, the child who recognizes he is loved by his parents is secure in his position and relationship with them. He has a heart that is purely motivated by desire to obey and please them.

"The apostles make no mention of merit" is a false claim

Throughout many of the epistles, we see a continual model where the first half of the epistle is doctrine and the second half is practice. Ephesians is the clearest example of this, with the first three chapters being orthodoxy (right teaching) and the last three chapters being orthopraxy (right practice) in light of one's position in Christ. There is a clear shift in chapter 4 with the first verse, "I therefore, a prisoner of the Lord, urge you to walk in a manner worthy of the calling to which you have been called..." Paul then goes on to describe the true believer's unity and changed life (chapter 4), how they should walk in love and love their spouses (chapter 5), and finally the further roles of parents, children, masters, and slaves along with the strength we have in the whole armor of God (chapter 6).

The apostles unanimously teach that our power to do right doesn't come from our striving obedience and good works, but rather such things are enabled and overflow as a result of what Christ has done for us. Often times people mistakenly reject the Gospel, because they feel they have to get their lives in order before they are ready to pursue their faith. The reality is that no one has anything to offer God or can even pursue Him apart from what He does for us. This is as absurd as a sick person believing they need to get healthy on their own before they can see a physician. Jesus uses this illustration in Luke 5:31-32 when He states, "Those who are well have no need of a physician, but those who are sick. I have not come to call the righteous but sinners to repentance."

It's important to note that sinners have nothing to offer God; they simply turn from their sinful ways and turn to God in faith. The great danger of religion and the emphasis of merits that are believed to be worthy of a reward is that they cause one to look to self rather than God. Those who boast in how religious they are, and who are dogmatic about how their many works are required by God, have pridefully aligned themselves with the Pharisees. In God's great plan of salvation, He gets all the glory. As we forsake everything we think we have to offer Him and depend on Him alone, we sound a trumpet for His glory. As true believers who are wholly dependent on His grace, demonstrating the change He has made in their lives, we lovingly bear much spiritual fruit, not out of obligation but out of love. Those that seek to abuse or take advantage of sanctifying grace put themselves in a very precarious place where one has good reason to question if they are truly saved (Romans 6:1-2).

"Righteousness is too easy" is a misunderstanding

This objection might be one of the most common misunderstandings by Catholics today. God's biblical plan of salvation sounds too easy for those who do not understand divine justice. What many fail to realize is that salvation is of such great value, that we could never merit it even if we tried. Salvation appears not to be fair in the sense that innocent One who was of infinitely more value than any man, would take on the wrath of God for the guilty and condemned who were living in rebellion to God (Rom. 3:10-18). But praise God that He provided a way to demonstrate His love and mercy by crushing His Son as a substitute for His people (Isaiah 53:4-5); He accomplished this in the only way His justice and righteousness would not be compromised (Psalm 97:2; Hebrews 4:13-16).

Those who believe salvation is easy have failed to humbly recognize the great sacrifice God has done for believers. Prior to salvation, our religious good works are like filthy rags (Isaiah 64:6) offered by a condemned felon before a righteous judge.

Obtaining the righteousness of God is not easy. We will never understand the full extent of what Christ had to endure on this side of eternity. Jesus said, "the gate is narrow and the way is hard that leads to life, and those who find it are few" (Matthew 7:14). When Nicodemus asked Jesus how to be born again (John 3:4), Jesus responded that "the wind blows where it wishes, and you hear its sound, but you do not know where it comes from or where it goes. So it is with everyone who is born of the Spirit" (John 3:7-8). Salvation is a work of the Lord from beginning to end.

In Ephesians 2:1-3 we get a glimpse of the natural man's spiritual condition before God. He is described as dead in sin, following Satan, sons of disobedience, following his passions and desires, and under God's wrath. For the religious individuals, who believe that we have much to contribute to salvation so that it is not so "easy", they must ask themselves, what does such a condemned person have to offer God? Ephesians 2:4-10, goes on to describe how God intervenes in the life of the born again believer; He has given such helpless individuals grace to receive salvation by faith. We have nothing more than faith to contribute and repentance from all in which we formerly trusted that opposed faith in Christ alone. Even the good works that verse 10 speaks of are "prepared beforehand" by God, not by man. The heart of a follower of Christ is one of overwhelming gratitude because they properly recognize that it is God, "who has saved us and called us with a holy calling, not according to our works, but according to His own purpose and grace which was given to us in Christ Jesus before time began" (2 Timothy 1:9).

While the majority of Pope Francis' message appears noble to us to be tolerant of one another's views, especially his, it is in fact a clever sleight of hand. What better deception could Satan put forth than to encourage kindness towards his false beliefs. Francis fails to address where true teachings can be found. From the beginning, Roman Catholicism has been opposed to the one true Gospel in God's Holy Word. While Francis calls anyone who opposes his "infallible" false Gospel as doing the work of the devil, it is in fact him and his organization who have long been pawns under the influence of Satan himself. The lesson to be learned from all this is to ensure that our disagreements with one another are always rooted in understanding what God's perfect holy Word says. Jesus said, "If you abide in my word, you are truly my disciples, and you will know the truth, and the truth will set you free" (John 8:31-32).

Catholicism's Defense of Justification by Works

Roman Catholics will often quote one verse to justify their position of justification by works. "You see that a person is justified by works and not by faith alone" (James 2:24). When this verse is taken out of context, it appears that James is teaching something inconsistent with the rest of Scripture. However, by studying the entire chapter to get the full context, James is not teaching how to be justified; he is contrasting two kinds of faith—a faith which saves and one which does not. There is spurious faith and genuine faith. There is intellectual faith and heart faith, a man-generated faith and a God-given faith. There is dead faith and living faith.

To fully understand this passage and the meaning of biblical faith, all of Scripture must be considered. The Bible clearly tells us that the only way to come to God is through faith in Jesus Christ. Jesus warned against false faith, or non-saving faith. He said,

Not everyone who says to Me, 'Lord, Lord,' will enter the kingdom of heaven; but he who does the will of My Father who is in heaven. Many will say to Me on that day, 'Lord, Lord, did we not prophesy in Your name, and in Your name cast out demons, and in Your name perform many miracles?' And then I will declare to them, 'I never knew you: Depart from Me, you who practice lawlessness.' Matthew 7:21-23

Saving faith should not be confused with faith in a profession, or faith in faith, or faith in a decision, or faith in a prayer. The people Jesus referred to in the above passage did not possess true, saving faith.

Non-saving faith is temporal and usually is found in a person's head but not their heart. It is faith based on a historical event that Jesus is the one true God who died for the sins of the world. Many have this head knowledge, but this kind of faith cannot save. The demons exercise this kind of faith, and they certainly are not saved! "You believe that God is one. You do well; the demons also believe, and shudder" (James 2:19). Professing Christians who merely acknowledge the historical facts of Jesus Christ without repentance are not saved.

Temporary faith lasts for a while, then fades away because it does not have any roots (Matthew 13:18-23). Jesus describes this in the parable of the sower, in which the Word of God is sown upon shallow soil. But because of the shallow soil, there are no deep roots and the life is only temporary and quickly withers. Temporary faith is also like the seed which was sown on rocky places. This is the man who hears the Word, and immediately receives it with joy; yet he has no firm root in himself but is only temporary, and when affliction or persecution arises because of the Word, immediately he falls away. Some people have a religious experience or make a public profession of Christ, but their faith fades away when the demands of the Christian life confront them.

James wrote, "You see then that a man is justified by works and not by faith alone" (James 2:24). The Greek word for justify also means "vindicate, to defend or uphold." In other words, James is saying: "You see then that a man is vindicated (or defends and upholds his living, saving, God-given faith) by his works and not only by a mere profession of faith." The word vindicate could also mean to clear from suspicion. In no way is James teaching that sinners are justified by works, because he has already made the point that salvation is a gift from God according to God's will, not the will of man (1:17-18).

James is asking professing Christians, who have not shown evidence of their new life in Christ, to "show me your faith" (James 2:18). But faith is invisible to man. It is an unseen relationship between man and God. Since faith cannot be seen, the best way to prove one's faith is to be "doers of the word and not merely hearers" (James 1:22). Those who do the Word of God will live a righteous life in obedience to God. That is why James said: "I will show you my faith by my works" (James 2:18). James is saying that justifying faith will be evidenced by works.

Saving Faith

True saving faith is a gift of God that will persevere. "For by grace you have been saved through faith; and that not of yourselves, it is the gift of God; not as a result of works, that no one should boast" (Ephesians 2:8-9). True faith is based on what God has revealed in His Word. The object of saving, or justifying faith, is Jesus Christ and what He has accomplished on behalf of sinners through His substitutionary death and resurrection. It is granted by God when the sinner, under the conviction of the Holy Spirit, is humbled in godly sorrow for his sin. When God gives him grace to believe in Jesus Christ and what He accomplished on the cross, that person is transformed by the same power that raised Christ from the dead.

Saving faith is exercised when a person comes to the end of himself, recognizes his hopelessness before God, and turns from his sin and self-righteousness to the Lord Jesus Christ as the ONLY One who can save him. This repentance involves a change of mind such that the person turns away from his life of rebellion toward God and casts himself wholly upon the mercy of God to save him (Acts 2:38; Luke 13:3; Mark 1:15). The Apostle Paul described this work in his own life in Philippians 3:8-9.

More than that, I count all things to be loss in view of the surpassing value of knowing Christ Jesus my Lord, for whom I have suffered the loss of all things, and count them but rubbish in order that I may gain Christ, and may be found in Him, not having a righteousness of my own derived from the Law, but that which is through faith in Christ, the righteousness which comes from God on the basis of faith.

Saving faith also involves a total reliance upon Jesus Christ and His work on the cross. This belief in Christ goes beyond a mere head knowledge of Jesus to a trust in Christ and Christ alone for salvation. Faith means:

Forsaking
All,
I
Trust
Him.

The Apostle Paul never boasted about anything he did in order to be saved, because he realized that it was all of Christ and none of him. "May it never be that I should boast, except in the cross of our Lord Jesus Christ, through which the world has been crucified to me, and I to the world" (Galatians 6:14).

Saving faith also involves receiving Christ Himself as your Redeemer, Savior, and Lord.

But as many as received Him, to them He gave the right to become children of God, even to those who believe in His name, who were born not of blood, nor of the will of the flesh, nor of the will of man, but of God" (John 1:12-13).

Faith alone justifies, but faith that justifies is never alone. Faith gives evidence of its existence by righteous living. Anyone who claims to have a right relationship with God will live a life of good works. Sanctification is thus, the observable evidence that justification has been granted.

You can see in this passage that James is concerned for professing Christians who have a dead faith which is idle, barren, and unfruitful (James 2:17). He is saying that dead faith cannot justify anyone and is useless (James 2:20). Only genuine faith is alive and bears fruit.

Faith without works is the faith of the devils, mere intellectual assent without repentance.

We can see from these passages that the Bible must be studied inductively, that is, not to prove our theology but to develop our theology. The adopted child of God enters into a living, dynamic relationship with Jesus Christ as his Lord. Jesus has redeemed him from the power of sin and has applied His blood and righteousness to his life and declared him to be righteous before God. Jesus has saved him from the wrath of God, and there is now no condemnation to fear (Romans 8:1). Praise be to God!

Catholics Should Believe Who They Think Was Their First Pope

The apostle Peter played a prominent role in the early church. Soon after he abandoned his career as a fisherman to follow Christ, he became a fisher of men. Several of his sermons were recorded in the Book of Acts, and his two epistles are included in the divinely inspired Scriptures. Since Catholics have been taught that Peter was their first pope, I have developed some questions to shed some light on his theology, ecclesiology, and soteriology. All of the answers come directly from his writings and sermons. It is my prayer that those of us who have been sanctified by the truth will share these glorious truths with our Catholic friends and loved ones.

Peter, were you the first pope and the supreme head of the first century church?

"As a fellow elder, I exhort the elders among you... to shepherd the flock of God" (1 Peter 5:1-3).

Are you the rock upon which Jesus would build His church?

Jesus is "a living stone rejected by men but in the sight of God, chosen and precious... The stone the builders rejected has become the cornerstone and a stone of stumbling, and a rock of offense. They stumble because they disobey the word" (1 Peter 2:4,7-8).

Were you infallible?

Paul opposed me to my face because I was not in step with the truth of the Gospel (Galatians 2:11-14).

Should we confess our sins to priests?

Repent of your wickedness and pray to God that your sins may be forgiven (Acts 8:22).

Should we pray to Mary and the saints?

Pray to God (Acts 8:22).

Can anyone be saved apart from the Lord Jesus Christ?

"There is salvation in no one else, for there is no other name under heaven given among men by which we must be saved" (Acts 4:12).

What would you say to Pope Francis who teaches that atheists can follow their conscience into heaven?

"There will be false teachers among you, who will secretly bring in destructive heresies, even denying the Master who bought them, bringing upon themselves swift destruction." "The ignorant and unstable twist Paul's letters to their own destruction, as they do the other Scriptures" (2 Peter 2:1; 3:16).

Can anyone be certain that they have inherited eternal life?

God has caused believers to be born again to a living hope through the resurrection of Jesus Christ from the dead to obtain an inheritance which is imperishable and undefiled and will not fade away, reserved in heaven and protected by the power of God through faith (1 Pet. 1:3-5).

Is it possible for God's grace or indulgences to be purchased for the remission of sins?

God ransoms us "not with perishable things such as silver or gold, but with the precious blood of Christ" (1 Pet. 1:18-19).

Can a person be born again through water baptism?

The only way to be regenerated is to be "born again, not of perishable seed but of imperishable, through the living and abiding word of God" (1 Pet. 1:23).

Should Jesus Christ be made a sin offering during the sacrifice of the Mass?

Christ suffered "once for sins, the righteous for the unrighteous, that he might bring us to God, being put to death in the flesh but made alive in the spirit" (1 Pet. 3:18).

Is the Catholic priesthood necessary to mediate between God and man?

Every believer, who is called out of darkness into Christ's marvelous light, is made a priest for the purpose of offering spiritual sacrifices to God and proclaiming His perfections (1 Pet. 2:9).

Should Jesus continue to be pictured as a dead man hanging on a cross or as a baby in Mary's arms?

The resurrected Christ has "gone into heaven and is at the right hand of God, with angels, authorities, and powers having been subjected to him" (1 Pet. 3:21-22).

What should we do in these days of great deception?

Take care that you are not carried away with the error of lawless people and lose your own stability. But grow in the grace and knowledge of our Lord and Savior Jesus Christ (2 Pet 3:17-18).

There is a profound contrast between the divinely inspired teachings of Peter and the fallible, ungodly opinions of Pope Francis. The enormous disparity between the instruction of these two men Catholics call "pope" shows how far the Roman Catholic Church has departed from the faith of the apostles.

Let us look at other Roman Catholic doctrines that show how far they have departed from the faith of the apostles.

The Sacrifice of the Mass

Central to the regular rituals and sacraments of Catholicism is the Mass which must be attended by Catholics every Sunday, and holy days of obligation, under the penalty of mortal sin. As described in the *Catechism of the Catholic Church*, the Holy Mass is "the source and summit of the Christian life". It is taught that the ordained priest calls the Lord Jesus down from heaven and consecrates the bread and wine into His body, blood, soul, and divinity. The sacrifice of Calvary is represented over and over again on the altar. But there is no biblical support for the Mass. Following are seven biblical reasons why the Mass is a Catholic tradition that violates the perfect sacrifice for sin that was offered once, for all sin, for all time.

1. Jesus was never a "victim" as Rome purports; He went to the cross willingly in humble obedience to His Father (Philippians 2:8).

2. When Jesus said we must eat His flesh and drink His blood, His words were spiritual and not to be taken literally (John 6:63). He was using figurative language, as He often did (John 16:25). His disciples were familiar with the figurative phrase "eating and drinking" to describe the appropriation of divine blessings to one's innermost being (Jeremiah 15:16; Isaiah 55:1-3).

3. Those who take "eating and drinking" literally must become cannibals to gain eternal life. Furthermore, consuming blood was forbidden; those who did were to be cut off. Jesus would not have asked the Jews to break the law (Leviticus 17:10-14). This also presents a dilemma, "What if a person eats and drinks but does not believe?", or "what if a person believes but does not eat and drink?"

4. The alleged change of bread and wine into flesh and blood is not a miracle but a hoax, because there is no change in appearance, substance and taste. True biblical miracles were real and observable.

5. Rome says the Mass is a bloodless sacrifice, but a sacrifice without blood cannot atone for sins (Leviticus

17:11; Hebrews 9:22). Jesus instituted the Lord's Supper as a memorial, not a sacrifice (Luke 22:19; 1 Corinthians 11:24).

6. Nowhere in the New Testament do we find priests offering sacrifices for sin or Masses for the dead. Catholic priests violate Christ's unique role as mediator between God and men (1Timothy 2:5).

7. To worship the elements of the Mass is to commit the sin of idolatry (Exodus 20:4-5).

Baptismal Regeneration

Baptism may be the most divisive doctrine in the professing church. Catholicism teaches the sacrament of water baptism is a sacrament of regeneration that causes people to be "born again" and became "members of Christ." Catholic priests are said to be able to do what only God can do, and that is, bring those who are dead in sin to life in Christ. As the priest sprinkles the water of baptism, the baptized is said to be reborn as a new creature, adopted as of son of God, purified of all sin and justified (CCC 1263-66). This false teaching violates the sovereign regenerating work of God. Those who become sons of God are born again, "not of blood, nor of the will of the flesh, nor of the will of man, but of God" (John 1:13). They are saved on the basis of God's purpose and grace (2 Timothy 1:8-9).

The word "regeneration" is found in only two places in the New Testament, namely, Matthew 19:28, and Titus 3:5. The new birth, or being born again, or born of God, is dealt with in several passages, particularly in John 3. Christ said, "Except a man be born of water and of the Spirit, he cannot enter into the kingdom of God" (John 3:5). If by the "water" He meant baptism, it means that not a single soul could be saved unless they are baptized with water! That would disqualify the repentant thief, who was crucified at the same time as Christ. If water baptism is what saves sinners then Jesus could not have been the Savior, because he did not baptize anyone (John 4:2).

Catholics still insist that their doctrine of water baptism is found in this Scripture: "Except a man be born of water and of the Spirit" (John 3:5). But in order to get the correct interpretation, we must refer to other Scriptures. The words in John 3:5, "of water and of the Spirit," could be correctly interpreted, "of water, even of the Spirit." Such a rendering would be fully in accord with Ezekiel 36:25-27, John 4:14 and 7:37-39, where the water is a metaphor for the Holy Spirit. Christ was explaining to Nicodemus that the new birth was entirely a spiritual one, which, like the wind, no man can control. In many places in the Bible, "water" is used figuratively for the Word of God as well as the Spirit of God. In Ephesians 5:26, we see the Word as a cleansing agent from defilement. In 1 Peter 1:23, we are taught that the Word of God is the seed that effects the new birth. We are born again by the Word of God, the incorruptible seed, that brings forth life. In James 1:18 we are begotten by the Word of truth. In verse 21, we are exhorted to receive the Word which is able to save your souls.

The two necessary agents to bring about the new birth are the Word of God and the Spirit of God. No priest can initiate spiritual regeneration. Physical water cannot raise those who are dead in sin to life in Christ.

Idolatry in the Catholic Religion

Many Roman Catholic traditions find their origin in paganism, but none as obvious as the use of statues, icons, relics, and images in worship. Historians report that statues of the Egyptian goddess Isis, with her child Horus, were renamed Mary and Jesus by pagan Rome. Today, shrines of the Black Madonna and Child are the holiest shrines in Catholic Europe. It should not surprise us that some of the titles and honor given to Mary by the Vatican, such as "Our Lady", "Eternal Virgin" and "Madonna", were the same titles attributed to Isis. Whether the idolatry is pagan or religious, the principle is the same. The worship and honor that is due to God alone is turned away from Him and given to that which is not God.

On a missionary trip to Mexico several years ago, I went into the Cathedral of Acapulco to share the Gospel with Catholics. The idolatry I witnessed there was so nauseating that it has grieved me to this day. In a transparent glass coffin there was a statue of Jesus lying face up with wads of pesos in his hands. In front of the coffin was an offering box with the words in Spanish: "For the holy burial of Jesus." I wept as I watched poor Mexican peasants kneel down and offer what little money they had so that Jesus could be buried (again).

The first two commandments of God clearly forbid two things: 1) creating and worshipping an image of the true God and 2) worshipping anyone other than God (Exodus 20:1-5). In other words, our worship must be directed only to the true God and not through any object. Thus, to worship, venerate, kiss, adore, lift up, pray to, speak to, or make religious use of man-made images of God and saints is a sin of the most serious kind. God could not have made this any clearer when He commanded: "You shall not make for yourself and idol, or any likeness of what is in heaven above or on the earth beneath or in the water under the earth. You shall not worship them or serve them; for I, the Lord your God, am a jealous God" (Exodus 20:4-5). Yet, the Roman Catholic Church has laid aside this commandment of God, teaching instead the traditions of men (Mark 7:8). This is a most deliberate and willful defiance of God's holy law. The one who refuses to listen to the law must know this: "Even his prayer is an abomination" (Proverbs 28:9). God has made it clear that those who continue in the sin of idolatry will not inherit His kingdom (1 Corinthians 6:9-10). "Their part will be in the lake that burns with fire and brimstone, which is the second death" (Revelation 21:8).

Almighty God is never to be worshipped using man-made images, because it is impossible for images to capture or display His divine attributes. How could man ever create an image that displays God's transcendence, holiness, majesty, eternality, sovereignty and His glory which fills the earth? To portray God in the form of an idol crafted by man reduces the Creator to the substance of creation. No wonder the infinitely glorious, all-powerful and omnipresent God of heaven and earth hates being approached by worshippers who distort His character with flawed images crafted by mortal men.

True and False Worship

Jesus said, "God is spirit, and those who worship Him must worship in spirit and truth" (John 4:24). One does not have to formally deny the Triune God in order to be an idolater. Reverence for the God of the Bible coupled with the ungodly sin of idolatry is common place. The Israelites never renounced God when they fashioned a golden calf. Instead they said, "This is your god, O Israel, who brought you up from the land of Egypt." Afterwards Aaron built an altar in front of the idol and proclaimed: "Tomorrow shall be a feast to the Lord" (Exodus 32:4-5). The Lord, who is a consuming fire and a jealous God, did not let this wicked sin of idolatry go unpunished. He ordered those who helped create this god of gold, and who did not repent, be put to death (Exodus 32:26-28). About three thousand idolaters were slain.

Lessons From History

Sadly, the Roman Catholic Church has not learned from biblical history and fled from idolatry. Instead Rome created a god of flour and water to be worshipped as the resurrected and glorified Son of God. It is idolatry to call what man's hands have made "God", and then worship it as deity. Like the Israelites, Catholics also build altars to celebrate (Eucharistic) feasts to the Lord.

As incredulous as this sounds, Catholicism teaches that the resurrected and glorified Jesus Christ returns daily to Catholic altars to be worshipped as a sin offering in the form of a wafer. Its priests are said to have the power to reach up into the heavens and bring Christ down from His throne to be offered again as the "Victim" for the sins of man. According to Father John O'Brien in his popular book, *The Faith of Millions*, "the priest speaks, and Christ, the eternal and omnipotent God, bows his head in humble obedience to the priest's command." This is not only a fatal lie but the most wretched form of blasphemy. The idolatrous worship of a wafer as the true Christ is no different than the idolatrous worship of a golden calf as the true God who delivered the Israelites out of Egypt (Exodus 32:4). Both are hated by God and are punishable by death. The Eucharist is irrefutably and undeniably a false Christ, because Scripture declares Jesus will remain in heaven until He appears "a second time, not to bear sin" (Hebrews 9:28).

There is little difference between worshipping a golden calf as the true God and worshipping the Eucharist as the Son of God. Both religions appear to have had the same objectives in creating their idols. It is the desire to give worshippers a sense of the physical presence of God in order to make use of His power and blessings. Both religions are guilty of the sin of idolatry, which will bring down the most severe judgments of God.

The Cause of Idolatry

The cause of all idolatry is the corruption of man's heart and his need for some kind of religion. The evidence of this is seen in the many false views of God and false ways of worship throughout the world. Ignorance of God, including a diminished understanding of His attributes and commands, characterize the religion of natural man. Man is eager to bring God down to his level, which leads him to create an image of God he can see, feel, and touch. Man desires to worship in the flesh with all of his senses instead of with a humble and contrite spirit (Isaiah 66:2).

Catholics Must See to Believe

Unbelievers, who are blinded by their religion, say you must see to believe. Their eyes cannot see the glory of Christ, because they are blinded by the prince of this world and the hardness of their own hearts (2 Corinthians 4:4, Ephesians 4:18). The unbelieving Jews, not seeing Jesus's glory, mocked Him with: "Let this Christ, the King of Israel, now come down from the cross, so that we may see and believe!" (Mark 15:32). Earlier Jesus had told them: "Unless you people see signs and wonders, you simply will not believe" (John 4:48).

Roman Catholic leaders also say you must see to believe. They teach Catholics to have faith in visible things for the appropriation of spiritual power and blessings. Catholics see and worship their god in the Eucharist, believing it has the power to wipe away their sins (*Catechism of the Catholic Church*, paragraph 1394). They see and eat the Eucharist, believing they have consumed the physical body and blood of Jesus (CCC 1377). They see and confess to their priest, believing he has the power to forgive sins (CCC 1461). They see and bow down to statues believing the saints, who are represented, will intercede for them (CCC 2683). They see and feel rosary beads, believing their repetitious prayers to Mary will remit punishment for sin (CCC 1471). These are just a few examples of how "seeing signs and wonders" is an undeniable part of the Catholic faith. Rather than worshipping by faith in things not seen, Catholics worship what they can see (Hebrews 11:1). They defend their practice by saying they are not worshipping Mary and the saints when they bow down and pray to them, they are merely venerating them. But according to Webster's Dictionary, veneration is a form of worship and reverence. This practice, along with prayer, is reserved for God alone.

Unbelievers Must Believe to See

The Lord said you must first believe before you can see the glory of God (John 11:40). Genuine faith is the assurance of things hoped for, the conviction of things not seen (Hebrews 11:1). Jesus said, "Blessed are those who have not seen and yet have believed" (John 20:29). So, we fix our eyes not on what is seen, but on what is unseen. For what is seen is temporary, but what is unseen is eternal (2 Corinthians 4:18). Faith does not come from things that are seen (the Eucharist), but from things that are not seen (the Lord Jesus at the right hand of God). Born-again Christians walk by faith not by sight (2 Corinthians 5:7). This faith comes, not from seeing something, but from hearing the Word of God (Romans 10:17). The natural man cannot see, because there is a veil that covers his heart and will remain until he turns to the Lord Jesus in faith (2 Corinthians 3:16). When God removes the veil, a person can see Jesus in every book of the Bible.

What does the Lord say about those who make statues and idols?

> They are altogether stupid and foolish in their discipline of delusion—their idol is wood! Every man is stupid, devoid of knowledge; Every goldsmith is put to shame by his idols; for his molten images are deceitful, And there is no breath in them. They are worthless, a work of mockery. In the time of their punishment they will perish. (Jeremiah 10:8,14-15)

> All mankind is stupid, devoid of knowledge...his molten images are deceitful, And there is no breath in them. They are worthless, a work of mockery. In the time of their punishment they will perish. (Jeremiah 51:17-18).

> They have no knowledge, [those] who carry about their wooden idol, and pray to a god who cannot save" (Isaiah 45:20).

The Levites, speaking for God in a loud voice, proclaimed: Cursed is the man who makes an idol or a molten image, an abomination to the Lord (Deuteronomy 27:15).

People who create and trust idols become like the idol they created, which cannot see, speak or hear (Psalms 135:15-18). They cannot see the glory of God nor hear His Word, nor proclaim His Gospel.

What does the Word of God command? "Do not be idolaters" (1 Corinthians 10:7). "Flee from idolatry" (1 Corinthians 10:14). "Keep yourselves from idols" (1 John 5:21). I pray Catholics will take these exhortations seriously and not participate in the sins of their church any longer. Even if, by the slimmest of chances, the Vatican were to remove all the objects of their idolatrous worship, it must still eradicate another form of idolatry. The idolatrous practice of making ordained priests as mediators between men and God, which gives the priests an honor which the Apostles flatly repudiate, must be ceased. Furthermore, this practice robs Jesus Christ of His unique office (1 Timothy 2:5).

God created us so that we would find our greatest joy in Him when He is our greatest treasure. In light of that glorious truth, there is nothing we should fear more than the wrath of an omnipotent, sovereign God who is angered when people show more reverence to idols. Many ignore the clear and present warnings in His Word to flee idolatry and to keep away from idols (1 Corinthians 10:14; 1 John 5:21). God is rightfully jealous of anything we value above Him. This is why His wrath is coming against all idolatry (Colossians 3:5-6).

All Bible-believing Christians who hold to the infallible truths of God's Word should be moved to share these important truths with Catholics in their circle of influence. You may be their only hope, since most Catholics do not read the Scriptures nor do they have faithful ministers to instruct them. May God increase your love for Him and your compassion for those blinded by religious deception. When the Lord Jesus Christ is clearly proclaimed, rightly known, genuinely believed, gloriously exalted and truly loved, He will set captives free from religious bondage!

Roman Catholicism's Exaltation of Mary

When considering the purity of the Gospel in light of numerous distortions that have occurred since the day our Lord walked this earth, it is important that we consider Catholicism's view of Mary, the mother of Jesus. The Mary of Catholicism is a twisted distortion of the Mary revealed in Scripture who also gave birth to James, Joses, Judas, Simon, and their sisters (Mark 6:3). Rome rejects the Scriptural proof of Mary's other children by infallibly declaring she remained a virgin throughout her life. This counterfeit Mary is said to be another sinless mediator, who is the cause of salvation for herself and the whole human race (*Catechism of the Catholic Church*, 494). Rome also ascribes attributes of God to Mary by calling her a sinless mediatrix, an advocate and a co-redeemer (CCC 491-494, 969).

What is most disturbing is the exaltation of the virgin Mary by Catholics, which is completely unfounded in Scripture. Outside of the Gospels, Mary's name is mentioned only once and that is when she is praying with her other children and other believers in the upper room (Acts 1:13-14). Information about Mary in the Gospels is also very sparse. After the narratives related to the birth of Jesus, there are only three other references to Mary. The first is at the wedding in Cana (John 2:1-5). Next is when she and the brothers of Jesus desired to talk to Jesus. Jesus responded that His mother and brothers are those who do the will of God (Matthew 12:46-50). One other reference is given when a woman in the crowd calls the mother of Jesus "blessed", but Jesus does not affirm her. Instead He said blessed are those who hear the Word and observe it (Luke 11:27-28).

Roman pontiffs have created a Mary that shares the divine attributes of the Lord Jesus Christ. They say she was conceived without sin, lived a sinless life, was bodily assumed into glory, is the mediatrix of all grace, is our advocate, and now reigns as the "Queen of heaven" alongside the King of kings. Pope Francis declared, "The Immaculate 'Virgin' becomes the sublime icon of Divine Mercy that conquered sin. To her I entrust the Church and all humanity, especially the city of Rome."

The idolatry associated with the Catholic Mary is evidenced in many ways, but primarily in the ungodly practice of praying to her. Prayer is one of the deepest forms of worship, because it acknowledges the divine power of the person to whom we pray. This is why we never see any God-fearing man praying to anyone other than God in the Bible. Yet thousands of Catholics pray to Mary, at the same time asking for her help. The only way Mary could hear and answer those prayers would be if she were omnipresent, omniscient, and omnipotent. Yet, she is only human like all of us.

As Christians, we esteem Mary as blessed among women, but to ascribe divine powers and attributes to her is blasphemous and idolatrous. Satan will use anything to persuade people to take their eyes off Jesus. Just as he deceived Eve by his cunning, Catholics who idolize Mary will be led astray from a sincere and pure devotion to Christ (2 Corinthians 11:3). All people in the Catholic church need to be warned of how God hates idolatry. We must call them to turn to God from idols to serve the living and true God (1 Thessalonians 1:9).

The Difference Between Religion and a Relationship

Our ministry, Proclaiming the Gospel, began when we invited all the Roman Catholics we knew into our home to watch a video called *Roman Catholicism: Crisis of Faith*. The video explained the difference between belonging to a religion and having an intimate relationship with God. Former priests and nuns shared how our Sovereign Lord opened their eyes to see and believe the Gospel of grace. Every Tuesday night we had a different group of Catholics watch the video. Their responses varied from one extreme to the other. Some stormed out of the house very upset and offended, but others stayed to ask questions. We invited the truth seekers to return on Wednesday nights for a Bible study on the Gospel of grace. Within three months we witnessed 17 Catholics exchange their religion for an eternal relationship of peace with their all-sufficient Savior. God was glorified as His Spirit and His Word brought forth new disciples for His Son!

We can be wrong about a lot of things in this life and still survive, but if we are wrong about the only way to obtain forgiveness from God, we will pay for that fatal mistake throughout all eternity. Our Creator provides only one way to redeem man from sin and He has revealed it in a divinely inspired message to mankind. However, it didn't take long for God's complete and perfect Gospel message to be corrupted by religious leaders. These men, who say they speak for God, have distorted and perverted this good news of God's mercy and grace. Their unstated goal has been to control people by keeping them in legalistic bondage to their authority. The Lord Jesus revealed the only way of escape from this bondage. He said: "If you abide in My word, then you are truly disciples of Mine; and you shall know the truth, and the truth shall make you free" (John 8:31-32).

Tragically, many Roman Catholics are like the unconverted Paul. They have a zeal for God but not according to knowledge. Many have a gratifying and stubborn-hearted knowledge of their religious traditions, but they do not know the all-sufficient Savior as He is gloriously revealed in Scripture. They seek to become righteous before God, because they do not know God requires perfect righteousness, which they can never achieve. Like the Jews who were "ignorant of the righteousness of God, and seeking to establish their own, they did not submit to God's righteousness" (Rom. 10:3). Being ignorant of God's righteousness, Catholics believe it is infused over time through the sacraments instead of imputed instantly by faith (Rom. 4:5). As fallen people, they are doing whatever they can to cover up their guilt by participating in the rituals of the Catholic faith in an attempt to gain a right standing with God.

The message in the video we shared with the all the Roman Catholics who came to our home stressed these distinctive points regarding the difference between religion and a true relationship with the living God.

The Exchange of Religion

The Apostle Paul's zeal for following the traditions of his religion led him to relentlessly persecute the church of Jesus Christ. Although as a Jew he was entrusted with the oracles of God, he was so indoctrinated with religious traditions that he tried to destroy Christ's church. He wrote: "I persecuted the church of God ... being more exceedingly zealous of the traditions of my fathers" (Galatians 1:13-14). The unconverted Paul bore witness to having a zeal for God but not according to knowledge (Romans 10:2). He had a superior knowledge of his religion, but not a spiritual knowledge of God, which God imparts only to those who exchange their religion for a relationship with Christ (1 Corinthians 2:14). His religious pride and arrogance had blinded him from the glorious light of the Gospel (Philippians 3:5-6; 2 Corinthians 4:4). When God gave him spiritual eyes to see the truth of His Word, he was miraculously transformed (Acts 9:8-22). No longer a merciless persecutor of the church, he was now a passionate evangelist for the church.

The apostle Paul not only exchanged his religion for an everlasting relationship with the Lord Jesus Christ, he considered all his religious accomplishments worthless rubbish. If anyone had reason to boast and be proud of his religious status, it was Paul, "a Hebrew of Hebrews; as to the Law, a Pharisee; as to zeal, a persecutor of the church; as to the righteousness which is in the Law, found blameless" (Philippians 3:5-6). Yet, he considered all this contemptible compared to changing his relationship with God from one of enmity and hostility to one of peace and harmony (Philippians 3:7-11; Colossians 1:20). The notable religious credentials, which he once thought profitable, were actually worthless and damning to his soul (Luke 18:9-14).

The Bondage of Religion

True disciples of Jesus are those who have been set free by the truth as they abide in His Word (John 8:31-32). Those who do not know the truth will continue to be enslaved to the bondage of religion. Throughout history, the goal of every religion has been to control people. This has been accomplished with religious traditions, legalism, pride and deception. One example of this fierce religious loyalty is a comment we hear so often from Roman Catholics: "I was born a Catholic, and I will die a Catholic." Yet, true conversion can only take place if they confess: "I was born a sinner and will die a saint." And what a way to die! By God's amazing grace, saints are elected in Christ (Ephesians 1:4), called to Christ (1 Corinthians 1:9), have believed the truth about Christ (Romans 10:14-17), have turned to Christ in repentance (1 Pet. 2:25), are justified by the blood of Christ (Romans 5:9), are united with Christ (Galatians 2:20), are being transformed into the image of Christ (2 Corinthians 3:18), are being kept and preserved by Christ (1 John 5:18) and will one day gain the glory of Christ (2 Thessalonians 2:14). Why would anyone choose to be enslaved to religion when they can become a blessed and privileged slave of the Lord Jesus?

The End of Religion

The Lord Jesus Christ never came to start a religion; in fact, He put an end to the only religion God ever ordained. Ironically, the rulers of this God-ordained religion had become so corrupt they plotted to murder their Messiah (John 11:53). There was no more need for religion after Jesus, the perfect and eternal High Priest, offered Himself, the perfect sacrifice, to a perfect God who demands perfection. The veil that once separated sinners from their holy God was torn open from top to bottom (Matthew 27:51). The one mediator between God and man provides access to the Father (1 Timothy 2:5). By faith in the shed blood of Jesus, repentant sinners can enter into the presence of God with confidence (Hebrews 10:19-22). No more religion, no more priests offering sacrifices for sin and no more religious rituals or ceremonies. In place of religion, the risen Savior mediates a relationship with God through faith in His one sacrifice for all sin, for all time (Hebrews 10:10-18).

Christianity in its purest form is not a religion but a Spirit-sealed relationship with the God of all creation. Catholicism is Christianity in its most debased form. It became corrupt when it denied the finished and all-sufficient work of Jesus and perverted His Gospel. This warped Gospel of works leads people to a Christ-less eternity. To avoid deception, Christianity instructs people to study the Bible and believe what God says. Religion, on the other hand, requires people to believe what man says God says. When people without discernment submit to men, who are naturally prone to error, they are easily deceived. Catholicism tries to overcome this by declaring its popes are infallible in matters of faith. Christianity is when God's children follow the Lord Jesus, the only one who is immune from error. I will never forget what my uncle, a Catholic priest of 58 years, said after I read to him Scriptures refuting Catholic traditions. He said, "God doesn't mean what He says there; let me tell you what He really means."

The Deception of Religion

When you ask most religious people what they are trusting to gain entrance into heaven, they rarely mention the name of Jesus. That's because their religion is ultimately the object of their faith. They trust their self-righteous clergy and their religious works and rituals to keep them heaven bound. Tragically, they cannot see the glory and sufficiency of Christ Jesus. They have been blinded from the truth of the Gospel by religious indoctrination, a most effective tool of Satan (2 Corinthians 4:4). His primary goal is to confuse people by corrupting and mangling truth as much as possible. Many victims of religious indoctrination are content to blindly trust their unregenerate spiritual rulers, who are willfully ignorant of biblical doctrine and are more interested in holding onto their power than seeking the truth. We have found that indoctrination is so powerful that many Catholics refuse to engage in conversations about spiritual issues with non-Catholics. I recall, as a young indoctrinated Catholic, how "lucky" and proud I was to be born into what I was told to be the one true church. I felt sorry for Protestants who were not as "lucky" as I was. Blinded by Catholic traditions, I did not realize my zeal was misdirected. I was honoring God with my lips, but I was submitting to another Lord—a pope.

The Attraction of Religion

One of the primary attractions of a religion is its appeal to the flesh. The world tells us that "seeing is believing," that we must see before we can believe. This explains why it is so easy for religious people to believe what they can see or touch. Catholics worship and consume the Eucharist, a "god" they can see. They go to a priest they can see to receive sacraments they can see to merit the graces necessary for salvation. They light votive candles as a visible sign of their offerings. And yes, they bow down and pray toward statues they can see.

Those who have a relationship with their Savior walk by faith not by sight (2 Corinthians 5:7). Since faith is the conviction of things not seen, we fix our eyes not on what is seen, but on what is unseen. For what is seen is temporary, but what is unseen is eternal (Hebrews 11:1; 2 Corinthians 4:18). Jesus said only those who believe will see the glory of God (John 11:40).

All religions teach that you must do things to appease their god or gods. Every religion has a works-based system of righteousness that instructs its followers as to what they must do to achieve spiritual blessings. This checklist mentality appeals to the natural man, but man's best efforts are but filthy rags in the sight of a holy God (Isaiah 64:6). Many do their good works because of their zeal for God but they are ignorant of what God's righteousness actually demands (Romans 10:1-4).

Christianity is set apart from all religions, because its founder has done everything necessary for repenting sinners to have a right relationship with God. Spiritual blessings are available by God's grace to all who trust what Jesus Christ has accomplished through His sinless life, death and resurrection. All religions say "DO", but true Christianity says "DONE." Those who desire an eternal relationship with God must trust in what has been done by the Lord Jesus, apart from anything they do for Him (Ephesians 2:8-9).

The Loyalty of Religion

Religion stirs up a passionate loyalty to its rulers instead of to the Lord Jesus Christ. Who can forget the images of Pope John Paul II's funeral? Thousands of misguided Catholics stood in long lines for up to 18 hours to venerate a dead man with an unbiblical rosary in his hands and a twisted crucifix by his side. What a sharp contrast to those who have an everlasting relationship with the only Holy Father. They refuse to listen to the voice of robbers who are out to steal and destroy their souls. They flee from them and instead follow the voice of the Good Shepherd who gave His life for His sheep and calls them by name (John 10:3-11). They come to Him for eternal life, mourning over the sins that nailed Him to the cross. They recognize their unworthiness to be in His presence, yet they rejoice in the hope they have in His Word (Psalm 130:5). Christ and His Word are so connected that one cannot have a relationship with Him apart from His Word (John 8:47).

Those who desire to have a relationship with the true God must seek Him from the only infallible source for truth. All religious teachings, including teachings in this book, must be tested for veracity by searching the Scriptures (Acts 17:11). Those who cling to religious teachings while rejecting God's Word will be condemned on the last day by the very Word they rejected (John 12:48). Conversely, those who believe the Scriptures have been born again through the incorruptible seed which is the Word of God (1 Peter 1:23). As children of God, it is their ambition to be pleasing to the one who set them free from the bondage of religion (2 Corinthians 5:9-10).

We must take the same approach Jesus did by refuting religious error and opposing those who spread it. Religion can never save anyone; in fact, it cuts them off from God and the saving power of the Gospel (Romans 1:16; 4:2-8). Let us exhort those who are enslaved to their worthless and empty religions to become privileged slaves of the Lord Jesus Christ.

Are Catholics Deceived?

Deception will always be exposed by Truth. Have you ever realized that you could be deceived and not even be aware of it? Those who are deceived will never know it unless they are confronted with the truth. Many go to their grave deceived about the most important issue we all face, and that is, locating the narrow road that leads to eternal life. Who are you trusting to show you the way and the truth to eternal life? What is your source for truth? Is it absolutely trustworthy? Will it protect you from the schemes and lies of the master deceiver? The prophet Jeremiah gave us wise counsel for choosing whom we should trust. He said if you trust in man you will be cursed liked a bush in the parched places of the desert. But if you trust in God you will be blessed. You will be like a tree planted by water always bearing fruit, whose leaves are always green. No worries or fears will come upon you in a year of drought or when the heat comes (Jeremiah 17:5-8).

Who will you trust? Many people disregard Jeremiah's advice and put their trust in religious leaders. As was shown earlier, Catholics believe that the Pope and the Roman Catholic Church accurately teach what Jesus and His Word reveal. This can be a fatal mistake. Those who disregard the objective truth of the Bible and rely only on the subjective teachings of men leave themselves open to deception. We know God would never deceive anyone, because He wants all people to be saved and come to a knowledge of the truth (1 Timothy 2:3-4). He gave us His Word so we could know, understand and believe the truth (John 17:17).

Would the Pope have a person believe what is not true? Maybe not intentionally, but what if he was deceived by previous popes who were also deceived? How do we know if any of the pope's teachings or the dogmas of the Roman Catholic Church are true? The only way we can be 100 percent sure is to do as the Bereans did—check everything with the Scriptures (Acts 17:11). If the apostle Paul's teaching had to be verified for its truthfulness, it stands to reason we must use the same standard for any religious leader. Unfortunately, the elevation of tradition, along with the supposedly infallible teachings of popes, to the same authority as Sacred Scripture has allowed deception to go unabated in the Roman Catholic Church. Popes and their teachings constantly change, whereas Jesus and His Word are constant and never change.

The Apostle Paul revealed the source of all deception, "The Spirit clearly says that in later times some will abandon the faith and follow deceiving spirits and things taught by demons" (1 Timothy 4:1). You may be familiar with some common deceptions taught by religious leaders today: heaven is a reward for those who live good lives...water baptism is necessary for salvation...purgatory purges and removes sin...the sacrifice of the Mass can turn away God's wrath on sinners...God's grace can be earned and purchased. Satan has used lies like these to become the greatest "soul winner" in human history. For two thousand years, the master deceiver has perverted the Gospel of salvation by grace. His ferocious wolves, disguised in sheep's clothing, preach counterfeit Gospels that seduce people who are ignorant of God's Word (Matthew 7:15). A counterfeit Christianity is Satan's ultimate weapon, so he can one day be worshipped as Christ. His worldwide religious system is taking shape, and unfortunately it includes many people in our churches today.

All this should come as no surprise to those who know the Scriptures. For this scenario was revealed by Christ and the apostles as a warning of things to come. Jesus announced that right before His second coming, the deception will be so convincing that even the elect might be deceived (Matthew 24:4,11,24). The deceit will come from false prophets, false teachers and false Christs, who will snare people from both inside and outside the church. Peter warned people of spiritual deception, "There will be false teachers among you. They will secretly introduce destructive heresies...and will bring the way of truth into disrepute" (2 Peter 2:1-2).

Satan uses deception to prevent people from being saved. God uses the truth to proclaim salvation to all who believe it. Man is either saved by believing God's truth (Ephesians 1:13) or condemned by believing Satan's lie. Satan blinds the minds of unbelievers by perverting God's truth through false religious systems (2 Corinthians 4:4). Any religion that teaches salvation is obtained through human effort and merit is nullifying the grace of God to its followers. We are saved by grace, "And if by grace, then it is no longer by works, if it were, grace would no longer be grace" (Romans 11:6).

The truth will set you free. How can we avoid falling prey to these subtle and scheming impostors? Our only defense is to experience the emancipating truth of Scripture (John 8:32). We must know and live the truth. All teaching must be filtered through God's Word. We are to use the Bible to lovingly correct and rebuke all teaching that contradicts God's inspired Word (2 Timothy 3:16). The Scriptures must become our ultimate authority in all areas of our faith. We must cling to Jesus who came to testify to the truth (John 18:37) and who is the truth (John 14:6). We are to stand firm with the belt of truth buckled around our waists (Ephesians 6:14). It is through living the truth that we are sanctified (John 17:17). Does the church where you worship submit to the truth of the Gospel? It is of vital importance to God that you worship Him in truth (John 4:24).

There are consequences for those who do not seek God's truth through His Word. Those people who blindly put their faith in religious leaders are most susceptible to deception. Many assume that religious leaders would never seduce anyone with a false plan of salvation. Yet Luke warned, "Even from your own number men will arise and distort the truth in order to draw away disciples after them" (Acts 20:30).

Other people choose not to let truth interfere with their lives. They turn away from it and listen to teachers who say what their itching ears want to hear (2 Timothy 4:3-4). Truth demands a response. The choice is to believe it and conform to it or reject it and go our stubborn way.

There are people who are devoted to God, but do not know Him personally because religious leaders conceal the source and authority of truth. People who have been indoctrinated with false teaching have difficulty believing the truth. They are always learning but never able to acknowledge the truth (2 Timothy 3:7). Acknowledging the truth requires a "turning away" from all unbiblical doctrines.

It was a lack of faith in God's purpose, plan and Word that separated Adam and Eve and their offspring from God. They chose to put their faith in the deceiver, which brought spiritual and physical death to us all. How divine for God to use the very instrument that separated us from Him "faith" to restore us back to Him. It is now through faith in God that we receive His gift of spiritual and eternal life (Ephesians 2:8).

The object of our faith determines who we are—a child of the devil (John 8:43-45), or a child of God (John 1:12); how we live—as slaves to sin, or slaves to righteousness (Romans 6:16-18); and how we will spend eternity—under the wrath of God, or in His loving presence (John 3:36). Faith in anyone other than Jesus, and in anything other than His Word will allow deception to creep into our lives. Those who follow the traditions, opinions and philosophies of men and reject Christ and His Word will be condemned on the last day (John 12:48). By contrast, how wonderful are the words of Christ that those who believe in Him shall not perish but have eternal life (John 3:16).

Jesus and His Word teach...

- You are saved by faith and not by works (Ephesians 2:8-9).
- All who rely on observing the law (commandments) are under a curse (Gal. 3:10).
- Salvation occurs at the moment you believe the Gospel (Ephesians 1:13).
- Jesus purifies sin (Hebrews 1:3).
- You can know for sure you are saved (1 John 5:13).
- The sacrifice of Jesus is finished (John 19:30).

The Pope and his church teach...

- You are saved by faith plus works.
- Obedience to the commandments is a condition for salvation.
- Salvation is a process from baptism through purgatory.
- Purgatory purifies sin.
- You are condemned if you claim to be saved.
- The sacrifice of Jesus continues in daily Mass.

As you can see these two teachings directly oppose one another. You must make the choice as to which is true and which is deception. Your choice will determine your eternal destiny.

Chapter 10

THE URGENCY OF THE GOSPEL

———◦◦◦———

The Lord Jesus declared there are only two roads that lead to eternity, but only a few will find the narrow way that leads to life. Everyone else will travel the broad way that leads to death (Matt. 7:13-14). The many people who are on the broad way will take comfort in knowing they are doing and believing what everyone else does and believes. They need to know, as far as salvation is concerned, there is no safety in numbers. Anyone entering the narrow gate must enter alone with empty hands of faith, trusting Christ *alone*. Thus, the urgency of the Gospel is paramount because billions worldwide seek salvation through other means rather than the only way provided by the one true, merciful God.

Why are there only a few who find the narrow way? It is because false prophets, dressed in sheep's clothing, are constantly directing people to the broad way (Matthew 7:15). These ravenous wolves are successful because the broad way seems right to man, but its end is death (Proverbs 14:12). This is why Jesus said, "Strive to enter through the narrow door; for many, I tell you, will seek to enter and will not be able" (Luke 13:24). Jesus is pleading with people to strive to enter God's Kingdom and be set free from a fallen world that is held captive by Satan to do his will (2 Timothy 2:26). Only the truth will set captives free, and only when they abide in God's Word will they know the truth (John 8:31-32). Then they will be able to discern truth from error and the narrow gate from the wide gate.

Many gullible people fall prey to false teachers because of their deceptive appearance. As servants of Satan, they "disguise themselves as servants of righteousness, whose end will be according to their deeds" (2 Corinthians 11:15). Like anything that is counterfeit, their goal is to fool people. False teachers mask their deceptive lies with an air of religious authority. They hide their fatal Gospel under a thin veneer of truth, such that the outer shell is believable, but what's inside is deadly poison. They often hide their blasphemies and heresies with illogical arguments and traditions of men. They have no fear of God and twist and distort His Word to their own destruction (2 Peter 3:16). They are not interested in saving souls, only in gaining more followers. They are not interested in building the Lord's church, but a church of their own.

Tragically, there are many who never take the time to consider on which road to eternity they are traveling. It is the responsibility of everyone on the narrow way to warn those who are in peril on the broad way. Let us encourage them to consider the many contrasts, listed on the next page, between the narrow way and the broad way before it is too late.

Both ways do have one thing in common: they both lead people to the Lord Jesus Christ. Many will meet Him as a sin-avenging Judge and hear Him say, "Depart from me, I never knew you" (Mat. 7:23). Others will stand before Him as their gracious and merciful Savior and sing His praises throughout eternity!

The most terrifying words a professing Christian could ever hear would be Jesus saying, "I never knew you; depart from Me, you workers of lawlessness" (Matt. 7:21-23). On judgment day those words will be heard by many who once made professions of faith and claimed to be followers of Jesus. The Lord Jesus will declare those horrifying words to many,

Narrow Way	Broad Way
Guided by pure truth (1 John 2:21)	Truth mixed with error (Galatians 1:6-7)
Directed by the infallible Word of God (2 Timothy 3:16)	Directed by the fallible traditions of men (Mark 7:7-8)
The path that sets men free (John 8:31-32)	The path that holds men in bondage (2 Timothy 2:26)
Follows Jesus, the true Shepherd (John 10:3, 14:6)	Follows wolves in sheep's clothing (Matthew 7:15)
By grace and totally undeserved (Ephesians 2:8-9)	By trying to merit God's favor (Titus 3:5)
Enters by repenting and believing the Gospel (Mark 1:15)	Attempts to enter by rituals and self-righteousness (Romans 10:3)
Enters by divine accomplishment (Hebrews 7:25)	Attempts to enter by human achievement (Luke 18:9)
Traveled by the humble who know they deserve hell (Ephesians 2:1-5)	Traveled by the proud who think they deserve heaven (Luke 18:11-14)
Arrives expectantly because of God's promises (1 John 5:13)	Tragically surprised at their lack of entrance (Matthew 7:23)
Leads to eternal life with the Creator (John 5:24)	Leads to the eternal lake of fire (Revelation 20:14)

not a few, who will boast in the many works they did in His Name. They called Him Lord but did not obey His first command to "Repent and believe the Gospel" (Mark 1:15). Yet very few Evangelical leaders appear to be concerned.

It is a sobering thought to realize that according to an ABC News poll, 83% of Americans profess faith in Christ, but only a few of them show evidence of being born again as new creatures in Christ. According to the research, many of them cannot even communicate the Gospel that has the power to save souls. Part of the blame must be placed on man-centered methods of evangelism such as, making a decision to "accept" Christ, or repeating a sinner's prayer, or asking Jesus into your heart, or coming forward for salvation. None of these methods are found in the Bible.

What happened to the God-centered method of evangelism that calls sinners to repent and believe the Gospel? For the last 100 years, people have been told to repeat a prayer, come forward, sign a card or get baptized to be saved. Many of them have lived with a false hope because none of these methods are found in God's Word. The deadliest deception of Satan is to convince a person he is saved when he is not. The devil's ongoing strategy is to corrupt the church by planting tares, or false converts, where God has planted wheat. He knows he can be more effective in attacking the church from the inside than from the outside. Jesus described tares as "sons of the wicked one." The one who sowed them is the devil (Matthew 13:38-39).

Well-meaning Christians who use a man-centered approach to evangelism by manipulating people to make a decision are helping the devil plant tares. They promote easy-believism with no call to repentance or discipleship, because it produces quick results that people can see and measure. The unanticipated results of their actions are devastating: God is not glorified, the sinner is not saved, the church is not sanctified and the devil is thrilled and delighted. The best way to produce true converts and reduce the number of tares coming into the church is to follow a biblical, God-centered method of evangelism. We must quit seeking quick results and instead glorify God by making disciples and faithfully proclaiming His Word until the sinner asks, "What must I do to be saved?"

The only *saving* response to the Gospel of Grace is to repent and believe on the Lord Jesus Christ (Mark 1:15; Acts 16:31). Part of the blame can also be placed on those who compromise the Gospel to make it more inclusive and less offensive (Gal. 1:6-10). Our churches are filled with people who are headed to hell and don't even know it. What lulls so many people into this cruel deception?

The Nature of Deception

The Lord Jesus also referred to the "many" when He spoke of the two paths to eternity. Many will travel the broad road to destruction instead of the narrow road to eternal life (Matt. 7:13-14). Rather than striving to enter the narrow gate by testing every man's teaching, they foolishly follow false teachers, who are wolves disguised in sheep's clothing (Luke 13:24; Matt. 7:15).

Scripture describes these false converts as victims of deception. They are either deceived by false teachers or they deceive themselves. Some are victims of a false Gospel or an unbiblical method of evangelism (Galatians 1:6-7). A false Gospel offers the natural man what he wants: good feelings, healing, riches and success. The true Gospel offers him what he needs: forgiveness of sin, redemption, perfect righteousness, reconciliation with God and the power to live a victorious life.

Those who deceive themselves are people who hear the Word of God but do not do what it says (James 1:22). Since obedience to the Word is a divine requirement of every believer, the disobedience of those who deceive themselves is marked by a lack of concern for God's will and His commands. They have little desire for God's people, His Word or His glory. They are self-absorbed and self-centered and love themselves more than they love God (2 Timothy 3:2-4). Paul gave a stern warning for the self-deceived who reject what the Word says: "The wrath of God comes upon the sons of disobedience" (Ephesians 5:6). They perish because they failed to love the truth (2 Thessalonians 2:10).

They are those who thought they could merit eternal life by the works they were doing instead of trusting in the work Christ had *done*. They also never turned from their sin to follow Jesus Christ in faith. Since they never obeyed the Gospel of Christ, they will pay the penalty of eternal destruction, away from the presence of the Lord (2 Thessalonians 1:9). Tragically, when Jesus declares to them, "Depart from Me," there will be no second chance, no excuses, and no blaming the false teachers who deceived them.

With so many false converts, the church has become a mission field. Many *professors* of Christ are not really *possessors* of Christ! They are strangers to the new birth. They have never passed from death unto life. They remain condemned, because they have not been justified. They remain enemies of God even though they profess to be His friends! They remain enslaved to sin because they have never been set free. They profess the Savior with their lips, but their hearts are far from Him. They deceive other people with their external righteousness, but they cannot deceive God! They are unaware of their pending peril, because they have never examined themselves to see if their faith is genuine (2 Corinthians 13:5).

Ignorance and Pride Can Be Fatal

Tragically, the many warnings given in the New Testament about spiritual deception are not taken seriously. People are so comfortable in their church or religion that they have no hunger for spiritual truth. Deluded by arrogance, they deny their ignorance of God's Word. Many Christians have only a superficial knowledge of the Gospel. They know Jesus died for the sins of the world, but they don't know why He had to, or why it pleased the Father to crush Him (Isaiah 53:10). They don't know the divine punishment for sin is death (Ezekiel 18:4). They don't know the only way God will forgive sin (Luke 24:47; Acts 26:18; Ephesians 1:7). They don't know God opposes the proud and justifies only those who know they are ungodly (Romans 4:5; Luke 18:9-14; James 4:6). Religious pride keeps people in spiritual darkness. Many hold to a form of godliness but deny the power (or the necessity) of the Gospel (2 Timothy 3:5). Their self-conceit leads to self-deceit, and their self-righteousness damns them to everlasting shame.

Strong and Weak Foundations

According to Jesus, true Christians build their houses (which represent their lives) on the solid rock of Christ and His Word (Matthew 7:24-27). False Christians build their house on shifting sand, which is made up of traditions, opinions and teachings of men. When the storms and trials of life come, a true Christian continues to trust and act on God's Word while a false Christian gives up and suffers shipwreck of his faith. When his faith is tested, it is exposed as shallow, spurious and short-lived. He is the man who hears the Word and immediately receives it with joy; yet when affliction or persecution arises, he falls away (Matthew 13:20).

Living and Dead Faith

Anyone can profess to be a Christian, but genuine faith will be evidenced by how a person lives. Likewise, people are known more by what they do than what they say. James asks the probing question: "What use is it, my brethren, if someone says he has faith but he has no works?" (James 2:14). He concludes that a faith which does not produce any evidence of a changed life is a dead, spurious, worthless faith. Those with empty confessions profess to know God, but they deny Him by their works, being abominable and disobedient (Titus 1:16). "Everyone who names the name of the Lord is to abstain from wickedness" (2 Timothy 2:19). In other words, it doesn't matter what you profess to be, what really matters is how you live. Those who have living faith are born of God. They are new creatures created in Christ Jesus for good works, which God prepared beforehand for them to do (Ephesians 2:10).

Right and Wrong Motives

Both true and false Christians follow Jesus, but for different reasons. Unconverted people seek Jesus for selfish motives or wrong reasons, usually for material blessings. Jesus said, "You seek Me, not because you saw signs, but because you ate of the loaves and were filled" (John 6:26). These false disciples with-hold true allegiance and submission to Jesus and retain control of their own lives. They allow their own opinions rather than Scripture to control what they do and how they do it. True converts respond to the Lord Jesus in adoration, praise and worship (Matthew 2:11; 14:33; 15:25; 28:9, 17). They submit to Christ as Lord and obey His Word out of love and gratitude for all He has done and is doing. They are known by how they respond to sin with conviction, sorrow, confession and repentance.

Christ is living water for those who thirst for righteousness (John 7:37). He is living bread for those who hunger for eternal life (John 6:51). He is the only mediator to those who want peace with God (1 Timothy 2:5). Jesus is the only redeemer for those who want to be purchased out of the slave market of sin (Titus 2:14). He is the way for those who are lost, the truth for those who are deceived and the life for those who are dead in sin (John 14:6). He is the only Savior for those who know their hopeless and helpless condition (Ephesians 2:12; Romans 5:6). His blood is the only cure for those who know their sin will end in eternal death (1 John 1:7). His perfect righteousness is the only passport to heaven for those dressed in filthy rags (Isaiah 64:6; 1 Corinthians 1:30). Jesus is the Sovereign Lord who reigns over His people in love and will rule over unrepentant sinners in terror on judgment day (Revelation 20:11-15).

The best way we can prove our faith is genuine is to examine it through the lens of Scripture. The apostle John wrote his first epistle so that those who believe in the Lord Jesus may know that they have eternal life (1 John 5:13). We also see many characteristics of false converts in God's Word. Some of them are listed below:

- You think you are a good person (Romans 3:12).

- You have a zeal for God without knowledge (Romans 10:1-4).

- You have knowledge of God without obedience (Titus 1:16).

- You do not pursue sanctification (Hebrews 12:14; 1 Thessalonians 4:3).

- You are self-righteous without repentance (Luke 18:9-14).

- You seek to establish your own righteousness (Romans 10:3).

- You think you can merit or earn eternal life (Titus 3:5).

- You are unwilling to forgive others (Matthew 6:15).

- You have no desire to follow Jesus (Luke 9:23).

- You call Jesus 'Lord' but do not do what He says (Luke 6:46).

- You do not love other Christians (1 John 4:20-21).

- You love your sin (John 3:19).

- You have not departed from iniquity (2 Timothy 2:19).

- You condone or promote things God hates (Proverbs 6:16-19).

- You are a mere hearer of the Word, not a doer (James 1:22).

- You are full of pride with no humility (James 4:6).

- You walk in darkness (1 John 1:6).

- You live according to your sinful nature (Romans 8:5).

- You do not love the truth (2 Thessalonians 2:10-12).

- You take Jesus as Savior but not as Lord (Romans 10:9).

- You desire Jesus as a priest to pardon sin, but not as a prophet to instruct you or a king to rule over you.

Please know the assurance that we are truly saved is not based on a past decision but on a present reality. What should you do if you are unsure about your faith and your salvation? The answer is found in God's Word:

- Abide in God's Word—then you will know the truth that will set you free from religious deception (John 8:31-32).

- Repent –with godly sorrow for your sins and cry out to God for mercy (Luke 18:13; 2 Cor. 7:10).

- Believe the Gospel—follow the Lord Jesus Christ in faith (Romans 10:9-10).

- Love God—with all you heart, soul and mind (Matthew 22:37; 1 Corinthians 16:22).

What should we do if we know someone who may be a false convert? How should we counsel those who say they have been sanctified by the truth but cling to false teachers? How can we help professing Christians who are not bearing fruit in keeping with repentance (Matthew 3:8)?

We must intervene, because a Christian who "turns a sinner from the error of his way will save his soul from death" (James 5:19-20). We must lovingly confront them with the truth of God's Word and encourage them to examine their faith. Then we must encourage them to consider the exhortation of James.

> Draw near to God and He will draw near to you. Cleanse your hands, you sinners; and purify your hearts, you double-minded. Be miserable and mourn and weep; let your laughter be turned into mourning and your joy to gloom. Humble yourselves in the presence of the Lord, and He will exalt you (James 4:8-10).

Ask them to share the events surrounding their conversion. If their conversion testimony does not line up with Scripture, ask them more questions. Speak the truth in love. Give them a Gospel tract, such as the one available through our ministry: *True Faith or False Hope—How Can I Be Sure?* to encourage them. Let them know eternity is forever!

We can be wrong about a lot of things in this life and still survive, but if we are wrong about our faith, we will pay for that mistake forever and ever. Repentant sinners, who bear the fruit of the Spirit, can be sure they will never hear terrifying words from Jesus (Galatians 5:22-24).

Only Two Kinds of People

As has been made clear throughout this book, there are only two kinds of people in this world. There are those who have been justified by faith in the Lord Jesus Christ and those who remain condemned in their unbelief. God's Word makes it very clear! "He who believes in Him is not judged; he who does not believe has been judged already, because he has not believed in the name of the only begotten Son of God" (John 3:18). Everyone who has ever lived belongs to one of these two distinct groups and will spend eternity in one of two places. From a human perspective, it is difficult to understand why an unbeliever refuses to believe the greatest news he will ever hear about the greatest gift he could ever receive. It is even more difficult to comprehend why anyone would remain an unbeliever after they have been confronted with the reality of being eternally punished in hell's lake of fire. There they will suffer soul-racking remorse, eternal torment, and dreadful agony with no hope of escape.

The Gospel is indeed the greatest news any convicted and condemned sinner could ever hear! That is because God offers a full pardon for sin to those awaiting judgment on spiritual "death row". Since our holy and righteous God cannot let sins go unpunished, a sinless substitute must take their sins and suffer the punishment (Exodus 34:7). The pardon is graciously offered as a gift of God's mercy to repenting sinners, because of a love story written in blood, on a wooden cross, 2000 years ago. Jesus Christ satisfied divine justice by paying a debt He did not owe because we had a debt we could not pay. Every sin that has ever been committed in the history of mankind will be punished by our Holy and Righteous God. He punishes sin's eternal debt in one of two places. Sinners can either trust the Lord Jesus as their substitute on Calvary's cross, or they can reject Him and pay the eternal punishment themselves. If they trust Jesus as their Savior, the eternal debt for their sins will be cancelled (Col. 2:13-14). If they reject Jesus, they will meet Him at the Great White Throne Judgment and be punished in the eternal lake of fire (Rev. 20:14).

Following are 10 vivid contrasts that describe believers and unbelievers. May we all grow in compassion for those who choose to remain in unbelief and separated from God.

UNBELIEVERS	BELIEVERS
Unbelievers are spiritually dead Ephesians 2:1	Believers are alive in Christ-Ephesians 2:5; 1 Corinthians 15:22; Colossians 2:13
Unbelievers love darkness because their deeds are evil-John 3:19-20	Believers walk in the light –John 8:12; 1 John 1:7; Ephesians 5:8
Unbelievers do not seek after God-Romans 3:11	Believers seek God for refuge-Psalm 141:8
Unbelievers are guilty and condemned Matthew 5:22; James 2:10; Mark 16:16	Believers are forgiven and justified Ephesians 4:32; Romans 3:28; Romans 5:1; Galatians 2:16
Unbelievers are under God's wrath John 3:36; Romans 2:5	Believers are under God's grace Romans 6:14
Unbelievers are hostile enemies of God James 4:4; Romans 5:10	Believers are adopted children of God 1 John 3:1; Romans 8:15
Unbelievers are hopeless and helpless Ephesians 2:12; Romans 5:6	Believers are hopefully assured Hebrews 11:1; 1 Peter 1:21
Unbelievers are controlled by flesh and in bondage to sin-Romans 8:6; 8:21	Believers live by the Spirit and are set free by Christ and His Word-John 8:31-36; Romans 8:13
Unbelievers are separated from God because of sin-Isaiah 59:2	Believers are reconciled to God through Jesus Christ-Romans 5:10; 2 Corinthians 5:18-19; Ephesians 2:13
Unbelievers are the many who are on the wide road to destruction and destined for eternal agony in hell-Matthew 7:13; Luke 12:5	Believers are the few who are on the narrow road to life and destined for joy in heaven-Matthew 7:14; 1 Peter 1:4

The Urgency of the Gospel in a Post-Christian Country

Historians agree that from the early days of the founding of America, this country was considered a Christian nation, having its beginnings rooted in religious freedom and built on Judeo-Christian principles. In a relatively short period of time in our nation's history, that has changed. Many now describe the United States as a post-modern, post-Christian country.

God Blessed America

Do you find it troubling when our government leaders close a speech with the overused expression, "God bless America"? Can we continue to ask God for blessings when our nation has blatantly turned its back on the one true God? As a nation, we have suppressed the truth of God in unrighteousness and worshipped every other god instead of the one true God.

When I see bumper stickers with *God Bless America*, I want to get a magic marker and write the letters "ed" after the word "Bless". God has blessed America, but of late our utter lack of gratitude has been shamefully appalling. We lead the world in every abomination known to man: abortion, violent crime, drug addiction, gambling, divorce, child abuse, and pornography. To make matters worse, we export our violence and immorality to other countries through movies and television programs. As a nation, we have also foolishly tried to redefine marriage, the God-ordained union between one man and one woman, to include same-sex marriages.

Our public schools have been prohibited from teaching about God and His creation, and instead pollute our children's minds with atheistic evolution. The teaching and promotion of Islam is now a required addition to many curriculums, but the teaching of Christianity is still forbidden.

As a nation, we have no right to ask God for more blessings. Instead, we must prepare for the judgment that we deserve for our utter rebellion against our Creator. Very few nations have ever been blessed so abundantly as America with its natural resources, oil, natural gas, coal, and rich soil for crops to flourish. Our rainfall is plentiful, and we have rivers of all sizes to distribute water, and transport people and products. God has poured out His blessings on America from its majestic mountains to the oceans white with foam. Yet, as a people we have not honored Him as our great God and Creator or given thanks for His many blessings. It is time that we drop the overused expression "God bless America." As a nation, we need to repent and plead, "God, have mercy on America!" The Lord Jesus Christ is our only hope, and His church must faithfully proclaim His Gospel.

As this country continues its descent into darkness away from God as the King of creation and Lord over all mankind, and as the message of the Gospel is increasingly ignored and scorned in all sectors of society, true believers must equip themselves to give an answer for the hope that is within us (1 Peter 3:15). When there is a vacuum of biblical proclamation in a lost and dying world, when fewer and fewer obedient souls are willing to stand in the gap to call sinners to repentance, we will continue to witness the devolution of this country into an ugly, godless culture where the unthinkable becomes common and accepted. God has blessed America, but at what point will God judge America?

Life Is Short, Eternity Is Forever

We all recognize that life is short in light of eternity. We also know that death is unavoidable, but the brevity of life should not be our greatest concern. More sobering is what God's Word warns will follow: "after this the judgment" (Hebrews 9:27). For born-again Christians, death is but a passage into the glorious presence of our Lord Jesus Christ. He declared victory over death for all believers when He was gloriously raised from the dead (1 Corinthians 15:55-57). Yet, I am often overwhelmed by the solemn reality of standing before my Lord and Savior. He is also my Creator to whom I must give an account for what I have done with the life He has given me. I know His love for me is unconditional, but the realization that I did not faithfully live every day for His glory and purpose will surely bring sorrowful tears that He will graciously wipe away (Revelation 21:4).

No one knows what tomorrow will bring. Our life is but a vapor that appears for a little time and then vanishes away (James 4:14). Compared with the endless ages of eternity, man's average lifespan is so brief. Yet very few consider their lives from an eternal perspective. Instead they foolishly pursue a life of pleasure, prestige, and power with little regard for what awaits them after death. There is no more chilling question in all of human history than when Lord Jesus Christ addressed this folly when He said, "What will it profit a man if he gains the whole world and forfeits his soul? Or what shall a man give in return for his soul?" (Mat. 16:26).

Living with an eternal perspective will motivate Christians to share the Gospel of Christ with others. Each soul we meet is an eternal being who will spend eternity either in God's presence or being tormented in the Lake of Fire. Soon after I finished seminary at the age of 44, God's Word impressed upon me a compelling truth that gave me a new purpose for living. I realized that only two things in this life are eternal: the souls of men and the Word of God. Everything else in the heavens and the earth will be burned up by fire (2 Peter 3:10-12). By God's grace I wanted to spend my remaining years focused on the two things that will last throughout eternity.

May God help us to keep this eternal perspective firmly planted in our hearts. Let us seek after those who will never seek after the true God (Romans 3:11). They are easy to find, because there are many who are traveling the broad road that leads to destruction. Their only hope is for someone to point them to the narrow way that leads to life everlasting (Matthew 7:13-14). It will be the greatest news they will ever hear, because it speaks of the greatest gift they could ever receive!

Even in the midst of affliction, persecution, or mistreatment, we do not lose heart, because momentary, light affliction is achieving for us an eternal weight of glory (2 Corinthians 4:16-18). Let us emulate Paul who said, "In the day of Christ I will have reason to glory because I did not run in vain nor toil in vain" (Philippians 2:16).

The Consequences of Deception

Tragically, there are many who go to their graves and a Christless eternity clinging to their arrogant pride. Others will meet the same fate having been deceived about life's most critical issue. They either embraced the lie that good people go to heaven, or a similar lie that heaven can be merited by good works or religious activity. The only hope for victims of this kind of deception is for them to be lovingly confronted with the truth of God's Word before it is too late.

The source of all spiritual deception is Satan, who is the god of this world, the master deceiver, and the father of lies. Rarely will anyone believe an outright lie, so he cleverly mixes truth with error to deceive even the elect if possible (Matthew 24:24). This is why so many evangelicals have been misled about Roman Catholicism. Many believe Roman Catholicism is a Christian denomination, instead of an apostate church that radically departed from the eternal Gospel of Jesus Christ. This deceitfully insidious religion, headquartered in the Vatican, has become Satan's greatest counterfeit. It hides its false and fatal Gospel with a thin veneer of truth that seduces undiscerning people. Whenever truth is mixed with error, it is no longer true. We need to heed the warning given by Dr. Harry Ironside, the former pastor of Chicago's Moody Memorial Church. He said, "Error is like leaven which leavens the whole lump. Truth mixed with error is equivalent to all error, except that it is more innocent-looking and, therefore, more dangerous. God hates such a mixture! Any error, or any truth-and-error mixture, calls for definite exposure and repudiation. To condone such is to be unfaithful to God and His Word and treacherous to imperiled souls for whom Christ died."

Those evangelical leaders who continue to promote ecumenical unity with Roman Catholics are being unfaithful to God's Word and to the sanctity of His church. As Ironside warned, "God hates such a mixture!" Those who say that Roman Catholics share the same faith as evangelicals are saying Roman Catholics do not need to be evangelized. This is a tragic position because it discourages Christians from sowing the seed of God's Word in the world's largest and most neglected mission field. What hope is there for 1.2 billion Catholics trapped in religious deception if evangelicals do not see the need to lovingly confront them with the true Gospel?

Deception Leads to Bondage

Former Catholics have described their experience of participating in the weekly Sacrifice of the Mass as a "prison sentence" that was, for the most part, repetitious and boring. They remember attendance at the Mass as being a requirement to avoid committing a mortal sin and incurring the penalty of eternal damnation. The expression on the long, drawn faces of many Catholics during Mass revealed their lack of joy for having to be there. They were not there to worship God in spirit and truth but to fulfill the unbiblical laws of their religion. According to the *Catechism of the Catholic Church* (CCC, para. 2180), "On Sundays and other holy days of obligation the faithful are bound to participate in the Mass." Why is this law so demanding? Why are Catholics compelled to participate in the mindless ritual of standing, sitting, kneeling and genuflecting, as priests perform their religious duties? Why are Catholics not given the freedom to attend religious services out of love and adoration for their god? The answers are found in the deceptive dogmas of the Catholic Church.

Catholics are taught they must attend the weekly sacrifice of the Eucharist in order for the sins committed during the previous week to be forgiven. According to the Catechism, "The Eucharist is a sacrifice because it represents the sacrifice of the cross...the sacrifice of Christ and the sacrifice of the Eucharist are one single sacrifice: The victim is one and the same. In this divine sacrifice...the same Christ who offered himself once in a bloody manner on the altar of the cross is contained and is offered in an unbloody manner...this sacrifice is truly propitiatory" (CCC 1366,1367). In other words, Catholics are taught that divine justice (for their sins) is satisfied every time the Eucharist is offered to God.

Catholics are also taught that their redemption comes through the ongoing sacrifice of the Eucharist. "Every time this mystery is celebrated, the work of our redemption is carried on" (CCC, para. 1405). This blatantly denies the testimony of Scripture. When Jesus ascended into heaven, He "entered the holy place once for all, having obtained eternal redemption" (Heb. 9:12).

Catholics are given no choice but to believe these deceptive teachings. If they deny the physical presence of Jesus in the Eucharist, they are condemned by their religion. "If anyone denies, that in the sacrament of the most Holy Eucharist, are contained truly, really and substantially the body and blood together with the soul and divinity of our Lord Jesus Christ, and consequently the whole Christ...let him be anathema" (Canon 1, Council of Trent).

I have a great love and compassion for Roman Catholics. They are in the same place I was for most of my life—believing I belonged to the one true church and on my way to heaven, yet destined for the eternal lake of fire. I would still be woefully deceived and on the wide road to destruction if I had not been confronted with the truth of God's Word. For this reason, I created Gospel tracts to challenge Catholics in their faith. The tracts force Catholics to make a choice between believing the teachings and traditions of their religion or submitting to Christ and His Word.

Roman Catholics are not the only group woefully deceived and blinded by the lies of Satan. Any church, synagogue, mosque, or religious institution that dilutes, distorts, denies, or lies about the true Gospel of Jesus Christ as revealed in His Word, is guilty of holding people captive in their deception. It is my prayer that more and more Christians will share the truth of God's Word that is able to set captives free from religious deception (John 8:31-32).

Chapter 11

THE PROCLAMATION OF THE GOSPEL

—❦—

How would you respond to a recruiting ad that read like the following:

> Men and women wanted for the difficult task of building Christ's Church. You will face constant attacks from an invisible enemy who will try to distract you from your objective and destroy your effectiveness. You will be persecuted, mocked and ridiculed by his ministers of unrighteousness. You will often be discouraged and misunderstood by apathetic and lazy people working with you. Whenever you are persecuted for the sake of your King, you will be asked to leap for joy. The results of your labor and your full reward will not come until after all your work is completed. You will not be able to boast or take pride in what you do and it may cost you your life. However, you will enjoy compelling advantages over all competition by tapping unlimited resources from your headquarters' support team. The fruit of your labor will last for all eternity. And most importantly, the incomparable retirement program is out of this world.

This recruiting ad is an accurate description of what every Christian experiences when they devote their lives to the Savior and His great commission. Jesus asked His disciples, "Who do the people say that I am?" (Luke 9:18). Following their responses, He replied:

But He warned them and instructed them not to tell this to anyone, saying, "The Son of Man must suffer many things and be rejected by the elders and chief priests and scribes, and be killed and be raised up on the third day." And He was saying to them all, "If anyone wishes to come after Me, he must deny himself, and take up his cross daily and follow Me. For whoever wishes to save his life will lose it, but whoever loses his life for My sake, he is the one who will save it" (Luke 9:21-24).

Have you ever wondered why religious people plotted to kill the Lord Jesus when He walked this earth? Why would devout Jews, who had a zeal for God, kill one of their prophets? It was not because He was so merciful (John 10:32; Luke 23:34). Nor was it because of His abundant grace and sacrificial love (John 15:13). So why did the religious leaders seek to have Jesus crucified? This may surprise you. It was because Jesus told them the truth (John 8:40). He proclaimed the truth about Himself and the truth about who they were (John 8:44). As the personification of truth, He declared His Word to be the truth (John 14:6; 17:3). He told them that He came from heaven to testify to the truth (John 18:37). He did not come to be a man-pleaser, but to do the will of God. This truth angered the Jews so much they plotted to have Him killed.

The self-righteous Jews became incensed when Jesus said, "Unless you believe that I am He, you will die in your sins" (John 8:24). Their religious pride, a powerful tool of the devil, had blinded them from the truth (2 Cor. 4:4). It is no wonder the proud oppose God, and God opposes the proud (Jas. 4:6).

In one of the Bible's curious paradoxes, people were put to death for telling the truth, but made alive for believing the truth (John 5:24).

Jesus said, "You seek to kill Me because My word finds no place in you" (John 8:37). The Jews would eventually deliver

Jesus to be crucified and killed by lawless men, according to the definite plan and foreknowledge of God (Acts 2:23). God used the truth that was rejected by stiff-necked, stubborn-hearted, religious people, to have the Lord of Glory put to death.

Following Jesus in the First Century Was a Life and Death Decision.

Telling the truth threatened the apostles with death. When they were brought before the High Priest and his council, they began proclaiming the truth, and the Jews became infuriated and wanted to kill them (Acts 5:27-33). Eventually, 11 of the 12 Apostles would all die a martyr's death for proclaiming the truth of the Gospel.

It was also the truth, spoken so boldly by Stephen, that had him killed. When the Jews heard his message of truth, they became enraged and stoned him to death (Acts 7:1-58). Throughout the New Testament, we see a fierce opposition and hatred of God's truth. After King Herod killed James with the sword and saw how it pleased the Jews, he made plans to arrest and kill Peter also (Acts 12:1-3).

The Jews have not been the only religious people who have killed God's people because of the truth. During the Counter Reformation, the Roman Catholic religion brutally murdered hundreds of thousands of Christians, who had been set free by the truth of God's Word (John 8:31-32). **The Gospel of Rome has not only been fatal for those who believed it, but also fatal for those who had the courage to expose it.** As the Reformers were calling people out of their apostate religion, many of them were tortured and burned at the stake by the Jesuits. Tragically, the truths they died defending are now being compromised by evangelicals who are uniting with Rome.

The Vatican's hatred for the profound truth that Jesus Christ died once for all sin for all time has been demonstrated by its blasphemous sacrifice of the Mass. In this abominable tradition, a counterfeit Christ is immolated on an altar as a propitiatory sin offering for the living and the dead. It grieves me to no end that over one billion faithful Catholics embrace this utter nonsense instead of believing the clear truth of God's Word (Heb. 10:10-18). Because of religious indoctrination, Catholics are denying and suppressing the truth of God's Word to their own destruction.

People who are woefully deceived by their religion will never know it unless they hear the truth. Their only hope is to be lovingly confronted by Christians who have been entrusted with the truth. As Ambassadors for Christ, we must proclaim the truth with boldness and courage. We cannot be man-pleasers and servants of Christ at the same time. Sadly, we already have too many man-pleasers who allow the truth to be trampled in the streets in order to be loved by all. We need more God-pleasers who are willing to die for the Gospel, which has the power to bring life to those dead in sin. We need to do what Jesus did by refuting error, opposing those who spread it, and contending earnestly for the faith! This means we must strive to be biblically correct instead of politically correct!

Tragically, many who are called by Him have not reported for active duty but have gone AWOL. Sure, they will gather in holy huddles on Sunday morning, but when the play is called, they go sit on the bench to watch others run the offense. They say they are too busy or not equipped or fearful. What they really need is some divinely inspired motivation to get them actively involved in building Christ's church. Following are seven motivational truths that should inspire every Christian to become a more faithful witness for the Lord Jesus:

Witnessing Glorifies Our Great God

Each time we proclaim the Gospel, we proclaim the excellencies of Him who called us out of darkness into His marvelous light (1 Peter 2:9). Even if we do not see many conversions while laboring in the fields white for harvest, we are still glorifying our great God and Savior every time we proclaim His Gospel.

Of course, we must also live our lives in a way that reflects the matchless love and heartfelt gratitude we have for our Savior. Our actions provide another notable testimony to unbelievers. When they see our good works, our heavenly Father is glorified (Matthew 5:16). For this reason, Paul exhorts us: "you have been bought with a price, therefore glorify God in your body" (1 Corinthians 6:20). Jesus said the mark of a true disciple is one who glorifies God by proclaiming the fruit-bearing Gospel. "By this is My Father glorified, that you bear much fruit, and so prove to be My disciples" (John 15:8).

Witnessing is a Divine Command

The Lord Jesus gave a command for every Christian to obey. "Go therefore and make disciples of all the nations, baptizing them in the name of the Father and the Son and the Holy Spirit, teaching them to observe all that I commanded you; and lo, I am with you always, even to the end of the age." The Greek word for "go" is "*poreuomai*" which means "on your way" Christians are to make disciples (not decisions) as they go from place to place. Jesus has given us this great responsibility of making His last command our first concern. When you break up the word "responsibility", we see it is our "response" to His "ability."

Witnessing is a Royal Privilege

All Christians are given the awesome privilege of being ambassadors for the King of Kings. One of the highest honors for an American is to represent our country as an ambassador. In the same way, the highest honor for a Christian is to represent King Jesus and to take His message of reconciliation to a lost and dying world. Every man in Christ is a new creature who has been given the ministry of reconciliation. God has recreated them for the privilege of reconciling the world to Him through Christ (2 Corinthians 5:17-20).

Witnessing is a Great Act of Love

I believe the primary reason many Christians do not faithfully proclaim the Gospel is because they do not grasp the sheer horror of hell. If we fully understood the reality of the everlasting torment and suffering that awaits those who die without Christ, we would do everything in our power to reach our loved ones before it is too late. Jesus lamented over Jerusalem, because He knew the dreadful terror the Jews would endure for rejecting their Messiah. Jesus said those who reject Him will be eternally punished in an everlasting fire (Matthew 25:41, 46). Paul, the compassionate evangelist of the first century warned unbelievers when he wrote: "Those who do not obey the Gospel of our Lord Jesus...will pay the penalty of eternal destruction, away from the presence of the Lord" (2 Thessalonians 1:8-9). It is a terrifying thing to fall into the hands of the living God (Hebrews 10:31).

Giving the good news of Christ's substitutionary atonement is indeed the greatest act of love we could ever do for those who are perishing. We have all heard of other great acts of love, such as when people donate one of their organs to another. As great as this sacrifice is, it only takes care of their temporal problem. When we share the Gospel with them we are giving them a cure their eternal sin disease.

Our love for the lost is often coupled with our deep compassion for them. The word "compassion" is not a passive word but a word of action. It means "sorrow for the [pending] sufferings of another accompanied by an urge to help."

Witnessing is also a compelling demonstration of our love for Jesus. Our love for God should reflect His merciful love for us. God demonstrated His love for His children by sending His only Son to die in their place (Romans 5:8). "He died for all, that they who live should no longer live for themselves, but for Him who died and rose again on their behalf" (2 Corinthians 5:15). One of the most consistent ways we can show our love for God is live for Him in obedience to His Word by proclaiming His Gospel (1 John 2:5).

The Gospel is a Message of Hope to Be Believed and Obeyed

Peter proclaimed, "there is salvation in no one else; for there is no other name under heaven that has been given among men, by which we must be saved" (Acts 4:12). There is no other Savior, no other mediator and no other Gospel (John 14:6; Galatians 1:6; 1 Timothy 2:5). If there were many ways to paradise, then the Gospel message would not be that important. However, the Gospel of Jesus Christ becomes the most important message anyone could ever hear, because it communicates how sinners can receive the greatest gift ever offered—everlasting life in the presence of our gracious Creator and merciful Savior. Those who do not share the Gospel are only helping the devil's cause. Satan uses everything in his power to thwart access to Scripture, because he knows that the living and abiding Word of God is the imperishable seed that brings forth eternal life to those he is holding captive with his lies (1 Peter 1:23).

The Gospel is presented as an announcement to be believed. On the night of Jesus' birth, the angels arrived and announced to the shepherds the good news of the Gospel, "there has been born for you a Savior, who is Christ the Lord" (Luke 2:11). The Gospel is a simple announcement to be believed. The Gospel is also presented as an invitation to be accepted. Paul declared as ambassadors for Christ, "we beg you on behalf of Christ to be reconciled to God" (2 Corinthians 5:20). It is a divine invitation to be reconciled to God. The Gospel is also a command to be obeyed. Paul warned that judgment will come on "those who do not obey the gospel" (2 Thessalonians 1:8). So, we can see the Gospel is an announcement to be believed, an invitation to be accepted, and a command to be obeyed.

Witnessing is Evidence of a New Life

Those who were converted in the first century could not stop speaking about what they had seen and heard (Acts 4:20). After our Lord finished His earthly mission to seek and to save the lost, He passed the baton to His disciples (Luke 19:10). Knowing this, we must seek after those who will not seek the true God (Romans 3:11). Bearing fruit for the glory of God is living proof that you are His disciples (John 15:8-16; 1 Peter 1:7).

Christians are born again to reproduce! Whenever I see repentant sinners respond to the Gospel in genuine saving faith, the very first thing they want to do is share the good news with all their loved ones. One dear lady in particular, who exchanged her Catholic religion for a relationship with Jesus, put together 17 three-ring binders with all the Scriptures that we shared to set her free. She immediately sent them to all her family members in the hopes they too would follow Jesus in the newness of eternal life.

Another friend, who left the Catholic Church after trusting Christ as her all-sufficient Savior, asked if we would start teaching her son and his fiancée all the Scriptures we shared with her. This new life, that is given by God as a gift, will indeed be evidenced by a desire to see others come alive in Christ. Paul wrote, "Every Christian has been created in Christ Jesus for good works, which God prepared beforehand, that we should walk in them" (Ephesians 2:10). A most important work God has prepared for us to do is to build His church by making disciples of Jesus Christ.

Followers of Jesus Will Fish for Men

Jesus said, "Follow Me, and I will make you fishers of men" (Matthew 4:19). Jesus gave this command to those who were professional fishermen. They had been successful in catching fish that were alive; now they were being asked to catch men who were dead. The only way to catch men who are dead in their sin is with the life-giving power of the Gospel (Romans 1:16). A disciple of Jesus will follow Him, and to follow Jesus is to be a fisher of men.

There is no greater cause for rejoicing than to see those who had been enslaved to Satan, sin and death, be set free by the power of God! The redeemed rejoice and all the angels in heaven rejoice when sinners repent!

May Christians everywhere develop a greater desire to glorify God through the proclamation of His Gospel. As our love for our Savior grows, might His wondrous mercy, sovereign grace and unfailing love flow from our hearts to our lips. And may we never refrain from proclaiming our Lord's sin-repelling holiness, His inescapable justice and His perfect righteousness that is required for entrance into paradise. In the power of the Holy Spirit, motivated by our matchless love for Jesus, and to honor and glorify His holy name, let us all emulate the early church: "Day after day, in the temple courts and from house to house, they never stopped teaching and proclaiming the good news that Jesus is the Christ" (Acts 5:42).

Fishing in the Depths of Fallen Humanity

Evangelism was of utmost importance to our Lord Jesus. He began and ended His ministry with a call to spread the Gospel. From the very beginning of His ministry, His plan was to use disciples to make disciples. He called his first disciples, who were fishermen, to become fishers of men (Mark 1:17). Instead of continuing to cast their nets into the sea, He directed them to cast their nets into the depths of fallen humanity.

He gave them a new purpose for living with an eternal perspective, because the difference between fishing for fish and fishing for men is profound. When you catch fish, they are alive, and then you watch them die. When you catch men, they are dead in sin, and then you watch them come alive in Christ.

The keys for effective fishing are similar whether you are fishing for fish or for men. Following are seven biblical principles for success!

1. Know Their Nature. As we fish for men, we need to know that they are spiritually dead (Ephesians 2:1). The natural man does not accept the things of the Spirit of God; for they are foolishness to him (1 Corinthians 2:14). They cannot see the light of the Gospel for "the god of this world has blinded the minds of the unbelieving, that they might not see the light of the Gospel of the glory of Christ" (2 Corinthians 4:4). It is no wonder the disciples asked Jesus "Who then can be saved?" Jesus said, "With man this is impossible, but with God all things are possible" (Matthew 19:24-26).

2. Be Properly Equipped. As we fish for spiritually dead men, we must be equipped with the Word of God, which is the seed that is needed to make them alive in Christ (1 Peter 1:23). We also need to be equipped with doctrinally-sound Gospel tracts to give away after we share the Gospel.

3. Go Where They Are. Just as fish live in water and won't come to us, we must seek the lost because they are running from the true God. Many love the darkness or all that the world has to offer. Others are content in their apostate religions and will never seek the truth. This is why we go to Catholic Churches to evangelize on Resurrection Sunday and Christmas Eve.

4. Use the Right Lure. The only lure for catching fallen humanity is the Lord Jesus. He said, "When I am lifted up from the earth, I will draw all people to myself" (John 12:32). If you use any other lure, you will only catch false converts.

5. Cast Your Line. This means sharing the Gospel and telling others about Jesus as He is revealed in His Word. Nothing can be caught until we do. "Faith comes from hearing, and hearing through the word of Christ" (Romans 10:17).

6. Be Patient. Fishing takes time. Don't give up. Trust God to draw the lost into the Gospel net. Jesus said, "No one can come to Me unless the Father who sent Me draws him" (John 6:44). Wait on the Spirit of God to use the Word of God to bring conviction of sin, righteousness, and judgment (John 16:8-11).

7. Reel in Your Catch. Reel them in by calling them to "repent and believe the Gospel" (Mark 1:15). Don't hook them and let them swim around without proclaiming the only saving response to the Gospel. Give them a sense of urgency! Today is the day of salvation; God doesn't promise anyone tomorrow!

May we all live with this eternal perspective. The only two things in this life that are eternal are the souls of men and the Word of God! Everything else will be destroyed in the end. In light of this, let us spend more time seeking and evangelizing the lost for the glory of God. There is no greater joy than to see those who are dead in sin come alive in Christ! As we fish in the depths of fallen humanity, let us remember that God has only called us to be faithful. We can only take the Gospel from the Bible to the human ear. God must take it from the ear to the heart and bring forth life.

Biblical Evangelism

Many Christians have substituted God's blueprint for evangelism with methods of their own, in order to fabricate a greater number of decisions. Instead of following the biblical model for evangelism, demonstrated by the early disciples who were trained by the Lord Jesus, the modern church has invented its own traditions. Rather than calling sinners to repentance and faith in Jesus Christ, evangelicals are asking unbelievers to repeat a prayer, sign a card, raise their hand, come forward or "accept" (rather than trust) Jesus as their Savior. None of these modern traditions have any biblical foundation. Not only do they dishonor the Savior, but they often mislead souls into a false hope of salvation. No one has the right to lower God's entrance requirements into His Kingdom. Unless we evangelize God's way, we run the serious risk of deceiving people about their eternal destiny. True saving faith always involves repentance (Acts 20:21).

Biblical evangelism requires making disciples, not decisions. This involves teaching people to observe all that Christ commanded (Matthew 28:18-20). His first command was to "Repent and believe the Gospel" (Mark 1:15). Repentance is a change in mind that is granted by God and leads to a knowledge of the truth (2 Timothy 2:25). It results in turning from idols to God, from dead works to faith, from sin to righteousness and from the traditions of men to Christ and His Word (Acts 26:20; 2 Corinthians 12:21; Col. 2:8; 1 Thessalonians 1:9; Hebrews 6:1). The importance of calling sinners to repentance is also confirmed in the last command Jesus gave: "Repentance for forgiveness of sins should be proclaimed in His name to all the nations" (Luke 24:47). Remember, Jesus did not come to call the righteous, but sinners to repentance (Luke 5:32). Those who respond to the Gospel with repentance and faith will depart from the kingdom of darkness and follow the Light of the world (John 8:12). They will gladly get off the broad road to destruction and enter the narrow way that leads to life everlasting (Mat. 7:13-14).

Biblical evangelism also requires teaching people the attributes of God. The God who created us is also the One who will judge us. He is majestic in holiness (Exodus 15:11). Righteousness and justice are the foundation of His throne and He will not let sin go unpunished (Psalm 97:2; Romans 6:23). He is sovereign, and everyone is accountable to Him (Daniel 4:35;

Hebrews 4:13). The Father demonstrates His love by sending His Son to die for His people (Romans 5:8). God opposes the proud but extends His grace to the humble (Luke 18:14; James 4:6). By His mercy, He saves believers from the eternal lake of fire (Titus 3:5). Modern evangelism puts too much emphasis on God's love and too little on His holiness and righteous justice. This is a stark contrast to first century evangelism where, in the Book of Acts, the word "love" is never even mentioned. Clearly, without a true and balanced knowledge of all God's attributes, sinners will not know Whom they have offended. Nor will they know Who condemns them with eternal punishment or to Whom they must call to be saved. The world is perishing for a lack of the knowledge of God.

When we obey our Lord's last command and follow His directives for biblical evangelism, we can proceed with confidence that He will produce the results (1 Corinthians 3:6-8). He is the Lord of the Harvest (Luke 10:2); and may we all be His faithful laborers.

A Biblical Defense of the Faith

Have you ever considered how biblical your approach is to handling objections when you witness for Christ? It doesn't help that a great majority of apologetical resources encourage unbiblical methods. Whether the individual you engage is a skeptic or a false convert, they need to be confronted with the depravity of their sin, the authority of God's Word and the exclusivity of Christ. This is because their positions are the same and their objections are similar. They are both without Christ, and they both appeal to their own authority to justify how they live.

Do such individuals need to be given better evidences to refute their objections? Do they simply lack a few key proofs that Jesus is Lord and Savior? Or does such an approach perpetuate a false notion that they are the judge, and God is on trial? Nowhere in Scripture do we find Jesus or His disciples giving more evidence for what skeptics reject. The biblical model begins with the fact that man is "without excuse" because "what can be known about God is plain to him, because God has shown it to them" in His creation (Romans 1:19-20). Despite man having this inherent truth about God, he suppresses it (Romans 1:18). For this reason, it is not wise to spend time arguing over evolution, the existence of God, or for that matter, anything opposed to the Bible. If God's Word says it, then it is true. If one rejects His Word, the problem is not a lack of evidence, but an unwillingness to submit to the authority of God and His Word. For this reason, we must defend the faith, not with extra-biblical evidences, but with the Bible alone. This is the best approach because God's infallible Word never returns void (Isaiah 55:11).

Some Christians compromise and seek a neutral source for truth when someone doesn't respect the Bible. Yet, there is no such thing as neutrality, for each person has their own presuppositions. They are drawn either from submitting to God's authority or an authority of their own choosing. When someone rejects the supreme authority of God's Word, how can appealing to a lesser authority be of any help (Romans 10:17; 2 Timothy 3:15-17; Hebrews 4:12)? If an unbeliever wins an argument using an extra-biblical source, they will still need to surrender to Christ's authority for salvation.

Proverbs 26:4-5 provides a wonderful model for answering objections. It states, "Answer not a fool according to his folly, lest you be like him yourself. Answer a fool according to his folly, lest he be wise in his own eyes." Verse 4 reveals the importance of responding with truth while verse 5 explains the importance of exposing untruth. In other words, don't answer a skeptic by using his faulty worldview, but rather stay centered on biblical truth. Show the futility of clinging to anything opposed to God's Word. Also, do not allow the unbeliever to steal components from your biblical worldview such as logic, reason, certainty, or morality, none of which can exist apart from God.

As an example, imagine a discussion with a Catholic who believes they are a Christian but has unknowingly rejected the Gospel. First, we should point them to Gospel truth as laid out in God's Word. The conversation might begin by asking how one hopes to get to heaven. After they have articulated an unbiblical understanding of salvation, ask, "If God's Word said something different would you want to know?" Then show them that they fall short of God's perfect standard. Show them that they must give an account to a holy and just God who cannot overlook sin. Show them their only hope is the Gospel and help them understand that grace, by its very nature, cannot be earned. Explain that it is by faith and repentance that the sinner is made right with God. Reinforce that to add anything else to this free gift is an assault on the gift itself (Romans 11:6). If the Catholic is humble and interested in the Gospel, then continue to engage them and exhort them to forsake everything else and trust Christ alone. To discern if there is biblical understanding, ask the Catholic about certain Catholic teachings which oppose the Gospel. Look for genuine understanding of biblical truth and repentance of previously held Gospel-opposed beliefs.

If, however, the conversation doesn't even get this far and the Gospel message is rejected, then we need to switch gears. We must transition from leading out with the truth (Proverbs 26:4), to showing the folly of the untruth that the unbeliever is currently trusting in (Proverbs 26:5). This would involve respectfully but honestly exposing why the Catholic teaching on salvation is problematic. Ask them about their authority and how they know what they are saying is true. Ask multiple "how" and "why" questions to dig deeper and reveal the root of what they believe and why. At some point, it will be exposed that they are either blindly trusting in man or their own authority. Demonstrate how this is a dangerous path to be on and what Scripture has to say about trusting man (Psalm 118:9, 146:3). Discuss why man always drifts to religion when he really needs a saving relationship with His Lord and Savior. Jesus' discussion with the very religious Nicodemus in John 3, and Paul's testimony of the value of his prior religion in Philippians 3, both would be great texts to make this point. Let them see by way of analogies from Scripture where they stand and let God's powerful Word bookmark your conversation in their minds.

When the Gospel is proclaimed biblically and backed up by a strong biblical defense to any objections, then the evangelist further removes himself from the conversation. This allows for the individual to rightly see their rebellion against a holy God before whom they must one day give an account (Hebrews 4:13). Because this defense of the faith rightfully stands on God's Word, which is compared to a powerful sword (Hebrews 4:12; Ephesians 6:17), we must be wise in how we use it. With the truth on our side, it is easy to make a fool of the unbeliever and put them in their place. However, doing so demonstrates wrong motives, a proud spirit, and a lack of compassion for those who are perishing. The apostle Peter reminds believers when they give a defense of the faith to do so with "gentleness and respect" (1 Peter 3:15). What good is exposing an unbeliever's false worldview if they are so turned off by your manner that they refuse to listen to you (1 Corinthians 13:1)? We must continue to demonstrate our love for the unbeliever and show them that the door is open for them to repent and enter. May we saturate both our Gospel witness and defense of the faith in prayer that our hearts would be right, that we would stay faithful to God's Word, and that He would be glorified.

Guiding Conversations Toward Spiritual Truths

One of the greatest difficulties people have in sharing the Gospel is directing a conversation towards spiritual truths. We have found that this stumbling block can be easily overcome by asking questions. Asking questions shows people that you care for them and you are interested in their responses. People really don't care how much you know until they know how much you care.

Asking questions is a great technique in witnessing, because unbelievers tend to get offended when anyone preaches to them without letting them respond. The Lord Jesus asked many questions in His earthly ministry to make His Gospel known and also to challenge people in their unbelief.

Consider some of the questions Jesus asked the religious people of His day. He challenged Nicodemus, a ruler of the Jews, about his knowledge of the Kingdom of God, "Are you the teacher of Israel and do not understand these things?" (John 3:10). He asked the stubborn-hearted Pharisees who were blinded by religious tradition, "If I speak the truth, why do you not believe me?" (John 8:46). Then He exposed how corrupt their religion had become with this pointed question, "Why do you break the command of God for the sake of your tradition?" (Mat. 15:3). Possibly the most important question that the Lord Jesus ever asked was: "Who do you say that I am?" (Mat. 16:15). Clearly, the response to this question carries eternal consequences because Jesus warned, "If you do not believe that I am [He], you will indeed die in your sins" (John 8:24).

A good acronym to use for guiding a conversation toward spiritual truths is **FIRE**.

F—is for family

I—is for interests

R—is for religious background

E—is for evangelize.

You can ask about **F**amily with questions like: "Where did you grow up?" Then you can transition to **I**nterests and ask about their work or career, hobbies and sports. Next ask about their **R**eligious background: "Where do you go to church?" or "What was your religious upbringing?" This will lead you into an opportunity to **E**vangelize with any of the following questions:

What is the greatest gift you've ever received?

What is the most important decision you face in this life?

Do you know where will you spend eternity?

What is your supreme authority for knowing truth?

If you were ever deceived, would you want to know the truth?

How does your church teach people to have any hope of heaven?

Are you trusting what Christ has done or what you are doing?

If you could ask God one question, what would it be and why?

Why did Jesus have to die?

Are you ready to meet your Creator?

Is purgatory necessary to purify or purge away your sins?

Why do priests continue to do what Jesus declared "is finished"?

There may be occasions when friends or family members no longer want to talk about spiritual issues. If this happens you might respond by saying, "If our roles were reversed, I would want you to keep pursuing me with the truth until I believed it." There may be other occasions when people may not be interested in talking about the truth of God's Word. Whenever this happens, I say with compassion, "We can be wrong about a lot of things in this life and still survive, but if we are wrong about what we are trusting for eternal life, we will pay for that mistake forever and ever in the eternal lake of fire."

Witnessing to Catholics

Many of the 70 million Catholics in America were born into their religion and have never examined their faith through the lens of Scripture. From infancy, they are taught that salvation comes through their church, as they merit saving grace through the sacraments and perform religious rituals and good works to be justified and re-justified. Roman Catholicism is often called the "plus religion" because of what it has added to the Gospel of grace. Catholic salvation is based on Jesus plus Mary, faith plus works, grace plus merit, Scripture plus tradition and the blood of Jesus plus purgatory. Catholics do not know that any addition to the Gospel is a denial of the sufficiency of Christ (Hebrews 7:25). Any addition to the Gospel also nullifies the saving grace of God, which is the only means by which God saves sinners (Romans 11:6). Catholics, who are victims of this deception, need to be evangelized with the true Gospel of grace.

As we witness to Catholics, we must persevere with patience to untangle the sticky web of religious indoctrination that holds them captive (Colossians 2:8). We must follow the instructions of Paul and "not be quarrelsome but kind to everyone, able to teach, patiently enduring evil, and correcting opponents with gentleness." We must pray for God to "grant them repentance leading to a knowledge of the truth," that they may come to their senses and escape from the snare of the devil, who holds them captive to do his will (2 Timothy 2:24-26).

The two most important biblical principles to remember as you witness are to:

- Establish Scripture as the supreme authority for truth (2 Timothy 3:15-17)

- Proclaim the Lord Jesus as the all-sufficient Savior (Hebrews 7:25; Acts 4:12).

Following are other important biblical principles as you witness to Catholics:

- Proclaim Jesus and His Word as the most trustworthy source for truth (John 14:6; 17:17; 18:37).

- Discuss how sin has condemned every man under God's righteous judgment (Romans 3:10-18; Hebrews 9:27; Revelation 20:14).

- Show that the Scriptures are sufficient for knowing and understanding how to be saved (2 Timothy 3:15).

- Define the Gospel and its divine power to save (Romans 1:16; 1 Corinthians 15:1-4; Ephesians 2:1-10).

- Warn of the fatal consequences for anyone who teaches or believes a different Gospel (Galatians 1:6-9).

- Show that no man or pope is infallible. Peter (who Catholics believe was their first pope) admitted he was wrong (Galatians 2:11-14).

- Warn of the danger of following non-apostolic traditions (Mark 7:7-8, 13; Colossians 2:8).

Explain the need to repent from what they have been doing to save themselves, including the sacraments, the sacrifice of the Mass, purgatory, indulgences, other mediators, good works and infant baptism. These nullify God's grace and deny the finished and all-sufficient work of Christ.

- Stay focused on the Gospel, avoid going off on tangents that are unrelated to salvation (1 Corinthians 2:2).

- Sow the imperishable seed of God's Word with Gospel tracts (1 Peter 1:23).

- Pray for their salvation (Romans 10:1-4).

Remember that every sinner must repent and believe the Gospel to be saved (Mark 1:15). The only way to heaven is through Christ, and the only way to come to Christ is God's way - with repentance and empty hands of faith.

Questions to Ask When Witnessing to Catholics

As discussed earlier, one of the most effective ways to communicate the Gospel of grace is to ask questions. Based on the teachings of the Catholic Church, there are specific questions that can be posed to any Catholic to confront their unbiblical views of the Gospel.

Where do you go to find the truth about life's most critical issues?

There is only one source that will never mislead you, never deceive you or try to control you. It is Christ and His Word (John 14:6; 17:17). Jesus said: "If you abide in My word...you shall know the truth, and the truth shall make you free" (John 8:31-32). Free from what? Free from the bondage of religious deception. Knowledge of the truth is necessary to escape from the snare of the devil, who holds people captive to do his will (2 Timothy 2:25-26). Satan uses deceitful workers who disguise themselves as apostles of Christ to blind people from the truth (2 Corinthians 11:13-15). An example of this is how Rome falsely declares its Bishops to be successors of the "apostles of Christ." According to the *Catechism of the Catholic Church* (CCC), "whoever listens to them is listening to Christ" (CCC 862). The apostles had only two successors—Matthias, who was chosen by the apostles, and Paul who was chosen by Christ (Acts 9:1-19). Catholic bishops do not meet the qualifications for apostleship given in Acts 1:21-26. God warns us: "Do not trust in princes, in mortal man, in whom there is no salvation" (Psalm 146:3). Why the warning? Because "savage wolves will come in among you, not sparing the flock; and from among your own selves men will arise, speaking perverse things, to draw away the disciples after them" (Acts 20:29-30). In light of these warnings, a most critical follow-up question must be answered truthfully: Are you trusting Christ and His Word or man and his religious traditions?

Did you know there is only one way to be saved?

God's Gospel is by grace through faith in one person (Ephesians 2:8-9). The gift of eternal life is given freely to those who trust the eternal God incarnate –Jesus Christ—His virgin birth, His perfect life, His atoning death and His glorious resurrection (1 Corinthians 15:1-4). The Lord Jesus is sufficient to save sinners completely and forever. Diametrically opposed to God's Gospel is the Catholic gospel, which offers salvation through baptism. New born babies, who receive the sacrament of baptism, are said to be saved apart from personal faith in Jesus. The Catholic priest believes he is replacing the sovereign work of God by administering baptism. The sacrament "not only purifies all sins, but also makes the neophyte a new creature, an adopted son of God who has become a partaker of the divine nature, a member of Christ and co-heir with Him and a temple of the Holy Spirit" (CCC, 1257, 1265).

Did you know those who distort the Gospel are condemned?

This includes apostles, priests, popes, pastors or angels (including apparitions of Mary) from heaven. The apostle Paul warned: "there are some who...want to distort the Gospel of Christ. But even though we, or an angel from heaven, should preach to you a Gospel contrary to that which we have preached to you, let him be accursed" (Galatians 1:7-8). Catholics need to be warned that their clergy is under divine condemnation for adding works and sacraments to God's Gospel (CCC, 1129).

Did you know that Jesus put an end to the ordained priesthood?

God's Word reveals that the veil of the temple that separated the Holy of Holies from sinful man was torn open by God (Matthew 27:51). Man can now come directly to God through faith in the shed blood of the Savior (Romans 3:23-26). Priests are no longer needed to offer sacrifices for sin (Hebrews 10:18). The only legitimate priesthood which remains on earth is the royal priesthood of all believers. They offer sacrifices of praise and thanksgiving for being called out of darkness into the marvelous light of the Son (1 Peter 2:9).

Do you really believe Catholic priests have the power to call the Lord Jesus down from heaven every day?

According to Roman Catholic priest John O'Brien in his book *Faith of Millions*, "The priest...reaches up into the heavens, brings Christ down from His throne, and places Him upon our altar to be offered up again as the Victim for the sins of man... Christ, the eternal and omnipotent God, bows his head in humble obedience to the priest's command."

Over 200,000 times each day, priests throughout the world believe they re-present Jesus on their altars as an offering for sins of the living and the dead (CCC, 1371-1374). Again, Catholics ignore God's Word, which declares that Jesus "having been offered once to bear the sins of many, shall appear a second time for salvation not to bear sin" (Hebrews 9:28). The Bible also tells us how and when Jesus will appear. He will return the same way he left, immediately after the tribulation, with power and great glory (Matthew 24:27-30; Acts 1:11). By the authority of God's Word, we must conclude that the Eucharist is a false Christ that is deceiving millions.

Why do Catholic priests continue to offer Jesus as a sacrificial victim when He said "It is finished" (John 19:30)?

God's Word says: Jesus appeared once and offered Himself once to bear sins. His offering is not to be done again (Hebrews 9:25-28). When Jesus "offered one sacrifice for sins for all time, [He] sat down at the right hand of God" (Hebrews 10:12). Disregarding the infallible Word of God, Catholicism teaches: "the sacrifice of Christ and the sacrifice of the Eucharist are one single sacrifice. The victim is one and the same. In this divine sacrifice, the same Christ who offered himself once...is contained and offered in an unbloody manner" (CCC 1367).

Did you know Jesus has already obtained redemption for believers?

Catholicism denies this by teaching: "The work of our redemption is carried on" every time the Eucharist is celebrated (CCC 1405). God's Word declares: "He [Jesus] entered the holy place once for all, having obtained eternal redemption" (Hebrews 9:12). "In Him we have redemption through His blood, the forgiveness of our trespasses, according to the riches of His grace" (Ephesians 1:7).

Why do you call Jesus the Savior when you must save yourself?

Catholicism teaches the sinner must "make satisfaction for" or "expiate" his sins. This satisfaction is also called "penance" (CCC 1459). "In this way they attained their own salvation and cooperated in saving their brothers" (CCC 1477). God's Word proclaims "There is salvation in no one else; for there is no other name under heaven given among men, by which we must be saved" (Acts 4:12).

Why do you believe a place called Purgatory can purify your sins?

God's Word says "when He [Jesus] had made purification of sins, He sat down at the right hand of the Majesty on high (Hebrews 1:3). "He gave Himself for us to... purify for Himself a people for His own possession" (Titus 2:14). "The blood of Jesus...cleanses us from all sin" (1 John 1:7). These verses destroy the myth of purgatory. Yet the Vatican continues to deceive Catholics by teaching they "must undergo purification [in Purgatory] to achieve the holiness necessary to enter the joy of heaven" (CCC 1030).

Why do you pray to Mary?

Nowhere in the Bible do we see believers praying to anyone except God. Jesus taught us how to pray in the Sermon on the Mount. He instructed us to pray to the Father and not to use meaningless repetition (Matthew 6:7-13). Yet Catholics are taught to pray the rosary, which is made up of over 50 meaningless and repetitious prayers to Mary.

Why aren't these Catholic traditions found in the 1st century church?

- Priests offering sacrifices for sins
- Indulgences remitting sin's punishment
- Church leaders forbidden to marry
- Infallible Popes and Bishops

Did you know that whenever you believe a doctrine, you must also forsake that which opposes it?

Scripture reveals that Jesus saves...

- by faith in Him, not baptism
- by His grace, not our merit
- by His finished work, not our works
- by His righteousness, not ours
- by His one offering for sin, not the Mass
- by His blood, not purgatory
- by His obedience, not ours
- by His Gospel, not man's perversion of it

Which Jesus will you trust?

The Jesus of the Bible promises eternal life, the complete forgiveness of sins, a permanent right standing with God and the power to live a victorious life. The Catholic Jesus is a Jesus that was never preached by the Apostles (2 Corinthians 11:4). This counterfeit Christ provides only conditional life, partial forgiveness of sins, an ongoing need for priests and mediators, uncertainty, fear and doubt. Those who reject the true Jesus, who is clearly and conclusively revealed in His Word, will be judged accordingly. The Lord Jesus Christ said, "The word I spoke is what will judge him at the last day" (John 12:48).

The Discussion of Heaven in Evangelism

Do you mention heaven when you share the Gospel? If you do, what specifics do you share about heaven? Many people in and out of the church have an inaccurate or wrong picture of heaven. Therefore, you need to prepare beforehand what you will say about heaven before your witnessing encounter. Here are ten key suggestions to keep you centered on the Gospel and Jesus Christ when discussing heaven.

1. One unforgiven sin or a life of disobedience without repentance will keep people out of heaven (James 2:10; Galatians 3:10, 5:19-21; Romans 6:23, 1 Corinthians 6:9-11)

2. Heaven is not for unbelievers (Revelation 20:13-15; 22:14-15)

3. There is only one way to heaven, and that is through the Lord Jesus Christ. (Matthew 7:13; John 3:16, 10:9, 14:6; Acts 4:12; 1 John 2:23)

4. Eternal Life in heaven is impossible without repentance from sin and faith in the person and work of Jesus Christ. (John 3:3; Luke 15:7, 10; Luke 24:46-49; Mark 1:15; Acts 2:38, 3:19; 11:18; 26:14-18; Luke 11:31-32; 13:2-5; 1 Thessalonians 1:9-10; 2 Timothy 2:24-26; 2 Peter 3:9; John 6:40; Romans 6:22-23; 1 John 5:11.

5. Citizens of heaven must be washed in the blood of Jesus Christ (Ephesians 1:7-8; Hebrews 9:13-15; 1 John 1:7; Revelation 1:5, 7:14-17)

6. Citizens of heaven must be in the Lamb's book of life (Revelation 3:5; 21:22-27)

7. Citizens of heaven will love God and obey His Word with glorified bodies (John 14:21; Phil. 3:20-21; 1 John 5:3-5)

8. Citizens of heaven will worship, praise and sing to God in heaven (Revelation 5:8-14; 15:3-4)

9. Citizens of heaven will serve God through eternity (Revelation 7:13-15, 22:17)

10. There are no second chances to get into heaven after you die (Hebrews 9:27; John 3:18, 3:36, 5:24, 8:24, 12:48; 1 John 5:12).

May your evangelism include calling people to repentance and faith in Christ as well as explaining the glorious hope of eternal life with Christ in heaven.

Why Evangelize if God Has Already Chosen Who Will be Saved?

This engaging question has prompted many discussions and debates over God's sovereignty and man's free will. In answering the question, I am aware of the stricter judgment that awaits me if I mishandle the Word of God (James 3:1). My passion is to always honor and glorify God and never misrepresent His character. Scripture reveals that our sovereign Lord not only chose to save certain sinners, but He also ordained the means by which He will convert them. God established His eternal decree to save His people when they hear and believe His Word (Romans 10:13-17). It is for this reason the Lord of the Harvest commissioned His church to proclaim His Gospel. Every Christian has been given the awesome responsibility and highest privilege to call people to repent and trust Jesus Christ alone for salvation.

God Promises Success in Evangelism

As an evangelist, I have come to love the doctrine of election. There is a sense of relief knowing that when I evangelize, the eternal destinies of souls are not dependent upon my persuasive ability to convert them. God guarantees success whenever His elect hear His Gospel. Jesus promised, "All that the Father gives me shall come to me" (John 6:37, 65). Not some, not most, but all. This sovereign act of God will eventually result in the conversion of those He has given to the Son. This occurred when Paul proclaimed the Gospel to the Gentiles in Antioch—"as many as had been appointed to eternal life believed" (Acts 13:48). The elect will come to Jesus as Christians proclaim the voice of the Good Shepherd. He promised that when His sheep hear His voice, they will follow Him (John 10:27). Whenever Christians sow the imperishable seed of God's living Word, He promises to bring forth life when the seeds fall on fertile soil (1 Corinthians 3:7; 1 Peter 1:23). Success in evangelism is therefore guaranteed by God's sovereign decree. What an encouragement it is to know that God causes those whom He has chosen to come to Him (Psalm 65:4). Man can never thwart God's predetermined plan and purpose.

Doctrine of Election

Election, as defined in Scripture, tells us that God, in eternity past, before all things were created, chose specific individuals to be saved by His unmerited grace. He chose them according to the sovereign good pleasure of His own will. Paul wrote, "God has chosen you from the beginning for salvation through sanctification by the Spirit and faith in the truth" (2 Thessalonians 2:13). In another epistle, Paul said, "He chose us in Him before the foundation of the world" (Ephesians 1:4). The Father chose His elect to be justified and totally glorified (Romans 8:29-30). In a general sense, God desires all men to be saved (1 Timothy 2:4). However, He decreed to save only some, and then He wrote their names in the Lamb's Book of Life (Revelation 17:8).

If the choice were left up to man, no one would choose God. Paul makes this clear without exception, "There is none who understands, there is none who seeks for God" (Romans 3:11; Psalm 14:2-3). Clearly, rebellious sinners could never choose Christ on their own free will; they choose Christ because He first chose them (John 15:16). Why does God choose some and pass over others? His purpose is hidden in the secret counsel of His will (Ephesians 1:11). God's purpose has been established, and He will accomplish it all for His good pleasure (Isaiah 46:10).

Man's Inability to Choose God

Scripture presents a clear contrast between God who is able to save and man who is unable. Man's inability is due to the corruption of his nature and his rebellion and hatred of God (Hebrews 7:25; Romans 8:7; Ephesians 2:1-7). God includes everyone in His invitations, but sinners exclude themselves because of their enslavement to sin. Their bondage to sin keeps them from coming to God. The Bible teaches that we are all born spiritually dead with a sin nature that corrupts our senses and limits our "free will." Opponents of divine election deny this and teach that man has the free will to choose God and come to Him for salvation. However, Scripture proves this is humanly impossible. We cannot know God (Matthew 11:27); we cannot please God (Romans 8:8); we cannot see the light of the Gospel (2 Corinthians 4:4); we cannot understand spiritual truths (1 Corinthians 2:14); we cannot hear the Words of Christ (John 8:43); and we cannot come to Jesus (John 6:44).

The unregenerate man lives in the lusts of his flesh, indulging the desires of the flesh and of the mind, and are by nature children of wrath (Ephesians 2:3). Only when God causes the spiritually dead to come alive in Christ can they see, hear, know and understand the Gospel, and thus, come to Jesus in faith (Colossians 2:13). No one can become a child of God by their own will or by the will of their flesh (John 1:13). There is nothing man can do on his own to be adopted into God's family. Only by God's will can anyone be brought forth through the word of truth (James 1:18). "So then it does not depend on the man who wills or the man who runs, but on God who has mercy" (Romans 9:16). Sovereign election underscores not only the inability of man but also the freedom of God to save sinners according to His own purpose and grace (Titus 3:5; 2 Timothy 1:9). Those who are not recipients of His grace will remain in bondage to sin, captive to their own fleshly desires and hostile towards God (Romans 8:7).

A Doctrine Hotly Contested

Although divine election is clearly presented throughout Scripture, it remains one of the most hotly debated doctrines in church history. Christians who reject the biblical doctrine of election do so for one of the following reasons: 1) pride—they believe man has the free will to release himself from the bondage and power of sin, and then come to Jesus; 2) man-centered evangelism - they enjoy taking credit for persuading people to "accept" Jesus; 3) fear—they refuse to accept that their loved ones may not belong to the elect; and 4) a distorted view of God—they say God is unjust by choosing to save some while passing over others. Paul anticipated these objections when he wrote, "Who are you, O man, who answers back to God...Does not the potter have a right over the clay, to make from the same lump one vessel for honorable use, and another for common use?" (Romans 9:19-23). Is man so prideful that, as a depraved sinner, he has a better plan than an infinitely holy and eternally righteous God? Scripture soundly rebukes this foolish idea! "For My thoughts are not your thoughts, neither are your ways My ways," declares the Lord. "For as the heavens are higher than the earth, so are My ways higher than your ways, and My thoughts than your thoughts" (Isaiah 55:8-9). Those who deny election are usurping God of His absolute control over His creation and the right to choose His own family. They wittingly or unwittingly rob God of His glory, which is a dangerous position to take.

God does not treat everyone the same, but He does treat everyone justly. Some receive justice, which they deserve, and some receive mercy, which they don't deserve (Romans 9:15). Election does not mean that God chose some for heaven and some for hell. Every passage of the Bible that reveals divine election deals with it in the context of salvation, not damnation. Nowhere is anyone elected for hell. The only support for such a view is human logic, not Scripture. Clearly, all of us deserve the eternal fires of hell as the just punishment for our sin. People end up in hell, because they rebelled against their Holy God and Creator. It is not man's love for God that is the motivating factor behind anyone being saved, but God's amazing, unfathomable love for fallen man (Romans 5:8; 1 John 3:1). We must never forget that God is glorified both when His righteous justice is executed on sinners as well as when His mercy is graciously bestowed on the elect. "Who will not fear, O Lord, and glorify Thy name? For Thou alone art holy...for Thy righteous acts have been revealed" (Revelation 15:4).

Divine Sovereignty and Human Responsibility

God is sovereign, but He made man responsible for his actions. To some, this appears to be a paradox. The two subjects are often set in opposition to each other, rather than harmonized together. Both are true and both are found in the Word of God. We see that all men are held responsible for what they believe. "For God so loved the world, that He gave His only begotten Son, that whoever believes in Him should not perish, but have eternal life...He who does not believe has been judged already, because he has not believed in the name of the only begotten Son of God" (John 3:16, 18). Yet we also hear Jesus saying, "You do not believe because you are not my sheep" (John 10:26).

The harmony of these two subjects are hidden somewhere in the infinite mind of God. They stretch man's ability to comprehend the perfect purpose of God (Ecclesiastes 11:5). This is good, since it gives us a greater desire to know Him, and, in turn, it causes us to dig deeper into His Word. We must praise God for who He is and honor Him for His sovereign grace.

Motivations to Proclaim the Gospel

We must be diligent in proclaiming the Gospel, because God is pleased to save those who believe it as His Spirit works in their hearts. The faithful Christian knows that God is in control and He moves us to do the work He has prepared for us. We evangelize because we are sent by God to reconcile the world to Himself through Christ. What a royal privilege it is to represent the King of kings as His ambassadors to a lost and dying world. Like Paul, we must "endure all things for the sake of those who are chosen, that they also may obtain the salvation which is in Christ Jesus and with it eternal glory" (2 Timothy 2:10). It is true we do not know who the chosen ones are, but we do know this: "Whoever will call upon the name of the Lord will be saved" (Romans 10:13). We also know that people will believe the Gospel as the Spirit of Truth reveals its glory and illuminates the Word to them.

The answer to "why evangelize?" is very simple—obedience! God has commissioned His saints to call the lost sheep to the Shepherd. No longer thundering from the mountain or from the burning bush, He uses Christians to accomplish His task of getting His Word to the elect. In closing, let us be motivated with this encouraging thought: Divine election is like a net cast into the sea—it does not drive the fish away, but draws them in. This should inspire us all to cast out the Gospel net more faithfully for God's glory!

The Need for Faithful Evangelists

When our Lord Jesus Christ appointed seventy-two men to go out and proclaim the Gospel, He said, "The harvest is plentiful, but the laborers are few" (Luke 10:2). We have been praying earnestly to the Lord of the harvest to send out more laborers into His harvest. The fields are indeed white for harvest (John 4:35). We are now looking for a few dedicated evangelists who have a compelling desire to make our Lord's last command their first concern. From the beginning of this ministry, we have developed some effective evangelistic resources that we make available at a minimal expense to those who are committed to distributing them.

It has been said that the Gospel is so simple that a young child can hear it, understand it and believe it, yet so profound that a theologian can spend a lifetime studying its glorious transcendent truths. It is the greatest news anyone will ever hear, because it offers a free and complete salvation from the punishment and power of sin and reveals a glorious inheritance in the everlasting kingdom of God. With such promises from the God of pardon, peace and protection, it should not surprise us that God's adversary has been using his false teachers to twist and distort the Gospel to keep people dead in their sins (Galatians 1:6-9). Knowing this, it is the God-given responsibility of every Christian to contend for it earnestly, guard it passionately and proclaim it faithfully (Jude 3; Matthew 28:18-20; 2 Timothy 1:14)

The largest and most neglected mission field continues to be the Roman Catholic Church. It represents more than 1.2 billion souls that need to hear the truth that will set them free from religious deception (John 8:31-32). Yet many Christians are neglecting this mission field, because a growing number of evangelical leaders are saying Catholics are already our brothers and sisters in Christ.

There is much confusion in the Evangelical Church regarding Roman Catholicism. A majority of evangelicals believe it is a Christian denomination instead of an apostate church that formally and dogmatically departed from the faith at the 16th century Council of Trent. The bishops pronounced over 100 anathemas on any Christian who would stand on the truth of God's Word rather than submit to the pope and his ungodly traditions. Those damning condemnations against Christians, who trust the perfect, finished, and sufficient redemptive work of Christ, are still in effect today and can never be rescinded.

Because of the growing confusion in the Evangelical Church, we realized the urgent need to educate Christians concerning the deceptive teachings of Roman Catholicism. This was our motivation for publishing the Gospel tract: *Rome vs. the Bible.* The tract offers 13 clear contrasts between God's Word and the *Catechism of the Catholic Church* regarding authority, regeneration, justification, salvation and the Lord's Supper. Anyone who reads this tract will see that Roman Catholicism has departed from the truth of God's Word and stands opposed to the faith of the Apostles. The tract not only exposes the errors of the Catholic religion, but also forces Catholics to make a decision: "Should I trust Christ and His Word or the teachings and traditions of a religion?"

One of our most popular evangelistic resources that has helped many people understand and protect the purity of the Gospel has been our set of 12 Gospel Cards. Each card defines and explains the most important words of the Gospel using Scripture. This has been a most helpful tool for Christians who feel they do not know the Gospel well enough to share it. These cards can not only equip and encourage people to gain a deeper understanding of the Gospel, they can also be used to evangelize the lost. When people use the cards in witnessing opportunities, they can be assured they will not leave out an important part of the Gospel.

There are many other ways the Gospel Cards can be used to equip and edify the saints and evangelize the lost. At the State Fair of Texas, we laid them out in our booth and asked people who visited to consider the 12 words. We asked them a probing question, "Since your eternal destiny may be determined by your understanding of these words, which one would you like to know more about?" It was interesting to see the card that was picked up most often. It was "Sin." Perhaps they were looking for a loop hole. After they read the definition and explanation of sin according to Scripture, they would continue picking up other cards.

We also use them at dinner parties with both believers and unbelievers. After dinner, we ask each person to take a card. Then each person, in turn, explains what their word means without looking at the definitions on the back. Then the rest of the table gets to offer their explanations. The card is then turned over and the four bullet points are read to see what was missed. At the end of the evening, our dinner guests have shared how the conversations were so rich and meaningful.

People have also used the Gospel Cards to teach their children and grandchildren or to share in their Sunday School classes and home Bible studies. Finally, the cards can be used as the biblical standard to discern the true Gospel from counterfeit Gospels. Take them with you in your pocket or purse and be ready for divine appointments.

We have additional resources to support you in your outreach ministry. A complete list of the resources we provide, and ordering information, can be found on our website: www.ProclaimingTheGospel.org. Remember, only two things on earth are eternal: the souls of men and the Word of God. Everything else will eventually be burned and destroyed with intense heat (2 Peter 3:12).

Chapter 12

THE RESPONSE TO THE GOSPEL

Using the authority of God's Word, we will see the utter importance of calling sinners to both faith and repentance to be saved. Jesus preached, "Repent and believe the Gospel" (Mark 1:15). He said, "unless you repent, you will all likewise perish" (Luke 13:3). He ended His ministry on earth with, "repentance for forgiveness of sins should be proclaimed in My name to all the nations" (Luke 24:47).

Certain responses to the Gospel are purposefully avoided by evangelicals such as the call to repentance and Christ's lordship. The say this is adding something to the offer of God's free gift. They make "faith" the only response to the Gospel. This has populated the church with many false converts whose hope hangs on "accepting Christ as Savior." Casually affirming Christ with their mouths, many deny Him with their deeds (Titus 1:16).

Clearly, repentance is a critical element of conversion. It is the work of God in a new heart that causes a change of mind which results in turning from sin and self to God (Eze. 36:26; 1 Thes. 1:9; 2 Tim. 2:23-25). Sorrow for sin that is according to the will of God produces a repentance without regret, leading to salvation (2 Cor. 7:10). When someone is truly converted, they will respond to sin with conviction, sorrow, confession and repentance. The change of mind produces a change of purpose as Paul said. They "turned to God from idols to serve a living and true God" (1 Thes. 1:9).

Paul said he testified "both to Jews and to Greeks of repentance toward God and of faith in our Lord Jesus Christ" (Acts 20:20-21). He declared to Jews and Gentiles, "to repent and turn to God, performing deeds in keeping with their repentance (Acts 26:20). Paul has made it clear that all must repent. To the men of Athens, Paul said, God "commands all people everywhere to repent, because he has fixed a day on which he will judge the world in righteousness by a man (Jesus) whom he has appointed; and of this he has given assurance to all by raising him from the dead" (Acts 17:30-31). Not calling people to repentance is a most grievous error. According to God's Word, repentance accompanies saving faith.

My heart is burdened for the many professing Christians who have never experienced the second birth (1 Peter 1:23). They are all tragic victims of a subtle yet potentially fatal deception. Unless they are confronted with the truth, they will one day hear the most terrifying words anyone could ever hear, when Jesus says: "I never knew you; depart from Me" (Matthew 7:23). These precious souls have either been led astray by a false Gospel or manipulated to make a decision by unbiblical methods of evangelism. The blame must fall on church leaders who have discarded God's blueprint for building His church and have created their own. These men have discovered they can gain a larger following by making the Gospel more appealing and more inclusive. By broadening the narrow road, they have found out they can build bigger churches for themselves. Little do they know, they are helping Satan plant his tares among the wheat (Matthew 13:38-40). The devil loves to see false converts deceiving and being deceived in the name of Christ.

The strategy of Satan has been consistent for 2000 years. He continues to raise up false apostles, who influence false teachers to teach false Gospels about false christs for the purpose of producing false Christians with a false hope. The apostle Paul saw this happening and warned us. The same serpent who deceived Eve by his craftiness also sends deceivers to preach another Jesus and a different Gospel (2 Corinthians 11:3-4). Satan hates the Gospel of grace and has been using men filled with religious pride to pervert the message ever since it was first announced. That is why Paul informed us that the Gospel he preached was not according to man's traditions or philosophy. He received it directly from God through a pure revelation of Jesus Christ (Galatians 1:11-12).

Some church leaders feel that the best way to win more people to Christ is to exchange God's Gospel for an "easy to believe" Gospel. This watered-down version of the Gospel is hardly worth living for and certainly not worth dying for. Yet, it is gaining popularity within evangelical circles and must be exposed and confronted. There are three major areas of compromise.

The Christ of the Gospel

There are some Christian leaders who have found the Gospel is "easier to believe" if they present a generic god without holiness and a partial Christ without authority. They say you don't have to make Jesus your Lord, as long as you believe He is your Savior. Such a teaching is foreign to the Word of God. Paul said, "Believe in the Lord Jesus, and you shall be saved" (Acts 16:31). Jesus Christ is repeatedly and resolutely revealed in Scripture as our Master, our Creator, our King, our Ruler and our sovereign Lord. Paul addressed Jesus as Lord over 200 times in his 13 epistles.

Still others deny that Jesus really is who He said He is. This is a fatal mistake, because Jesus declared, "Unless you believe that I am He, you shall die in your sins" (John 8:24). Jesus made it clear that He is the only way to the Father when He announced, "I am the way, and the truth, and the life; no one comes to the Father, but through Me" (John 14:6). The very words of Christ declare that He is the only valid object of saving faith. Yet there are some popular pastors and evangelists who foolishly teach that sinners can be saved apart from Jesus Christ. Why would anyone deny, discredit and dishonor the Lord Jesus in this way? Might it be so that they can be loved and admired by a greater number of people?

The cults deny the Christ of the Gospel by teaching that Jesus is not the eternal God of the Trinity. Mormons, for example, teach that Jesus is a created being (conceived by a physical sex act between God the Father and Mary) and is the elder brother of Lucifer, who became one of many gods.

There are other false religions who uphold the name of Jesus Christ but deny He is able to save sinners totally and completely. The Roman Catholic Church is the greatest offender by requiring sacraments (CCC 1129), indulgences (CCC 1498) and good works (CCC 2016) for the forgiveness and remission of sin. Catholicism also blatantly denies that the blood of Jesus purifies all sin (1 John 1:7). A safety net called purgatory is provided for Catholics. This fictitious place is said to purge away the sins that Christ failed to purge (CCC 1030).

Those who believe the Jesus of the Gospel will trust His righteousness, not their own; His finished work on the cross, not the Catholic Mass; His power to keep them, not the sacraments; His blood to purify sin, not purgatory; His Word to guide them, not the traditions of men; and His grace to save them, not their merit. Those who do not trust Jesus need another Gospel to tell them what they must do to be saved. Whenever Jesus is dethroned, denied or diminished, the promises of the true Gospel can never be realized.

Those Who Deny the Promise of the Gospel Are Denying the Gospel

Everlasting, never-ending, eternal life with the Savior is the glorious promise of the Gospel, yet the majority of professing Christians believe they can lose their salvation. This is because they do not know or trust the glorious Christ of the Gospel. Paul knew Him well, which prompted him to write: "I know whom I have believed and I am convinced that He is able to guard what I have entrusted to Him until that day" (2 Timothy 1:12). The eternal Gospel of our eternal God promises every believer eternal life and eternal glory in God's eternal kingdom (Revelation 14:6; Romans 16:26; 1 John 5:13; 1 Peter 5:10; 2 Peter 1:11). The Lord Jesus promises to lose not one that the Father gives Him (John 6:39). His promise to every believer is this: "I will never desert you, nor will I ever forsake you" (Hebrews 13:5). Neither sin nor anything else will separate a believer from God's love (Romans 8:38-39). This glorious truth is guaranteed, because God's forgiveness is given freely and completely at the moment of faith and is secured forever for all past and future sins (Colossians 2:13-14). Everyone who believes the promises of the Gospel possesses eternal redemption through the eternal Spirit who guarantees an eternal inheritance (Hebrews 9:12-15; Ephesians 1:14). God's promises to every believer are backed up by His eternal power (1 Peter 1:3:5). This is why Paul declared: "Your faith should not rest on the wisdom of men, but on the power of God" (1 Corinthians 2:5). The world, through its wisdom, does not come to know God. Tragically, many professing Christians choose to trust the wisdom of man rather than the promises and power of God revealed in His Gospel. Those who reject the promise of eternal life have believed another Gospel and trusted another Christ (1 Corinthians 15:2).

May we all examine our faith and practice to ensure that it conforms to God's Word. Have we trusted the Christ of the Gospel and believed the glorious and infallible promises of the Gospel? Are we calling people to respond to the Gospel God's way? Let us all obey from the heart the doctrine to which we were delivered (Romans 6:17).

Contemplate Our Wonderful Savior

As we meditate on our great God and Savior, the Lord Jesus Christ, let us ponder the majesty of His creation, the riches of

His grace, the cleansing power of His blood, the perfection of His righteousness, the necessity of His mercy, the faithfulness of His love, the blessings of His redemption, the greatness of His power, the authority of His word, the purity of His Gospel, the sufficiency of His atonement, the miracle of His resurrection, the need for His intercession, the promise of His inheritance, the assurance of His promises, and the glory of His second coming. Meditating on the Lord Jesus will keep our heart and mind stayed upon Him. As we behold the glory of the Lord, we "are being transformed into the same image from one degree of glory to another. For this comes from the Lord who is the Spirit" (2 Corinthians 3:18).

The more we contemplate the glory of Christ's incarnation and His sin-bearing sacrifice which satisfied divine justice, the more we will be compelled to tell others about His gracious offer of forgiveness and redemption. After all, He is the greatest man who ever lived who offers the greatest gift anyone could ever receive! There is no higher calling in this life than to serve the King of kings as His ambassadors. It is indeed a great privilege and an awesome responsibility to be His ministers of reconciliation (2 Corinthians 5:18-20)

ABOUT MIKE GENDRON

———◁᷁◦᷁▷———

For over 34 years, Evangelist Mike Gendron was a devout Roman Catholic and a strong defender of the "one true church." He was taught from a very early age to trust and rely on the church, its priests, the sacraments and his own good works for salvation. However, in 1981 while attending an evangelical seminar, he came to believe the Bible is the supreme authority for knowing truth. His new excitement and hunger for the inspired word of God led him to help organize the very first Little Rock Scripture Study at a Catholic Church in Dallas.

Mike soon realized that many of the teachings and traditions of the Catholic religion were not found in the Bible. After more study, he discovered the Roman Catholic plan of salvation was diametrically opposed to the Gospel of grace that is revealed in the Bible. When Mike discerned that God seeks worshippers in spirit and truth, he left the Catholic Church in 1984 for an evangelical church where Scripture is the final and supreme authority in all matters of faith.

In 1988, he left a successful career in corporate management to study at Dallas Theological Seminary. Three years later, during his last semester at DTS, Mike and his wife Jane's love for Catholics inspired them to begin a ministry that would point Catholics to Jesus Christ as their all sufficient Savior. Their hearts are now burdened for those who may be where they were for most of their lives - eternally condemned and not even aware of it.

Contact: mike@ProclaimingTheGospel.org

REFERENCES

I heartily recommend Mike Gendron's work in his book Preparing for Eternity as well as his continued ministry through Proclaiming the Gospel.

Dr. John MacArthur
President, The Master's Seminary

Mike Gendron presents penetrating insights into Catholicism based both on experience and biblical study. He does it with a spirit of love, for his motivation is not to condemn, but to provide deliverance from faith in religion to faith in Jesus.

Dr. David Reagan
Evangelist, Lamb & Lion Ministries

Mike Gendron is a man of insight and vision who has been used mightily of the Lord to lead Roman Catholics to a personal relationship with Christ by effectively proclaiming the good news.

Dr Ron Blue
President, CAM International

I applaud and endorse Mike Gendron in his courageous effort to proclaim the true Gospel by opposing both the counterfeit church and by implication, its insidious, burgeoning ecumenism. He ventures to go where most Christians fear to tread.

John Dwyer
College Professor and Author of Stonewall & Robert E Lee

I heartily recommend the Proclaiming the Gospel seminars. Mike was a blessing to our people as he contrasted Catholicism with truth in a clear, bold, sensitive way.

Tom Nelson
Pastor, Denton Bible Church

About Proclaiming the Gospel

The ministry was established in 1991 and is governed by a board of directors from four different churches. Over 30,000 subscribers, representing all 50 states and foreign countries, have received our newsletters and share our love and compassion for the lost. We are an independent evangelical mission working in and through local churches. The ministry is supported by seminaries, churches and Christians who share our vision. Donations are tax deductible. The ministry is incorporated in the state of Texas as a nonprofit 501(c)(3) corporation.

Ministry Purposes

To honor, serve and glorify our Lord Jesus Christ by proclaiming His death and resurrection as the only way of salvation and encourage others to do the same. (1 Cor. 15:1-4)

To make disciples by calling people to place their complete trust and confidence in the Lord Jesus Christ while forsaking all human works and merit, so that by grace alone, they can receive God's irrevocable gift of eternal life. (Matt. 28:18-20; Eph. 2:8-9)

To expose any doctrines or traditions that oppose or nullify the Gospel of grace, so that people can discern truth from error and not be deceived. (Eph. 5:11; Titus 1:10-16)

Ministry Seminars

Proclaiming The Gospel seminars are customized according to the particular requests of each church or seminary. Each seminar is complimented by Keynote or PowerPoint presentations and can address the following topics:

Evangelism for the Glory of God—Encourage and equip the saints to faithfully and effectively proclaim the Gospel of grace with biblical integrity. Provide biblical resources to help the saints evangelize God's way. Train people in practical evangelism by taking them into the community to engage people with the Gospel.

Apologetics/Discernment—Equip the saints to always be ready to give a reason for the hope that we have in Christ Jesus. Train people to have discernment by contrasting false religions and apostate Christianity with the true faith. Encourage evangelicals to earnestly contend for the faith of the apostles.

Bible Prophecy—Proclaim the soon return of the Lord Jesus Christ and instruct believers on the prophetic events surrounding His glorious return.

Discipleship—Provide a safe, loving, compassionate environment for truth seekers to investigate the person and work of our all-sufficient Savior. Encourage new believers in the faith who may be suffering persecution or guilt for exchanging their religion for a relationship with the Lord Jesus Christ.

Resources

Visit **ProclaimingTheGospel.org** to see all the resources available to equip and encourage Christians to be more faithful witnesses for our Lord Jesus Christ. Many of the resources, including doctrinally sound Gospel Tracts, Gospel Cards, DVDs, CDs and books, will help you share the glorious Gospel of God with the people in your circle of influence.

The website also has a wealth of resources that can be viewed or downloaded, including articles, streaming videos, debates, and lists of doctrinally sound churches.